God,
Where
Are
You?

God, Where Are You?

REDISCOVERING THE
BIBLE

Carlos Mesters

*Translated by John Drury
and Francis McDonagh*

ORBIS BOOKS

Maryknoll, New York 10545

The Catholic Foreign Mission Society of America (Maryknoll) recruits and trains people for overseas missionary service. Through Orbis Books, Maryknoll aims to foster the international dialogue that is essential to mission. The books published, however, reflect the opinions of their authors and are not meant to represent the official position of the society.

English translation copyright © 1995 by Orbis Books

Originally published in 1972 as *Deus, Onde Estás?* by Editôra Vega, S.A., Belo Horizonte, Brazil, and reprinted in 1987 by Editôra Vozes Ltda, Rua Frei Luís, 100, 25689 Petrópolis, RJ, Brazil

"Part I: The Old Testament" is a revised edition of *God, Where Are You? Meditations on the Old Testament*, published in English by Orbis Books in 1977.

Published by Orbis Books, Maryknoll, NY 10545-0308
Manufactured in the United States of America

Library of Congress Cataloging-in-Publication Data

Mesters, Carlos.
    [Deus, onde estás? English]
    God where are you? : rediscovering the Bible / Carlos
Mesters ; translated by John Drury and Francis McDonagh.
       p. cm.
    ISBN 0-88344-998-6 (pbk.)
    1. Bible—Criticism, interpretation, etc. I. Title.
BS511.2M49 1995
220.6′1–dc20
                                94-44034
                                   CIP

Contents

v

Part Two
THE NEW TESTAMENT

INTRODUCTION
Finding God in the Bible

"God, where are you?" The question is hardly a new one. Many before us have asked it. It is the kind of question that calls for an answer that will have a profound impact on the direction we take in life. Hence there is some value in having someone around who might be able to point us in the right direction as we look for a response.

Among the many responses already given to the question, there is one that is recorded in history and that still continues to make an impression on people today. It is the response of the Bible, which has become a best-seller in over a thousand different languages and which has sold over a billion copies.

The Bible is like an old family album containing all sorts of pictures and snapshots. Some record important events: weddings, newborn babies, baptisms, the house newly purchased. Other photos record events of seeming unimportance: for example, a family picnic on the weekend, with no date attached.

The standards for judging whether a particular photo is important or not are quite relative. A photo of a smiling baby lying naked on a bearskin rug, taken with an old, cheap camera, can be far more important than an expensive family portrait taken by a professional photographer. Both are useless when one registers for working papers; they do not serve that particular purpose. All the

---

The Introduction and chapters 1–10 were translated by John Drury. Bible citations are from *The New English Bible*.

1

pictures are useful for the album, however. It preserves them all, organizing them in its own disordered way according to the rhythms of family life and thus offering us a faithful portrait of the family in question. It is a pleasure for the children and grandchildren to leaf through the pages of the album. They learn who they are and where they came from. Indeed all the photos are important in terms of this purpose, even though they might not seem to be at first glance.

Such is the Bible. It has a little bit of everything: formal official portraits and snapshots of casual moments. Some items were meant to provide explicit documentation; others have no purpose except to draw a smile from the reader. The Bible is the faithful portrait of a people preserved in organized disorder. The children and grandchildren can leaf through its hoary pages to learn who they are and thus fashion an awareness of their own membership in that people.

But why is it that this album should be so important for us? Wouldn't the complex and varied history of our own country be enough for us today? In one sense it certainly does provide us with enough material. But the point is that many of us at least go through life with certain questions for which we cannot find an adequate answer in our family and national albums. Where is God? In what way, if any, does our national history have anything to do with God? And if God is somehow present in the midst of it all, what criteria do we have so that we can discover God's presence? How are we to determine and give direction to the course of history that we are putting together? We all seem to have our own ideas about the future. Where are we to find some means of discriminating among them and knowing that we are relying on something certain insofar as the future is concerned? These are some of the serious questions that arise in the minds of people who really ponder life. The direction we take in life will depend in no small measure on our answers to these questions.

The people of the Bible, living in their particular time and historical situation, raised these same questions and tried to formulate answers. The direction they took in life was based on the answers they fashioned. They were on a journey and, to the wonderment of all, they arrived at their destination: the resurrection of Christ. The photos preserved in the Bible deal with this journey, tracing its course from beginning to end.

We Christians believe that the route followed by the people in the Bible is a sure route, indeed, the route of God. Hence Christians read the Bible and offer it as an indispensable tool for reflection. They see it as a great help in the attempt to analyze reality and find answers for the questions raised by life. They see the history of the people in the Bible as a pattern of action that provides certainty and that is guaranteed by God. Hence they study the Bible, not just to find out what happened in the distant past, but also and primarily to get a better grasp of the sense and purpose of what is happening today in our history. It is this sort of Bible study that is taking on prime importance today, more so than it ever did before.

Never in history has the Bible been subjected to such close exegetical and hermeneutical scrutiny as it has been over the past hundred years. Practically every phrase and word of the Bible has been closely analyzed to discover its correct meaning. The literature is now so extensive that one feels compelled to specialize in some particular sector of biblical exegesis.

As time went on, however, something seemed to go wrong with this immense panoply of scholarly apparatus. The field of biblical study with its ever growing areas of specialization is like the case of the electronic computer that was not working. There seemed to be some defect that the professional technicians could not pinpoint. They formulated their questions, fed them into the machine, and pressed the button; but nothing happened. The computer would not respond. The defect actually was simple: the computer was not plugged in. It had not occurred to the professionals to check this simple but basic point. They checked every piece of equipment in the computer but could not find anything wrong. Then one morning a janitor cleaning up noticed the problem.

In the field of biblical interpretation, something has not been functioning as it should in the great complex of scholarly machinery. The professionals press the button, but they get no response to the questions life raises. The professionals are trying to pinpoint the defect, and a host of books have appeared to show people "how to read and interpret the Bible." Again the defect is simple and serious: biblical interpretation is not plugged into real life. It is almost wholly preoccupied with the past, with telling us exactly what took place back then. It does not tell us anything about the meaning and purpose of what is happening here and now. It is like a person given a microscope who spends a whole lifetime examining how the microscope is put together, without ever studying anything under it.

If it were simply a matter of learning what happened in the past, we would have no need of the Bible. Many things happened in the past of which there is no trace at all in the Bible. Our interest in preserving all that happened to the people of the Bible hinges on the belief that these people and their experiences have something to tell us about our lives today. This would seem to be the proper and principal reason for reading and interpreting the Bible: so that we may cull the message it contains, and thus be aided in answering the questions posed to us by life.

As in the case of the electronic computer, it was not the professional experts who first noticed the defect in biblical interpretation. It was simple people trying to sweep up the corridors of life. From the wisdom they had acquired through living, they posed certain questions of their own, thus making it clear that there was little sense in restricting biblical interpretation and exegesis to the study of the past. They put a simple but serious question to exegesis: "What does all this have to do with our lives today?" And thus they managed to plug the apparatus of scholarship back into the wall socket, once again connecting exegesis with the current of real life.

Hence our main concern in this book will not be to elucidate what happened in the past. Instead, by studying past happenings we shall try to find an answer to questions that we raise about life here and now. We shall try to restore to the word of God the function that it ought to have, which is to serve as a light on the pathway of life, as a help to our own reflective analysis of present-day reality in all its complexity. Then the word can help to insure life's movement toward the resurrection in which we believe and whose power is already operative in those who do believe (see Eph 1:19–23).

Today, however, we are faced with a lack of communication. There is a short-circuit between us and the Bible. We do not understand each other. The Bible speaks, but its words are foreign to us. Where does the fault lie: in us or in the Bible? When two people can no longer understand each other, one tends to place the blame on the other. We tend to do the same with the Bible. In biblical interpretation we start from the premise that the cause of the difficulties lies in the Bible, not in ourselves. Our ignorance and our inability to understand the Bible are apparently due to the fact that it is such a difficult book. Hence any introduction to the study of the Bible should clarify the difficulties the Bible contains and thus reestablish the communication that has been interrupted.

My point of view in this book is quite the opposite. The principal problem is not in the Bible but in ourselves, in the way we approach the Bible. My aim will not be to clarify the difficulties in the Bible for the reader. There are many good books around that tackle that task. My aim here is to correct the flaw in our own sight; to change the tint of the glasses with which we read the Bible; to show that the alleged beam in the Bible — that is, the difficulties it contains — is really nothing more than a speck of dust (see Mt 7:3).

I entered the world of the Bible through a gateway that was opened through long years of study. Living with other people, however, has taught me that there is another gateway into the Bible, which is in fact a much older one, used quite often by the Fathers of the Church. Today, however, it is often locked up or even completely forgotten. Yet it enables us to discover quite directly what the Bible is trying to say to us. I should like to provide the key to this gateway in the pages of this book.

Many generations of Christians passed through the gateway in question. It was well-worn with constant use. But it was new to me, giving new value to what I had studied and placing it all in a new light. I do not mean to suggest that my studies were a waste of time; they were not. My studies were in fact valuable. The only problem was that they shed very little light on the corridors of here-

and-now life. But thanks to the faith and life of simple people, the corridors are now much more brightly lit.

I did not really do anything special, except to open my eyes and ears to the sounds and sights of real life. Sharing life with other people, I entered the real world of people and events today as well as the real world of the people in the Bible. I discovered that while these two worlds are truly different, the lives of the people in them have the same roots and prompt the same questions. Life helped me to get a better understanding of the Bible, and the Bible helped me to gain a better understanding of life. In this book, which arose out of a series of talks in my neighborhood, I shall try to shed some light on life today by showing what the lives of the people in the Bible have to tell us.

"God, where are you?" Before we learn anything about God, we must know something of ourselves. We know that we are here. We feel that we know something about the path of life on which we are traveling. We are aware of the situation that prompts us to raise certain questions. It is the fact that *we are here* that prompts us to ask: "God, where are you?" Our dialogue with God starts from the reality of our life here, and that is the point from which the reflections in this book start.

In the chapters of this book we shall consider aspects of the life of the people in the Bible, aspects that are still part of our lives today. We shall see how the people of the Bible, with their feet on the ground and their heads in the clouds, managed to sense and grasp the appeals of God that emanated from life. They took their cue from those appeals, pointed their lives in a certain direction, and, as a result, managed to arrive at the resurrection. Perhaps their example can help us to do the same today. Perhaps we too can hear the summons of God emanating from the reality around us, let it become an integral part of our own lives, and allow it to lead us to an authentic resurrection that is guaranteed by the resurrection of Jesus Christ. We shall consider features of life that posed questions to the people in the Bible long ago and that now pose questions to us. The people of the Bible found solid answers for those questions that still challenge us.

PART ONE

The Old Testament

1

PARADISE

Myth or Reality?

Present-day science propounds evolution as a highly probable hypothesis. The Bible, on the other hand, presents the creation of humanity as the direct work of God: "Then the Lord God formed a man from the dust of the ground" (Gn 2:7). Which is right?

In the first account of creation (Gn 1:26), the human being is the last to be created. In the second account of creation (Gn 2:7), the human being is the first to be created. How are we to explain this contradiction?

Many myths and legends of antiquity speak familiarly of a "tree of life" (Gn 2:9), a "serpent" (Gn 3:1), and a paradisiacal era at the beginning of time. Can the language of the Bible be regarded as mythical and legendary?

In Paradise there is a river that feeds four streams: the Tigris, the Euphrates, the Nile, and the Ganges (Gn 2:10–14). Where can we find a geographical point that would contain such a source?

How could God make all human misery depend on the sin of a single couple? How could woman be formed from the rib of a man? How could man be formed from "the dust of the ground" (Gn 2:7)?

Such questions arise in our minds because we, perhaps unwittingly, regard the Paradise account as providing historical information. We are of the opinion that the author wrote these verses in order to tell us something about the course of real events at the very start of human history. But this mental outlook, which lies behind our reading and evaluation of the Paradise account, does

9

not correspond to the intention the author had when he put these details in writing.

The Viewpoint of the Biblical Author

The biblical author lived hundreds of thousands of years after the events he purports to describe. He was not at all interested in the past for its own sake, but he was deeply concerned about the situation in his own day. Something was wrong. The future seemed jeopardized, and something had to be done. That was the problem that preoccupied him and that led him to write his account. He was a thoroughgoing realist.

The intention of the biblical author, which will be explored in this chapter, can be summed up in five points: (1) He perceives the disastrous situation of his people and wants to denounce the evil in clear-cut terms. (2) He is not content with a general denunciation; he wants to point up where the responsibility lies. He wants the reader to discover the "origin" of the unfortunate situation, the evil that lies at the root of it all, the "original" sin. (3) Since people have lost sight of the responsibility involved, the author wants his description to raise the consciousness of his readers regarding the blame that might be theirs. (4) The author wants to arouse them to action, so that they will tackle the evil at its roots and thus transform the unfortunate situation into a state of overall well-being. He is trying to effect what elsewhere in the Bible is called "conversion." (5) Finally, he wants to assure them that this transforming and practical action and the will of God that serves as its guarantee are greater than the force that maintains the evil situation. Thus he will awaken people's will to fight against the evil and help to instill hope and courage in them.

The Situation to Be Denounced

Perception of evil depends to some extent on the level of culture. Lack of water is a great evil for us, but it is not such a great evil for the Bedouin in the desert. Thus the biblical author perceives evil in accordance with his culture, his own level of awareness, and his sensitivity. First of all, he notes a general ambivalence in life: (1) Human love, so good and beautiful in itself, has been turned into a tool for domination (Gn 3:16). Why? (2) The procreation of new offspring, designed to augment joy between human beings, entails the pangs of childbirth (Gn 3:16). Why? (3) One's own individual life is ambivalent. One wants to live and go on living, but death awaits (Gn 3:19). Why? (4) The earth is designed to produce nourishing food for human beings, but instead it produces only "thorns and thistles" (Gn 3:18). Why? (5) There is something incomprehensible about work, which is meant to provide us with the necessities of life. Much effort is expended for a very meager return (Gn 3:19). Why? (6) Enmity exists between human beings and other animals. Life is not safe and secure. Snakes are a real threat. Why does life fight against life (Gn 3:15)? (7) God is our creator and friend, but in fact God is a cause for fear (Gn 3:10). Why?

The biblical author also testifies to the existence of an extraordinary amount of violence. Cain slays Abel. One individual fights with another, taking vengeance seventy-seven times (Gn 4:24). There is also a diminution in the life of faith, which is now little more than ritual and an admixture of magic and superstition. The divine and the human are confused (Gn 6:1–2). Finally the biblical author sees a total disintegration of humanity. People do not understand each other; they are always fighting with each other and trying to get the upper hand. People live on the defensive in a state of siege (Gn 11:1–9).

This is the situation the author ascertains around him: complete chaos. The majority of his contemporaries do not understand this situation and even help to compound the confusion. The biblical author wants to awaken others to the danger that is facing them if they continue along the same lines. He is basically a "nonconformist." Why?

He is convinced that the blame cannot be placed on God. Nor does he think it is right to say: "Relax, we'll manage somehow. It is God's will." He would be the last person in the world to look to

God or religion for some way to justify a false patience that only worsens the present state of affairs. His faith tells him that God does not will the present state of affairs. And so he is faced with two questions: How would God like the world to be? If the world is not what God would like it to be, then who is responsible for the mess that exists? His faith in God makes him an aware and conscientious person who simply cannot accept the present situation. It prompts him to resist, to look for some solution, and to raise the consciousness of others to the same level that he is operating on. His feeling is: "If God does not want things to be this way, then I must not do anything that will perpetuate the world as it is."

Paradise as God's Ideal

The biblical author himself does not know how the world ought to be either. But he does know that God is good, just, and truthful. He thus imagines a situation in direct opposition to the one he knows first hand. It is a situation of thoroughgoing well-being: Paradise. This Paradise is described by the author (Gn 2:4–25): (1) The wife is no longer dominated by her husband; she is his equal and companion (Gn 2:22–24). (2) Life goes on forever because a tree of life exists (Gn 2:9). (3) The land produces trees and fruit in abundance, and there is no desert (Gn 2:8–9). (4) Work is not oppressive but easy; its yield is abundant because it is easy to take care of a garden with flowering trees (Gn 2:15). (5) The fertility of the soil is guaranteed by an abundance of water that cannot be found on any part of the present-day earth (Gn 2:10–14). (6) Instead of being hostile to people, other animals obey and serve them (Gn 2:19–20). (7) God is the friend and intimate companion of human beings; God takes walks and engages in conversation with them (Gn 3:8). (8) There is no violence, no magical abuse of divine things, no abusive domination of others.

It is a picture and a situation of total harmony: of God with human beings, of one human being with another, of human beings with the world of animals and nature. Complete order prevails, in direct contrast to the chaos the author sees and experiences in his day-to-day life. There is no ambivalence whatsoever.

That is what God wants. Paradise is, as it were, the model of the world that God wants. God entrusted construction plans to us so that we could fashion our own happiness. It was really possible for us to live forever and be immortal, to be happy and devoid of suffering, and to live in harmony with God and be sinless. Indeed it still *is* really possible because God has not changed the divine plan. God still wants that Paradise.

That Paradise should exist. In describing it the biblical author denounces the world he knows. Enlightened by the author's description, the reader is then led to ask certain questions that mark the first step on the road to "conversion": If that is the case, then why is the world exactly the opposite of what it should be? Who is responsible? The author's response to this question is provided by his account of "original sin."

Responsibility for Evil

The author speaks a language that is alien to us but that was quite clear and realistic for the people of his own day. The command not to eat of the fruit of "the tree of the knowledge of good and evil" may seem arbitrary to us. For the biblical writer and his people, however, the wisdom that served as a guide through life was often represented by the image of a tree. Wisdom told us what was good and evil, informing us whether a given course of action led toward fullness of life with God or not. God had given this knowledge through the law. If human beings chose to determine on their own what led to life (good) and what did not lead to life (evil), they would find anything but life; they would meet death. Thus the prohibition in the Genesis account speaks against those people who have chosen not to follow the law of God any longer but rather to decide for themselves what the criterion of moral behavior in life is. It speaks against those who have set themselves up as the sole and absolute criterion, who no longer regard life as a gift and a duty but rather as their own exclusive possession having no connection or relationship with any value outside themselves.

For the biblical author, the law of God is the instrument of order and progress. Observance of this law enables us to attain peace and to fashion Paradise. Disorder is rooted in the fact that his contemporaries have been disregarding this law, this declaration of human rights and duties. The forbidden fruit is the abusive use of liberty against God, and hence against human beings themselves.

What was the cause of this? Why were human beings abandoning this basic orientation in their lives? The cause was the serpent and its lures. The serpent was the symbol of the Canaanite religion, an agreeable religion entailing cultic ritual of a sexual nature and devoid of ethical commitments. It demanded little more than the observance of certain rites. This religion was a great temptation for the Hebrew people. It invited them to take refuge in easy ritual and to give up the harsh exigencies of the law. For the biblical author, the sin of his people was concretely rooted in that temptation.

Through this presentation the biblical author prodded his contemporaries to make a serious reexamination of their lives. Their world could be different if they did not follow this "serpent." Thus the biblical author was not thinking primarily of what had taken place in the distant past; he was thinking of what was going on around him, and perhaps even within himself. His account is a public confession of guilt. "Adam" and "Eve" can be translated as "a man" and "a woman" representing all. They are a mirror offering a critical reflection of contemporary reality and thus helping people to see in themselves the mistake pointed up in Adam and Eve. They should not ask: "Why are we all suffering because of one man and one woman?" The purpose of the account is not to allow people to shift the blame to others. It is to get the readers to admit that they act like that, that all of us share responsibility for the evil that exists. The biblical author is not a sentimentalist lamenting the good old days. He wants everyone to wake up to their personal responsibilities, to tackle the roots of evil in themselves. They can overcome this evil because God wills that they do so.

The author's description of the origin of evil does not end with this description of the "original sin." The initial error is only the beginning of the disgraceful mess: (1) Abusing liberty, human beings detach themselves from God and then from each other. Cain kills Abel, Cain representing all those who mistreat or kill their fellow human beings. (2) There is an alarming increase in violence, and vengeance is multiplied many times over (Gn 4:24). (3) Now separated from both God and other people, human beings go on the defensive; they look to flight and rite and magic for salvation. Pursuing this line of conduct, humanity eventually grows obdurate and starts to disintegrate. It becomes impossible for people to live together and act in common (the tower of Babel). Despite all this, the biblical author is hopeful. He foresees victory over the evil that stems from the serpent (Gn 3:15).

The Author's Solution

It is humanity that is responsible for everything. Hence we should not simply be revolted by evil, of whatever sort it may be; we should also struggle and fight to bring about its disappearance. We have the mission and the capacity to do this because God wills it. Paradise continues to exist as a real possibility because God did not destroy it. God simply placed an angel before the entrance in order to halt our improper advance (Gn 3:24). The future is still open.

Speaking in popular terms, the author shows that God has not abandoned humankind. God makes clothes for the couple (Gn 3:21), protects Cain (Gn 4:15), and saves Noah from the flood caused by humanity's evil (Gn 6:9–9:17). When humanity eventually disintegrates to the point where joint action is no longer possible, God summons Abraham in order to reach all others through him (Gn 12:1–3). Thus begins salvation history.

The human grouping that begins with Abraham might be considered "God's party" in the world. This group believes it is possible to eliminate evil with the power of God, to transform the world and fashion a Paradise of total peacefulness. Its roots are solid and true because it lives with God (Gn 17:1–2). It eliminates opposition and forms a people, the "people of God" (Ex 20:1–7). It does not exercise domination, nor is it protected for that purpose. Its purpose is service, and that is why it is called a "kingdom of priests" and a "holy nation" (Ex 19:5). The readers of the biblical account are members of this people. The author wants them to realize what it means to belong to the people of God. This people must be active in the world, recognizing the true meaning and purpose of life and carrying life forward by resistance to evil and transformation of existing conditions. It keeps up its hope, which is guaranteed by God's will for good.

With the coming of Jesus Christ, God's plan took on concrete form. Paradise became a fact in Jesus' resurrection. That is why Paul regards Jesus as a "new Adam" (see Rom 5:12–19), and why the author of the book of Revelation describes the future awaiting us in images derived from the earthly Paradise (see Rv 21:4; 22:2–3).

Response to the Difficulties

Is the Paradise account myth or reality? It is reality insofar as it talks about the destiny of humanity. The harmony described in the Paradise account is a real possibility, guaranteed by the power of God that was manifested in the resurrection of Jesus Christ. It is myth insofar as the author used the mythical language and imagery of his day to express and transmit this reality to his readers.

Is it historical or merely a figment of the author's imagination? There is no reason to think that any Paradise once existed in the terms described in Genesis 2:4–25. What existed then, and still continues to exist today, is the real possibility for us to realize perfect harmony and peace when we allow ourselves to be guided by God's light and power. It makes no sense to ask: "Why didn't God give Adam and Eve a second chance?" God is continually offering this second chance to humanity, right up to our own day. The problem does not lie with God or with Adam and Eve. It is our problem now. Paradise will exist, will become a "historical" reality, when we will it and work for it. The only expedition that will ever be able to discover Paradise is the one that sets out resolutely for a better future.

The Bible says nothing positively or negatively about evolution. The Bible is rather concerned with the human problem and seeks to offer us God's view of life. There is neither contradiction nor agreement between the two accounts of the creation of the human being (Gn 1:26, the human being created last; and Gn 2:7, the human being created first). These are two different narratives, each with its own objective.

What about the river that feeds the four major streams in the world of that age (Gn 2:10–14)? It is a literary device to express the ideal fertility of the earth. The formation of the human being from the dust of the ground is another literary image designed to show that in God's hands the human being is like a piece of clay in the hands of a potter: wholly dependent on God and very fragile (see Jer 18:6). The formation of woman from the rib of man is a concrete way of visualizing a popular Hebrew saying: "bone from my bones" (Gn 2:23). It is a way of explaining the divine origin and mystery of sexual attraction, which we should not abuse.

What about the serpent as the concretization of the devil? This is mentioned in the book of Wisdom (2:24). Humankind's original error was the abuse of liberty, disobedience of God's law as expressed in the Ten Commandments.

What concrete form did that first sin take? No one knows, and the Bible does not say. What the Bible does tell us is that at the time the author was putting together his final narrative, the root evil took the concrete form of succumbing to the false religion of the Canaanites. We today must do what the biblical author did. We must look around us to see what concrete form is being taken by that "original sin," what today is the "serpent" enticing us to be unfaithful to God and human beings.

If the biblical author were alive today, his description would be quite different. He would closely scrutinize our present-day situation, try to pinpoint the source of contemporary evils, and then probably offer a different description of the ideal world.

For example, he might present it as a developed nation in which everyone was paid an adequate wage and worked a forty-hour week; in which all owned their own home, shared the profits of economic enterprise, and knew how to read and write. In this modern Paradise social and individual well-being would take complete priority over greed for profit. There would be no exploitation or violence or foreign domination. There would be no speeding or accidents on the highway, no slums or shantytowns, no generation gap or educational problems. Life and safety would be a sure thing, so that there would be no need for the army or police. In short, the world would be in complete harmony, very different from what it is now.

This Paradise should exist. It is possible to construct such a future. And so we are faced with the same questions that were posed to the readers of the Genesis account: Why isn't the world like that? What stops our progress toward such a future? Who or what is responsible? How are we to act so that the world can be transformed into the world as it should be? The Bible thus attempts to raise questions that are far more serious and complex than questions of a purely historical nature. Historical questions can even distract us from the really important issues and alienate us from the world around us.

The biblical description of Paradise is a public confession, a manifesto of opposition, a cry of hope, and a summons to transform the existing world.

The author does not "prove" the existence of an "original sin." He simply verifies its existence and tries to determine what form it is taking in his own day. He is not concerned about elaborating a theory as to how evil entered the world; he is trying to present a strategy for getting it out of the world.

The doctrine of original sin was later clarified by Paul (Rom 5:12–19; 1 Cor 15:21–22). Sin affects us down to our very roots, but it does not eliminate our capability for doing good. Insofar as our personal sins multiply, we ratify that original sin. We eat the forbidden fruit and add to the "culpable" evils of humanity. Future generations will inherit the evil we have helped to maintain and intensify.

Baptism makes us capable of facing up to evil. It involves us with that group of people who believe in God's plan and who are trying to carry it out in history; they hope in God and expect God to help them in and through Jesus Christ.

2

ABRAHAM

In Search of the Absolute

Genesis 12–25 deals with Abraham. His life was not an easy one, but he enjoyed the advantage of having God close by his side. God stepped in, spoke to him, and gave direction to Abraham's life. But what about today? Where is that same God? Has God changed or have we become worse?

If the story of Abraham is merely meant to offer me an example upon which to reflect as I try to draw conclusions about my own life, then I would prefer to recall such figures as Pope John XXIII, Martin Luther King, Jr., and Mahatma Gandhi. These people were closer to my life here and now. Abraham lived in a totally different situation.

Moreover, Christ has already come. Abraham prepared the way for his coming. Why should we continue to focus our attention on the old when the new has already arrived? After all, when the building is finished we take away the scaffolding.

There is also the danger we might use our purported concern with the life of Abraham as a subterfuge and an excuse for in-activity. Confusing such concern with an interest in religion, we might talk ourselves into believing that we are good people who are carrying out our duties. In reality we may be completely failing to do what has to be done to change the world for the better.

These questions and difficulties are serious ones. They call into question the usefulness of the figure of Abraham for us today. How can the ancient texts really help us to solve our present-day problems and find God in the reality of everyday life? We repeat what was said earlier regarding the Paradise account: our customary way of approaching the figure of Abraham does not correspond with the aim of the biblical author.

The Bible's Viewpoint on Abraham

These are varied ways of commemorating a historical fact. If we consider them closely, we will soon realize that none of them gives a precise version of the original fact itself, which is lost in the obscurity of past history. People have different opinions as to what actually happened back then.

Picture a monument, for example, that has been constructed section by section over a long period of time. Since its various sections have been added at different points in history, the end result is a heterogenous affair that does not seem to be all of one piece. Each part tells us something about the vision of freedom and independence held by those responsible for that particular section. The biblical narratives about Abraham are very much like that.

Abraham lived somewhere around 1800–1700 B.C.E. With him began something that may have been small in itself, but that the Hebrew people came to value more and more. The descendants of Abraham recorded and celebrated this basic fact in accordance with the significance that it had for their own lives. As each succeeding century went by, descriptions were elaborated to fit the outlook of those living at the time. Finally, in the fifth century B.C.E., someone worked up the final edition of the story we now find in the Bible. It contains elements from four previous descriptions, as scholars have documented over the past fifty or sixty years. Thus the biblical narrative on Abraham is disconnected and heterogenous.

It is therefore difficult for us to know exactly what happened, because the Bible is not interested in that. The biblical writers wanted to present the figure of Abraham to the people of their day in such a way that they could learn from him how they might discover God and journey with God through life.

But doesn't this amount to a falsifying of history? No, not really. You can take a snapshot photo of someone or you can take an x-ray. The photographic plates will reveal two completely different things. Most history books try to take photographs of past facts and events. The Bible takes x-rays of the same events. Though different, the two sets of pictures are authentic.

Moreover, the full import and scope of an event is not always appreciated when the event is actually taking place. Only at a distance, over a long period of time, does the event show up clearly. When you start to round a big curve, you do not always notice the size of the curve at first. Only later can you look back and see how much of a curve it was and where it began. When Abraham started on the "curve" that would change his whole life, he himself probably did not pay too much attention to it. But later, when the Hebrew people looked back from a distance, they became aware of the fact that their existence as a nation belonging to God began back there with Abraham. The Bible does not describe the event as Abraham lived it, but rather as the Hebrew people saw it much later in and through the problems of each succeeding age.

Abraham's Life

These remarks may raise questions in the reader's mind: What, then, was Abraham's life really like? What exactly happened when God entered our life? What was the concrete happening in which the Hebrew people experienced the start of God's active intervention? Knowing the answer to such questions will help us take an x-ray of our lives and thus find the signs of God's presence and involvement with us.

We know Abraham lived in approximately the nineteenth or eighteenth century before Christ. At God's bidding he left Ur of the Chaldees (in present-day Iraq, near the Persian Gulf) and went up as far as the city of Haran in Assyria (present-day Syria). Then he came down to Palestine, continued on to Egypt, and finally returned to Palestine. There he died in the town of Hebron. Abraham was in continuing contact with God, and he acted upon God's bidding. This is clear to anyone who reads the pertinent chapters in Genesis (12–25).

Here two factors should be mentioned that will clarify the matter from a historical point of view. (1) In those days there was a large migratory movement that brought people from the Persian Gulf area up through Syria and then down to Palestine and Egypt. Abraham was one of those many migrants, indistinguishable from the rest. (2) All the peoples and tribes involved in these migrations in search of better land had gods of their own. They were "family gods" for the most part, and everything done by those peoples was done at the bidding of their gods.

Looking at the facts from outside, then, one might be inclined to draw the conclusion that Abraham was in no way different from the other migrants, not even in terms of his faith, that he was just another face in the crowd.

What did those people of antiquity mean when they spoke of "God"? What type of God was it: the God of the Bible or another god? To some extent at least, the religion shared by all those desert peoples had grown up in the following manner: It was evident that life depended on harmony in nature and the universe. Welcome rain came in the spring; the seasons followed their regular cycle each year; the animal herds were replenished when the animals went into heat; a plentiful supply of water irrigated the fields; and the continuing round of sun and moon, day and night, helped to ensure life from day to day. People could find in nature the things they needed for subsistence. It was obvious, however, that life was constantly threatened by unpredictable forces: storms, floods, diseases. People realized that it was impossible for them to exert much influence over those forces for harmony or those for disorder. The forces were stronger than the people, and the people did not have any explanation for them. People came to feel that those forces were unearthly or divine. If life was to continue, the forces would have to be beneficent. People thus began to worship those forces, and religion came into being. Hence if people wanted to live a decent and secure life as *human beings,* they would have to honor the gods. Woe to those who did not! They would jeopardize their own life and that of others, because the gods might grow irritated and stop maintaining the forces of harmony and order.

Those "gods" were not God in fact. They were expressions of fear and hope, of the desire to go on living. The worship rendered to the gods was an expression of the *will to succeed and prosper in life*. Abraham was a sincere human being, an authentic man of his own day. He sought to prosper in life by worshiping the God he had inherited from his father (see Judith 5:7).

Today science has destroyed that ancient outlook on harmony and disorder in the universe. These realities are not the result of divine forces. The sun does not rise because God pulls it up in the sky. Our whole view of the matter has changed, thanks to modern science. But one thing has not changed. *We still have a persistent wish to succeed and prosper in life.* Human beings still want to preserve life, to be faithful, to do what their consciences bid them. In Abraham's day people did this by worshiping various divinities and using cultic magic. Today many people still do the same, looking for anything that might give meaning to their lives.

Abraham was looking for an ideal in life, for some *absolute value*. He was searching for something that would have supreme value, so that everything else would be relative by comparison. And he sought this value in the realm of religious living, as many people still do today. In our day, however, there are also people who look elsewhere for such a value. They do not consider religion, or God, or any divine element. Instead they put value on their work to benefit their family, on their efforts to build a more humane world, or on their professional life as a doctor, lawyer, or whatever.

Our conviction is that this is the way we find fulfillment in life and prosper as human beings. The basic preoccupation is still the same, even though it may take quite different forms today. In Abraham's day people related in a vertical way with "the deity." Today many people have a horizontal relationship with "humanity." They want to work for others and to contribute to the welfare of all.

God's Entry into Life

In telling us how God entered Abraham's life, the Bible focuses a strong x-ray beam on our own lives. It shows us the precise point where God breaks through into the life of a human being. It tells us that God enters life and is revealed to us precisely when and where we make a conscious effort *to be real human beings,* i.e., to fulfill the ideal proposed. That is precisely how God entered the life of Abraham.

This breakthrough is hardly perceptible at the start. God, traveling incognito, gets on the bus of life and pays the fare. God shoulders through the standing passengers and strikes up a conversation with Abraham. God does not walk up with a business card reading "Creator" and then spell out everything to be done. Instead God dons a disguise, sidles in, and gradually wins a place in Abraham's life.

The ancient deities were generally projections of humankind's deepest fears and desires. In and through the concrete forms that life took, the outline and visage of *Someone* took concrete form. Abraham and his people came to perceive an *active presence* in and beyond those forms. It was not identical with the forms themselves, and it gradually made its presence known and felt by the weight of its own evidence. No longer was it a deity that was basically dependent on human beings. It was Someone on whom human beings depended. Gradually, as time went on, this Someone would correct our ways of living. Abraham had now started out on a wide and decisive curve whose full dimensions would be discerned only much later by the Hebrew people. In and through the forms of worship people used to honor the impersonal divine forces, there gradually appeared the lineaments of the true God. The latter grew out of the former, much as a flower blooms from the bud.

The great lesson to be learned from all this is one that answers an important human question: Where is God? Where can I find God? The answer is that God enters human life and is discovered wherever human beings are trying to be faithful to themselves and others, wherever they are looking for an absolute value and trying to live it. It is there that we too must look for God today. It is there that we must try to discern the features of this *Someone* in whom we believe. God is not to be found first and foremost in cultic worship. Our worship has value only insofar as it embodies what we are living in our day-to-day lives.

Abraham accepted this presence and allowed it to have an influence on his life. Seen from the outside, nothing apparently had changed. On the inside, however, a light had begun to shine. Gradually it would begin to cast its glow all around, illuminating every corner of the universe. People would come to see that this *Someone* was God, the Creator of heaven and earth. That is why the figure of Abraham was so important and meaningful for those who would come after him.

But if all that went so unnoticed at the beginning, then how does one explain the constant dialogue between God and Abraham that is recounted in the Bible? Well, dialogue is communication established between two people, and it can take countless forms. When a married man takes a trip, he takes things with him that remind him of his wife. There is a dialogue between them because of the *presence* of his wife in his life. Only he senses and appreciates this presence, because only he lives in the friendship and love shared between him and his wife. When you love someone, everything around you can evoke recollections of that person. The dialogues put in terms of human language in the Bible are concrete expressions of the feelings that the Hebrew people had for God. They lived in friendship with God, and the dialogues helped to express what they had perceived about God. When people accept the presence of God in their lives and believe in God, then dialogue is established that has its own laws. It may seem strange to someone on the outside, but it is perfectly understandable to the person who is living in the presence of God.

When we read the story of Abraham, we see a human being just like us. He too is trying to prosper in life. In and through this effort he came to encounter the true God. But God was no closer to Abraham than God is to us today. Why, then, do we not encounter God today? Perhaps it is because our sight is bad. We are so preoccupied with a particular image of God that we feel that something else cannot possibly be God. Our receiving set is not tuned to the same wavelength that God is using to send out the summons. The God who was revealed to Abraham, our God, is a God of human beings. Moreover, God is not afraid to hide. You may not see a butterfly when you are out hunting eagles; you may overlook the flowers if you are looking for trees.

God is present and is revealed in many things: in a mother's dedication to her family, in the labor of a working man for his children, in the struggle of young people to create a more humane world, in the joy produced by the presence of a friend, and in the mutual interchange of understanding and consolation. It is in such things that we discover the presence of God and gradually trace the lineaments of God's face.

Conclusions

God enters the life of a human being silently. God enters calmly and quietly through the ordinary events of everyday life. It is there that God is revealed to those who have eyes to see. When a person finally takes note of God's presence, God has probably been there a long time already. But then why does the Bible depict God's entrance into Abraham's life as a brusque and almost violent affair (Gn 12:1–4)? The reason is that it is easier to see the beginning of the curve, and the about-face it requires, from a distance. Even though God enters a human life imperceptibly, the fact is that God wants a total "conversion," a complete break with the past, a transformation of one's life.

God will be Abraham's future: "I will fulfill my covenant between myself and you and your descendants after you . . . to be your God" (Gn 17:7). Abraham, in other words, is to give up the other deities he had been following in his search for a prosperous life. The God of the covenant will be his guarantee of success. Thus God's entrance into Abraham's life confronts him with an either/or option. He must abandon the gods of the past and choose God alone (monotheism). If Abraham agrees to follow this new God, then he must travel the road of life as this God wants him to travel it (the ethical aspect of revealed religion); and his future will be assured by the fidelity and power of this God (hope in the future, messianism).

The difficult thing is to accept God's conditions and walk in faith. Abraham is presented to us as a man who did just that. He had to leave his homeland in order to obtain a new homeland, but he owned little more than a burial plot when it came time for him to die. He had to give up his family and native people in order to become the father of a new nation, but at the time of his death he had only one son. At the time that God promised him a large posterity, Abraham did not have any children and it did not seem that he would be able to have any. It was hard to believe in God's word because there was little proof. Then Isaac was born, and God eventually asked Abraham to sacrifice him. Abraham was ordered to kill the one and only hope he had of becoming the father of a great nation. But Abraham was willing to do that, to rely wholly on the word of God (Gn 22:1–18; Heb 11:19).

God's attitude seems to be contradictory at times. God promises Abraham a large posterity, then orders him to kill his only son. God tells Abraham to leave his homeland for another, yet Abraham did not gain a real homeland while he was alive. At the same time Abraham, through his faith and his absolute confidence in God, became God's close friend and confidant (Gn 18:17–19).

This description of the figure of Abraham is not meant to correspond to the real life of Abraham, but rather to the ideal of faith in the era of the biblical author. This was how his fellow Hebrews must live if they were to be worthy members of the nation founded by Abraham.

Response to the Difficulties

Where is God? As the exposition in the preceding pages would indicate, the story of Abraham is meant to provide us with an answer to that question. The story does not allow us to draw many conclusions about our own life today, or even about Abraham's life. Its purpose is to invite and encourage the reader to be another Abraham, to truly make the effort to prosper in life, to be sincere with self and others in order to discover the active presence of God.

Christ has already come, it is true. But he has not yet come for many people, perhaps not even for us. No one lives wholly in and with Christ. The important thing today is that people find out how they are to live, so that they can find their complete fulfillment in Christ. The story of Abraham tells us how to do that. The first step is to live a sincere life, to love truth, and honestly to seek the absolute: "All who are not deaf to truth listen to my voice" (Jn 18:37; see Jn 3:17–21; 8:44–45). If people take that pathway in life, then they will encounter the face of God.

The aim of the biblical account is not to have us analyze the story of Abraham solely in terms of historical happening, to find out how he actually lived and rest content with that. In seeking out answers to difficulties and problems of a historical nature, we are faced with other difficulties that are far more complex and important. Do I look for God where God can be found, or do I prefer to stay somewhere where it will be very hard to find God? Do I look for God in real life or elsewhere? If other people know nothing about God, are we Christians not guilty of failing to reveal the true face of God to them in and through our own lives?

3

EXODUS

God in the History of Liberation

The story of the Exodus seems to be one continuing miracle from beginning (the call of Moses) to end (the crossing of the Jordan after forty years of wandering in the desert). Without denying the reality of the miracle, one must admit that it seems strange we do not run into similar miracles today when so many people and nations need the same sort of liberation. Has God changed or have we become worse? Where is the miracle?

We believe in a liberator God. But where is that God today? Liberty is dying in the hearts of human beings, of both the rich and the poor, for a variety of reasons that we ourselves have helped to produce. Where is our God and God's liberty?

Many people have grown tired of waiting hopefully and have moved into action designed to bring about liberation. We have seen this happen in Czechoslovakia, Hungary, Vietnam. We have seen it happen among blacks in the United States. National Liberation Fronts have sprung up as workers and others on the margin of society take cognizance of their situation and move toward concrete action. Does all that have something to do with our God? People involved in such movements usually block God out. They don't think about God, and they don't seem to have any need of God.

The following accusation is often leveled against Christians: You say that you are free, when in reality you are bound by laws and traditions that have been imposed by your so-called liberator God. You talk about liberty, but you don't display it in your own lives.

You are like poor bums who go around claiming to be the descendants of a Roman emperor. We, on the other hand, are truly free because we have liberated ourselves from that God of yours. Of what advantage or use is it to believe in your liberator God?

These are serious questions and difficulties. They raise problems about what the Exodus account has to say concerning the process of liberation.

The Bible's Viewpoint on the Exodus

There are many descriptions of the Exodus in the Bible. We find them in various books (Exodus, Numbers, Deuteronomy, and Wisdom 10–19; Psalms 78, 105, 106, and 135; and in passages of the prophetic books, particularly Isaiah 40–55).

However, the various books that recall the Exodus event were written by different people at different points in history. Every sort of literary genre is used to describe the Exodus: prose and poetry, history and prophecy, hymn and narrative, liturgical text and wisdom literature. This would suggest that we are dealing with an event that was of the utmost importance in the life of the Hebrew nation. They recounted it and commented on it throughout their history. What was the reason for this great and enduring interest in the Exodus?

We can uncover this reason if we look at the many ways in which they spoke of the Exodus. In their descriptions of the event we find certain particular features that call for some consideration and explanation. First, there are frequent repetitions in the book of Exodus itself, and some incidents are recounted twice: the story of the manna, the quail, and the water struck from a rock; the call of Moses; the handing down of the decalogue. Second, there are obvious exaggerations in the accounts of the Exodus at various points: for example, in the poetic song of Exodus 15 and in the account of the plagues in the book of Wisdom. Third, we are faced with disconcerting uncertainties—about the plagues for example. Psalm 78 recounts seven plagues, Psalm 105 recounts eight plagues, and the book of Exodus mentions ten plagues. We also know that the book of Exodus was composed from three older traditions that did not agree on the number of the plagues. The Yahwist account, dating from the tenth century, had seven plagues; the Elohist account, dating from between the ninth and eighth centuries, had five plagues; and the Priestly account, dating from between the sixth and fifth centuries, had five plagues, which do not correspond to the five enumerated in the Elohist account. Fourth, the miraculous aspect of the whole event is gradually accentuated with the passage of time. The Yahwist account says that only water drawn from the Nile turned to blood (Ex 4:9); the Elohist account says that all the water of the Nile turned to blood (Ex 7:20); and the Priestly account says that all the water in Egypt turned to blood (Ex 7:19). Much later the book of Wisdom, composed around the first century before Christ, says even more fantastic things about the plagues.

So what were the plagues in reality? It seems that the author or final editor of the book of Exodus decided that ten was a good number. But what really happened? How exactly did water turn to blood? Is it possible to find out how things really happened?

These peculiar literary details, uncovered by modern exegesis, indicate that the biblical authors had certain basic concerns and a particular viewpoint. The basic concern is not primarily to narrate history and give a journalistic report of what happened during the Exodus. The primary concern in describing the event is to convey its import for the life of the people, a life constantly evolving. The biblical account is not a description of the event; it is an *interpretation* of it. Hence in reading the Bible we cannot accept everything as literal fact, because that would involve us in contradictions. The biblical account itself is not primarily interested in the material aspect, nor does it take everything literally; for the various accounts reveal repetitions, exaggerations, and uncertainties. The basic point in which the Bible is interested, the sense that it derives from the facts of the Exodus, is that in the Exodus God was revealed to the Hebrew people and became their God. This contact resulted in a commitment by the Hebrew people: the commitment of the covenant.In its description of the event, the Bible wants to bring out this divine dimension and to show that God was present and operative in the Exodus events. This helps to explain why the miraculous aspect was stressed as time went on. It was a suitable way of helping the reader to realize that there was a divine dimension at work.

The example I've used before may help to clarify this point. History books are like photographs; they describe what might be seen with the naked eye. The Bible is like an x-ray; on the exposed plate we find things that cannot be seen with the naked eye. On our own we cannot see or touch the operative presence of God (Jn 1:18), but the x-ray of faith perceives and reveals God's presence. The viewpoint of the historians is different from that of the Bible. Their instruments of observation and measurement are not the same, and hence the results of their inquiry are different. While their results do not contradict one another, they are different aspects of one and the same reality. The biblical description tries to present the facts in such a way that the readers will see the divine dimension in the past and thus be able to perceive and shoulder responsibility for the divine dimension in what is taking place around them. Hence if the readers are to grasp the message of the Bible, they must try to develop the same outlook the author had in describing and presenting events.

Modern Science and the Bible

Adopting a historian's perspective and applying the criteria of modern scholarship to the Bible, we obtain a more accurate historical knowledge of the events that actually took place. This has been done, and we can conclude the following: The plagues were natural phenomena that took place in the Nile region. The crossing of the Red Sea was made possible by a low tide, which was helped along by a strong wind (Ex 14:21). The manna was some form of edible resin. These conclusions seem undeniable and certain, for such phenomena could occur in Egypt even today. Thus scientific scholarship can explain the events in purely natural terms and show that there was nothing extraordinary about them. What took place was a successful human attempt at liberation, like many others that have taken place before and after the time of Moses. At first glance such conclusions bewilder us.

The results of historical research, however, are in the category of photographs. The Bible does not deny them; it presupposes them as the basis for its x-ray analysis. It probes deeper and concludes that God was at work in the events described. Historical scholarship, for its part, cannot deny the conclusions of the Bible because such a denial would exceed its premises and the capabilities of its observational tools. The tools of scientific scholarship cannot register God's activity. God's presence is perceptible only to the person open to it in and through faith.

Thus the Bible shows a certain lack of concern and interest in the material aspect of events as history. Biblical authors get involved in useless repetitions, exaggerations, and even contradictions. They add details or take away certain features, changing perspective as they deal with facts. It does not bother them to do this, for their main concern is to communicate the deeper message lying buried in the facts and events. The point of the Exodus account is that God was present and at work in that successful human effort at liberation. The biblical writer wants to open the eyes of his readers to what is happening around them in their own day. He wants us to realize that God is involved with the many liberation movements springing up around us today.

I cannot see microbes with the naked eye, but I can verify their existence and activity in the pains of a disease. And if I have the right instrument, I can even see them. Mere reasoning may not enable me to see the God of Exodus in today's world, but I can ascertain the results of God's presence: people becoming freer, more human, more aware and responsible. And if I possess the proper instrument, that is, faith, I can see the sign of God's presence in all this.

What happened in the time of Moses is still happening today and will continue to happen throughout history. Events have a fourth dimension not visible to the naked eye. If people become overly impressed with one viewpoint on things, they may become insensitive to other possible viewpoints. If people are interested only in the "scientific" view of things, they may suffer a diminution in the ability to perceive the hidden aspect of things, to profit from the insights of literature, art, music, philosophy. When human beings lock themselves up inside their scientific achievements and their own selves, their openness to God may atrophy. Eventually they may cease to give any importance to the divine dimension of events that is revealed by faith. In many instances, however, the fault is not that of science or scholarship, but that of those who profess but do not really live the faith. The way they live their lives seems to prove that faith does not have much to contribute to the progress and growth of humanity.

Seen in this perspective, the Bible can be a light that will help us to discover the hidden divine dimension in our lives. To be specific, the Exodus account can reveal the operative presence of God in certain sectors of human life where we do not usually look for it.

The Divine Dimension of the Exodus

If we examine the Exodus event solely in terms of human criteria, we would have to say that it was a successful attempt to obtain liberation from the yoke of oppression that the pharaoh had imposed on the Hebrews. It was a successful quest for freedom and independence, like that undertaken by many other people before and after Moses. People continue to seek the same liberation today because the yearning for liberty is a very powerful one.

The Bible looks at this same event in the light of faith. It relates the historical events, but it does not put its main stress on the material reality of the events that took place. Rather it stresses the concrete experience the people lived through and their unshakable conviction that God was present and at work in it. The Bible views that struggle for liberation as a manifestation of God's presence among human beings and as the start of a journey that leads to Christ and his resurrection. Through its description the Bible draws a lesson that is meant to help us perceive the divine dimension in events taking place today. Where there is a sincere effort at liberation, be it group or individual, there we hear the friendly voice of our liberator God calling out to us. In such efforts lies the road leading human beings to Christ and the fullness of the resurrection.

But is it possible, we might ask, that the biblical view of the Hebrew people's liberation from Egypt was the result of group autosuggestion? That certainly is possible, but then how would one explain the results? I can deny the presence of microbes, but if I do then I must explain the illness in some other way. The results of the Exodus account are such that no explanation seems to be quite as satisfactory as the one offered by the Bible. In this particular case, historical scholarship finds it impossible to find one cause that will adequately explain the results. This seems to speak in favor of the authenticity of the interpretation offered by the people who lived through the events that were part of their liberation from Egypt.

The end result, which history can verify but cannot satisfactorily explain, is this: As the Hebrew people continued on in their journey toward liberation, they became freer and more responsible. They became more sensitive to human problems, more aware and more loving. They found more strength and courage to keep moving on the road of life, to keep their heads held high where others might have despaired. All this is stated in the Bible and verified by historical investigation. It was evident to the Hebrew people. They saw it as a consequence of the Exodus and as a by-product of God's activity. Now if this vision of life rendered such great service to human beings where other visions had failed, then it merits confidence. A real-life experience with God was at the origin of the Hebrew people, and it enabled them to attain their liberty. It hardly seems right to classify it as some form of group autosuggestion.

The Initial Episode of Liberation History

We find two currents running parallel in the history of the chosen people. On the one hand there is a growing awareness of oppression. You cannot liberate people who are unaware of the oppression under which they are living. They would not know what liberty is, and hence they could not avail themselves of it. Running parallel to this growing awareness of oppression, we find a progressive process of liberation. Once their consciousness has been raised regarding their situation, the people commit themselves to action on behalf of liberation. They see it as their inalienable task. The Bible makes it clear that both these currents have something to do with God.

In that sense the Exodus was just a starting point. Consciousness-raising began at the point where the oppression was most keenly felt. The people first noticed their cultural and political oppression. But the consciousness-raising work of God continued after the Exodus itself. Through God's chosen leaders it continued to work on the people, moving toward the ultimate root of all oppression: egotism, which closes us up within ourselves and tempts us to create oppressive structures at every level of life.

The task of liberation did not stop either. Begun at the Exodus from Egypt, it continued on through the history of the chosen people. Finally, the root of oppression was eradicated through the liberating love preached by Jesus Christ. The true liberty that God envisions for humankind is that which is born of love for God and one's fellow human beings. The Exodus initiated by Moses reached its destination in the resurrection of Jesus Christ to true life. It is summed up in the gospel message: "Whoever cares for his own safety is lost; but if a man will let himself be lost for my sake and for the Gospel, that man is safe" (Mk 8:35).

God has no need of our liberty. God is not interested in giving us liberty as if it were a present. God is free. It is contact with God that frees us and puts in our hearts the seed of true liberty.

This seed was sown in the hearts of the Hebrew people at the time of the Exodus, and it grew from there. They had lived in Egypt for a long time (Ex 12:40) before they realized the oppression from which they were suffering. Only when it became intolerable did they take cognizance of it and give expression to their desire for liberation (Ex 1:1–2:25). Then God responded to their plea, summoning Moses to carry out the task of liberation (Ex 3:7–10, 6:2–8).

Although the activity of God in the Exodus is greatly stressed, because the biblical writer sees events in the light of his fuller faith, the artifices used by Moses to obtain his objective are clearly brought out. The ruse was that the Hebrews wanted to make a three-day pilgrimage into the desert (Ex 5:1–3; 7:16; 9:1; 8:25–27). To avoid perilous encounters with the pharaoh's army, Moses led the people south toward the Red Sea (Ex 13:17–18). He managed to cross the river because a strong dry wind held back the tide (Ex 14:21) and whipped up a sandstorm in the desert so that the visibility of the Egyptians was hindered (Ex 14:19–20).

But all the stratagems of human calculation were not the most important thing. Most important for them and for us was the new faith that was born of that experience. The people came to believe that God was journeying with them and that Moses spoke to them as God's own interpreter (Ex 14:31). The biblical account seeks to stir up the same faith in its readers, to stimulate them to the same liberative effort, and to get them to celebrate God's liberative presence in their midst: "Sing to the Lord, for he has risen up in triumph" (Ex 15:21). Thus the Exodus account sheds light on a journey that began in Egypt and has not ended yet. It is the journey of us all toward the promised land where the full liberty of God holds sway.

This vision of life offers us a new perspective on the true import of the events that are taking place today. It is in the concrete and careful plan of liberation that God has always been made known to us and we have been led to Christ. Today this plan may take many varied forms. We overcome our personal limitations by work and study. We strive to overcome some vice or fault that is weighing down on us. We undergo psychotherapy to free ourselves of complexes and unfortunate conditionings. A doctor frees fellow human beings from the oppression of bodily ills, a teacher helps to overcome the ravages of illiteracy, a skilled technician teaches people how to take care of their health or plant a garden. Nations try to free themselves from colonialism and imperialism, workers unite to protect their rights, international bodies formulate declarations about the basic rights of human beings. People in general try to overcome all the varied forms of egotism, denounce injustice and torture, and promote international development. The awesome work of liberation takes countless forms.

In and through all these efforts the human race journeys painfully through its own Exodus in search of total liberty. We all have our own Exodus to make from childhood to adulthood, as does each societal group and nation. Humanity as a whole is immersed in its Exodus; as Vatican II put it, it is radically and wholly immersed in "the paschal mystery of Christ." In this whole process there is an opening through which God enters, makes this presence felt, and acts on behalf of human beings. We can find God there if we will. From the outside there is nothing special to be seen, but the eye of faith can discern the underlying divine dimension in everything that human beings suffer and live through.

Must we conclude, then, that everything done in the name of liberty is endorsed by God? Such a conclusion goes far beyond the premises. There are so-called liberation movements that actually lead to greater oppression because they produce hatred and egotistical concentration on the narrow interests of one particular group. How are we to distinguish them from authentic liberation movements? What is the criterion for proper discernment?

The Exodus Story as a Basis for Discernment

Moses was educated at the pharaoh's court (Ex 2:5–10). It was customary in his day to do this with children of the nobility from occupied countries. They were brought to Egypt and educated there so that later they would serve the best interests of Egypt. Moses did not follow through with this planned career. Revolting against the degrading situation in which his people found themselves, he slew an Egyptian soldier (Ex 2:11–12). The deed may well have been connected with an attempt at liberation that failed. In any case Moses had to flee (Ex 2:14–22). In exile God approached him a second time and bade him to return to Egypt and free his people (Ex 2:23–4:18). After putting up a great deal of resistance, Moses obeyed and undertook this mission.

The liberty for which he was now going to fight steadfastly was no longer defined in purely negative terms, i.e., freedom from the political oppression of the pharaoh. It now had positive content as well. If people are fighting just to be free from something, then they know only what is not wanted. Lacking any criterion or standard to direct their action forward, they move into the future with their eyes turned backward. The liberty that now appeared on the horizon for Moses, however, was part of a larger plan that God had in mind: God meant to free the Hebrew people from Egypt so that they might be God's people and God might be their God (Ex 6:6–8). The Hebrew people were to be free for something, free for a covenant with God. They would know what they did not want because they would know what they did want in life. They had a criterion for acting and moving into the future.

This objective would give direction to the activity of Moses and the Hebrew people throughout their history. It would give solid content to the freedom for which they yearned. If something did not contribute toward this objective, then it would not really contribute to their liberty. Thus it is clear that God's entrance into the lives of human beings is a light that provides both correction and orientation. The first correction, or conversion, took place in the mind of Moses; he was turned from killing to consciousness-raising.

Not everything done in the name of liberty leads to the liberty that God has in mind for the people. By the same token, the effort to attain liberation does not always take place in a peaceful, nonviolent way. The first reaction to Moses' attempt at liberation was a hardening of heart on the part of the pharaoh and intensified oppression of the Hebrew people (Ex 5:1–18). This in turn led the Hebrew people to revolt against Moses, since he had whipped up the Egyptians and given them further cause to kill the Hebrews (Ex 5:19–21). Moses protested the intensified oppression (Ex 5:22–6:1), but the pharaoh only stiffened further (Ex 7:12, 22; 8:15–19; 9:7, 12, 35; 10:20, 27). Moses had to overcome the fear and apathy of his own people, to convince them that the stiffening of the pharaoh was part of God's action to pave the way for their liberation (Ex 7:3–5; 9:35; 10:20, 27). The work of Moses essentially involved trying to make the Hebrew people aware of their oppression so that they would choose to work for liberation as a task imposed on them by God. Moses interpreted various signs and happenings as God's summons to the people and God's actions on their behalf. Moses let facts and events do the talking for him.

The pharaoh finally gave in, and the Hebrew people started out from Egypt (Ex 12:37). They began the journey to liberation as a task willed by God. But that journey was, as it always is, an ambiguous one. On the very threshold of freedom everything seemed to fall apart. Cornered between the sea and the Egyptian army, the Hebrew people lost heart and rebelled against Moses (Ex 14:11–12). Moses appealed to their faith, the people continued forward, and freedom came into being (Ex 14:30). In that we see revealed the faith of the leader in the cause that he was defending and promoting. He saw it as a victorious cause. Moses was not the one who provoked the violence. It was the pharaoh who did that because he did not want the Hebrew people to set out on the journey to freedom. It was much more convenient for him to have an enslaved people at his bidding.

Celebrating the Liberation Granted by God

The great experience of the Hebrew people was that God had liberated them and that they were God's people (Ex 19:4–6). Everything that befell them was viewed in the light of that fundamental faith. God was present in everything, arranging for the good of the people. Human shrewdness led the fleeing Hebrews to choose the less dangerous route heading toward the Red Sea, but they saw in this the guidance of God (Ex 13:17–18). They saw the hand of God in the strong wind that blew all night and kicked up a covering cloud of sand (Ex 14:20–21). This phenomenon helped to reduce the tide on the one hand and to provide a covering smoke screen on the other. The natural plagues, which are customary in Egypt, helped to create a general climate of confusion that abetted the flight to freedom. Seen in the x-ray light of faith, however, they became a revelation of God's liberative activity on their behalf. The Hebrew people and their leader managed to grasp the "signs of the time" and to carry out the objective of God, using artifice and stratagem when necessary.

The Exodus occurred at Passover, which was a customary pastoral feast of spring. The blood of a lamb was sprinkled on the doorpost to ward off the influence of evil spirits. It was on the occasion of that feast that the Hebrew people left Egypt; or they may have left to celebrate it in the desert. In later years the Passover ceased to be a feast designed to combat evil spirits; it became a commemoration of the people's liberation. A reminder of what God had done on their behalf, it gave them another chance to make a personal commitment to the further work of liberation. It helped to keep alive their hope for complete liberation in the future. The Hebrew feast of Passover (Hebrew *pesah*) was called *pascha* in Greek. This is why the life of those who believe in God and God's promise is sometimes called a "paschal" life. In other words, it is a life that involves a "passover" from oppression to liberation. The *pascha* of Christ was the authentic one because he passed over from death to enduring life with God, and it is there that we find true liberty.

The effort to achieve liberation and a continuing concern to celebrate that victory deeply marked the history of the Hebrew people and became its most characteristic feature.

SAMSON AND DELILAH

Folklore or Something More?

The story of Samson occupies a relatively large place in the book of Judges (chapters 13 to 16), approximately one-fifth of the whole book. It deals with his birth (Jgs 13), his marriage (Jgs 14), his exploits and battles with the Philistines (Jgs 15), and his tragic but glorious end (Jgs 16). It is one of those episodes in the Bible about which we don't know exactly what to think.

Samson's attitudes did not conform to moral and ethical norms. Instead he did not seem to have any such norms; he followed his own impulses: the Bible mentions three women he was fond of. He killed people without the slightest scruple. His exploits and quarrels, most of them connected with love affairs, discomfited both his compatriots and their enemies. Samson did what he pleased and acted in accordance with the way he personally saw things. Is it really possible that the Bible can see the Spirit of God at work in his way of using force? What are we to think of the whole story? Wouldn't it be better suited to an X-rated movie? It could be unwise and even dangerous to imitate Samson, and yet the church continues to read the story of Samson today. Of what real use is it to us?

The Viewpoint of the Biblical Author

The book of Judges, written many years after the events it describes, is a patchwork quilt. The author constructs a new building

43

out of old bricks. The final editor or author of the book of Judges lived in the seventh century B.C.E., at a time when many people were talking about the need for thoroughgoing reforms in the life of the Hebrew nation. (This whole reform movement will be discussed in greater detail in chapter 6 below). Many people felt there would be complete chaos unless such reforms were enacted.

King Hezekiah (716–687 B.C.E.) tried to reform the life of the nation but the attempt foundered. Things went from bad to worse under the reign of Manasseh (687–642 B.C.E.) and Amon (642–640 B.C.E.). Then a young king, Josiah, took over the reins of government in 640 B.C.E. He had the sympathy of the people, and he was determined to pick up the urgent work of reform that had been neglected. At this time international tension had abated with the decline of Assyria. Thus a broad-based movement for national reform came into being, supported by government figures, the clergy, the prophets, and much of the population. It sought to implement the real constitution of the nation: the law of God. A new edition of that law, elaborated in what is now the book of Deuteronomy, had been composed around this time, having allegedly been "found" in the Temple.

During this period of general reform, someone had a clever idea. He decided to take advantage of all the popular traditions that had come down from the past in order to abet the reform movement. His basic theme was this: If someone reforms the life of the nation or paves the way for such reform, that person paves the way for a better future and helps to ensure its arrival. He was of the opinion that the general situation of moral and physical decay derived precisely from the fact that the Hebrew people were neglecting to observe the rights and duties spelled out in God's law. The people had to realize that fact, and he wrote his book to help them do it. His work is the book of Judges, in which we find the story of Samson.

The biblical author took all the ancient traditions of the era of the Judges and arranged them within a fixed schema that embodied his fundamental message. (1) When the Hebrew people stopped following the law of God during the period of the Judges, they lost their freedom and were oppressed by foreign powers (Jgs 2:1–3, 11–15; 3:7–8, 12–14; 4:1–2; 6:1–2; 10:6–8; 13:1). (2) When the Hebrew people repented for their sins and reformed their national life, God always raised up some leader on whom the power of the Spirit was bestowed in order to liberate the nation (Jgs 3:10, 15; 4:3ff; 6:7ff; 10:10ff). (3) This repentance and charismatic leadership resulted in a period of peace and tranquility in which the Hebrew people enjoyed liberty (Jgs 3:11–30; 5:31; 8:28). (4) When the Hebrew people once again abandoned the law of God, oppression returned and the same process was repeated.

That is how the biblical author saw the story of the Judges. The Judges were charismatic leaders raised up by God in response to the good will of the Hebrew people. It was God's consistent response to personal conversion and national reform. Thus the reader could be sure that such divine intervention was possible once again. The people simply had to pave the way for such intervention by adopting a thoroughgoing reform of their national life. Their God was the God of the Judges, and the power of God's Spirit would once again guarantee the success of their reform efforts. Thus the long-distant past of the Judges came to life for the writer's contemporaries. The point was simple: if things are to change for the better, we must do what our forebears did. The Hebrew author inserted the already existing story of Samson into the general context of his book. To make it fit into the general perspective and objective of his own work, he added a brief introduction: "Once more the Israelites did what was wrong in the eyes of the Lord, and he delivered them into the hands of the Philistines for forty years" Jgs 13:1). He also added a concluding sentence about Samson: "He had been judge over Israel for twenty years" (Jgs 16:31; see also Jgs 15:20). Thus an old story, without sacrificing any of its popular flavor, began to serve an important and useful function for the people of the writer's own day. It became a summons to them, challenging them to face their own situation with realistic faith and to pave the way for the manifestation of God's power. It raised a question in the reader's mind: "Who will be our Samson today? What leader deserves our support because the power of God is manifestly at work in him?" The biblical author clearly intended his readers to deduce that the young King Josiah was the man they were looking for.

Touchups to the Story

Some questions still remain, however. What about this story of Samson? Did it really happen? Is it true that God really approved of all that is recounted? Of what use are these questionable accounts of murder and love affairs? What really happened? Can we possibly know?

At this point two things should be mentioned. First of all, we are dealing here with popular or folk literature. Second, the stories arose in a very specific context, that is, in an age when the Hebrews were subject to the oppression of the Philistines.

Popular literature does not adhere to the rules of newspaper reporting. It is not interested in giving a photographic version of the facts. Such folk literature is very open to "gossip" that expands the narrative to suit the interests that hold sway at a given moment. Furthermore, since this particular literature arose in a context of oppression, it gave expression to the longings of the Hebrew people. They wanted to overthrow the Philistines and regain their freedom.

To give an example of the process at work, we can cite what might have happened during World War II. European Resistance fighters might have blown up some small bridge in a Nazi-occupied country. People would tell the story in hushed tones, and it would gradually spread. They would enjoy telling the story because it would relieve their tension and quicken their hopes. It would prove that there were forces at work for regaining the freedom that they all longed for. But as the story spread, the size of the bridge might grow to enormous dimensions and other phenomenal details might be added.

Something similar happened in ancient Israel. The Philistines overran the country and the Hebrew people suffered greatly. There were various heroes in its resistance movement against the Philistines. One of them was a figure named Samson, who put his stamp on a whole epoch. He was a man of great strength and courage and brutal audacity. Somehow he managed to keep alive the hopes of the Hebrew people and to pave the way for David's eventual over-throw of the Philistines many years later. Samson gradually became a legend. His story was touched up as it passed from mouth to mouth. It is now no longer possible to know exactly what he really did, just as it might be hard to find out the actual size of that bridge that was blown up.

The story woven around the person of Samson did have a real basis in history, but it was not designed to be an informational narrative about what actually happened. It came from a different source and it had a different objective. It arose as a way to give ex-pression and support to the hopes of the harried Hebrew people. It served as an escape valve, enabling the people to breathe a sigh of relief. The Hebrew people wanted to go on living their own lives and hoping for freedom. The story of Samson told them that it was possible to have hope and courage, to go on resisting the Philis-tines, because they had an even greater force on their side: the Spirit of God.

This concrete objective prompted them to add wondrous and miraculous details to the basic story. It is a patriotic rather than a historical narrative, designed to raise the consciousness of the He-brew people, keep them alert, and make sure that they do not give in to accommodation with the Philistine conquerors.

The Story of Samson

Samson's birth (Jgs 13). The description makes it clear that this child will be great. His father's name is Manoah ("tranquil"). The mother is supposedly sterile (Jgs 13:2), yet she gives birth to a boy child whose name means "fire." This suggests that God intervened in a special way. The story describes what happened as if Samson's birth had been foretold by an "angel of the Lord." This angel tells the mother that her child is to be consecrated wholly to God; thus she must observe certain rules (Jgs 13:4). The child himself is never to cut his hair (Jgs 13:5). Already, then, the reader can glimpse something of Samson's destiny and also the origin of his strength. It is rooted in his total dedication to God, which opened the way for the manifestation of the Spirit. In the Bible, prior annunciation of a birth is part of a general framework that tells the reader that the child to be born has a very special mission in the carrying out of God's plan. Such is the case with Jacob (Gn 25:21–26), Samuel (1 Sm 1:1–28), John the Baptist (Lk 1:5–25), and Jesus Christ (Lk 1:26–37).

Samson's marriage (Jgs 14). Samson was a nonconformist. He had a hankering for a Philistine woman, one of his people's enemies, and he decided to marry her. No one could dissuade him from that course (Jgs 14:1–3). Later on the Hebrew people saw the hand of God in this, mysteriously arranging everything for their benefit. It was Samson's betrothal to a Philistine woman that served as the occasion for the victorious struggle against the Philistine rulers (Jgs 14:4). In other words, God writes straight with crooked lines, and God's ways are not our ways. Verses 5–20 of this chapter are clearly a legendary accretion to some fact that we cannot pinpoint precisely. Samson slays a lion but does not tell his parents. He proposes a riddle during his wedding feast, but he loses the wager because his wife keeps pestering him for the answer and tells her compatriots when she gets it. Samson then has to pay up with thirty lengths of linen and thirty changes of clothing. He goes out and kills thirty Philistine men to get the clothing. The Bible says that "the spirit of the Lord suddenly seized him" (Jgs 14:19) just before he set out for this murderous work. Then Samson returns to his father's house and Samson's wife is given in marriage to the one who had been his best man.

Combat with the Philistines (Jgs 15). When Samson went to see his wife sometime later, he learned that his father-in-law had betrayed him by giving his wife to another man. In a rage he went out and grabbed three hundred foxes, tied their tails together two by two, fastened torches to each pair of tails, and then set the foxes loose in the cornfields of the Philistines. All their cultivated land was burned up (Jgs 15:4–5). The Philistines took revenge by burning Samson's wife and her father. Samson struck back by killing many Philistines in "a great slaughter" and then hid out in a cave (Jgs 15:6–8). The Philistines followed with a general attack on Samson's people, much to their puzzlement and dismay. Fearing worse problems, they sent out a posse of three thousand men to seize Samson and turn him over to the Philistines. Samson permitted his capture and surrender to the Philistines. But just as he was being handed over, the "spirit of the Lord suddenly seized him," He burst his bonds, picked up the jawbone of an ass, and slew a thousand men. Weary and thirsty after this exploit, he asked God for water. God spilt open a huge rock and water flowed out of it. God rewarded the slaughter of a thousand men with a miracle!

A tragic yet glorious end (Jgs 16). Samson went to Gaza, a Philistine city, and entered a house of prostitution. The Philistines, hoping to entrap him, locked the city gates. But Samson merely ripped up the locked doors of the city gate and the gateposts and carted them off with him to the top of a hill east of Hebron — a considerable distance from the city (Jgs 16:1–3). Then Samson developed a passion for another Philistine woman named Delilah. The Philistines worked up another plot against Samson in which Delilah would play the key role. She was to find out the secret of Samson's strength. Three times Samson led her astray with his answer, but the fourth time he revealed to her that the secret of his strength lay in his seven enormous locks of hair, which had never been cut. They were a mark of his consecration to God. The Philistines cut his hair while he was asleep, and so he did not have the strength to resist them when they came to capture him. They gouged out his eyes and imprisoned him.

The underlying lesson is that when we allow a third party to interfere between us and God, when we stray from God, we lose our strength and courage and become the hapless prey of human malice.

The Philistines had planned a great festival in honor of their god, Dagon. In the meantime Samson's hair had been growing back and his strength returning. In the midst of the festival Samson brought down the Philistine temple, killing himself and more Philistines than he had slain during his entire lifetime (Jgs 16:30).

The Point of the Story

The reader of these episodes cannot help but feel both repulsion and admiration: repulsion for the crimes that Samson committed and that the Bible does not cover up; admiration for Samson's bold-ness and authenticity. Samson is sincere, forthright, and completely free. He challenges convention and does not lie. He will not tol-erate duplicity and so even slays his own people when they try to serve the interests of the Philistines.

The Bible does not approve of Samson's crimes and weaknesses. It simply recounts the popular legend about him and indicates the way that led from oppression to liberty. Moreover, it consistently stresses the qualities that mark that journey from start to finish: sin-cerity and love of freedom. Thus it provides a clear bit of warning and advice for the reader: do not be led astray by the talk of a frivolous woman, for that can lead to chaos. It can even bring down a strong man like Samson.

These are popular stories, stories of a grateful people who are not unaware of misdeeds but who also know how to forgive. Sam-son was an outlaw, but he also incarnated a sacred ideal of the Hebrew people: love for liberty. He helped to bring about the full recovery of Hebrew freedom in the age of David. Looking back to the era of Samson from a later age, the Hebrews saw the hand of God at work in that strange story and realized that God works in strange ways.

There is much folklore in the story of Samson and Delilah, but that does not diminish its value. There is something more to the story than merely colorful folklore, and that is why the Hebrew people were deeply interested in it: It expresses the hope of the Hebrew people in a better future, thanks to God's help. It expresses their love of freedom and sincerity. It expresses their firm faith that God is with the people in all circumstances. It expresses disapproval of those who choose accommodation, trying to get rid of the one who is truly free.

Further Conclusions

The Samson story gives a glimpse into the way the Bible came into being and was shaped. It did not happen in a day. The process was a slow one, paralleling the gradual growth in awareness of the Hebrew people. With the help and enlightenment of God, they gradually came to an awareness of their responsibilities.

So we find that in the Bible, and even within a given book of the Bible, there are different layers of thought coming from different epochs. The story of Samson, for example, is presented from two different viewpoints: the viewpoint of the writer living in the time of King Josiah, and the viewpoint of the Hebrew people who lived under Philistine domination for hundreds of years. Thus the book of Judges seems to be a new building made out of old bricks. When we study it, we realize that the aim of the Bible is not simply to preserve the old stories and traditions for their own sake, but rather to preserve them in such a way that they might offer readers a concrete, faith-imbued view of their own situation. The aim of the Bible is to keep the Hebrew people alert and awake, fully conscious of their responsibilities.

The story of Samson also reveals the honesty of the Hebrew people in presenting their past history. They do not cover up or hide anything. Without approving of errors that may have been committed, they try to perceive the good contained in them. It is for this reason that the Bible is meaningful even today. One need only take a cursory look at human history to realize that all human activity is an ambivalent mixture of good and evil. Sometimes a deed looks good on the surface but is evil at the root. Jesus condemned this kind of acting as pharisaical, because surface appearance did not reflect the inner person. Sometimes a deed looks evil on the surface, but is basically good at the root. This latter kind of deed pleases God much more than the former. Jesus himself welcomes sinners, publicans, and prostitutes.

Samson was a man who seemed to display much surface wickedness. But deep down there was something very good in him: sincerity, authenticity, and love of freedom. The history of the church itself is a mixture of good and evil. Terrible things have been done in God's name, as the Crusades, the Inquisition, and the persecution of heterodox people clearly indicate. We have no right to condemn Samson's attitudes, which force us to confront our own consciences. If we look at our own lives and deeds, we soon realize that there is a fine line between good and evil and that we are a mixture of both. But God does not leave us because of that. The Bible rips off our mask and confronts us with what we really are. Instead of covering up and justifying evil, it acknowledges and confesses it. It seeks to bring about reform and conversion.

The world does not like free human beings — people who do not follow the lead of the majority, who challenge and inconvenience everyone as Samson did. But very often it is people like Samson who bring about a better future. Like Samson, those who are fighting for a better future today have their bad points and make many mistakes. But if we fail to recognize and acknowledge in such people the positive element and the summons of God, we may well be guilty of what Jesus called "the sin against the Holy Spirit." Jesus himself was accused of being possessed by a devil because he inconvenienced many people and because he took away their peace of mind. To justify themselves, they said that the enemy of God was responsible for the things that God was doing for human freedom in and through Jesus Christ (Mk 3:23–30). This sin against the Holy Spirit cannot be pardoned because it blocks up the well from which we draw water to purify the evil in our lives.

5

THE PROPHETS

Where Is the God We Believe In?

How do prophets know that God has commanded them to say a certain thing? How does the vocation of the prophet arise? How can one distinguish between a true prophet and a false prophet, since both claim to speak in God's name? What is the prophet's mission? How do prophets operate? What do they teach us about God? Do prophets exist today? These are some of the questions that crop up in our minds as we read the prophetical books of the Bible.

In the Old Testament sixteen books are attributed to prophets. Four of them are considered to be books of "major" prophets: Isaiah, Jeremiah (together with Lamentations and Baruch), Ezekiel, and Daniel. The twelve other prophetical books are considered to belong to "minor" prophets: Hosea, the innermost depths of Joel, Amos, Obadiah, Jonah, Micah, Nahum, Habakkuk, Zephaniah, Haggai, Zechariah, and Malachi. The division into "major" and "minor" is based on the quantity of material that the prophet has left behind for us. There are other prophets in the Bible of whom we possess no written record, e.g., Elijah and Elisha.

Many of these men are little more than names to us. It is now impossible for us to know who they were, how they lived, and exactly what they did. But critical study of their writings and a knowledge of both biblical and secular history does enable us to get a fair picture of the complicated human situation in which they were obliged to live and to carry out their mission.

The words "prophet" and "prophecy" evoke connotations of "foretelling the future" in our minds. In reality the root word (Gr. *profemi*) means "to speak in the name of" someone. The prophets are people who speak in the name of God and who know they are speaking in God's name.

The Prophet's Vocation

It is difficult to get inside another person, to lift the veil of mystery that surrounds that person's life with God. The vocation of the prophet is framed within this sphere of impenetrable mystery. But if we ponder some of the hints that the prophets themselves have left us in their writings, we can form some idea of how the prophetic vocation comes into being. Let us look at two examples.

The prophet Amos was a plain man of the people, a common laborer and herdsman (Am 7:14). He lived in a period of economic progress that had been stimulated by King Jeroboam (783–743 B.C.E.) of the Northern Kingdom. Unfortunately that economic progress was grounded on the collective egotism of selfish classes and social groups. Self-interest led to unjust social divisions and the oppression of large sectors of the general population (Am 5:7; 2:6–7; 3:10). The Hebrew people, whom God had liberated earlier, had become enslaved once again — this time to their fellow Hebrews.

Amos's life was deeply enmeshed in the life of the Hebrew people. His faith and his good sense told him that such a state of affairs was contrary to the will of God. It was a paradoxical situation that gradually turned into a serious problem for Amos; he could not get his mind off it. Everything reminded him of the injustice in the nation, and he could not help but foresee the divine punishment that it would eventually provoke. A raging fire in the woods reminded him that God was going to consume and burn away all the existing injustices (Am 7:4–6), and a basket of ripe fruit reminded him that Israel was ripe for God's punishment (Am 8:1–3). Facts and events began to speak for themselves, turning into a summons and an appeal. Gradually Amos became more and more aware of the situation, finally deciding that God wanted him to speak out: "The lion has roared; who is not terrified? The Lord God has spoken; who will not prophesy?" (Am 3:8) He dropped everything and began prophesying without mincing his words (Am 7:10–17).

The story of Hosea begins with these words: "This is the beginning of the Lord's message by Hosea. He said, Go, take a wanton for your wife and get children of her wantonness" (Hos 1:2). The most likely explanation is this. Hosea married some woman who, though happily married, eventually left him and became a prostitute. But Hosea continued to love her, and his faithful and unselfish love made the woman realize what a worthwhile man he was; so she came back to him. In this way Hosea discovered that he himself was an example and a dispenser of the regenerating force of love. Living within the Hebrew people, he came to see that this personal experience — both painful and fruitful — had much broader significance. The Hebrew nation was abandoning its spouse, God, and prostituting itself with the worship of other deities. But just as he had continued to love his unfaithful wife, so God continued to have a faithful and unselfish love for the people. God's love could regenerate the people and bring them back to being God's faithful spouse and nation.

Hosea gradually became aware of his mission. He would remind the Hebrew people about the unrequited love of God, thus hoping to prompt them to conversion. His prophecies are forceful and violent precisely because jealousy is one of the most violent emotions that can exist in a human being.

These two examples show us that the prophet was a person in whom the conscious awareness of the people of God culminated in the conscious awareness of an individual person. The prophet perceives the call of God in and through his own personal situation in the midst of the Hebrew people. His clear-cut perception of God's demands leads him to see with equal clarity what the life of the people should really be. He is at once a "man of God" and a "man of the people." He deeply feels his involvement with God and with his people, and he realizes that he cannot keep silent any longer. He speaks with authority because his words find their source in God and in the age-old consciousness and tradition of his people. His vocation is born of a confrontation between the real and the ideal.

Severe punishments are reserved for people who claim to be speaking in God's name when in fact they have not been sent by God (Dt 18:20). To prove the authenticity of his mission, the prophet foretells the future. His prophecies are short-range ones, and their fulfillment proves that God is with him (Dt 18:21–22; Jer 28:9; Ez 33:33). In this way the false prophet is distinguished from the true one.

The mission and activity of the prophet is always conditioned by the actual situation of the people to whom he is addressing his message. The prophet is an instrument in God's hands. He is to help the people to keep moving toward the objective to which they committed themselves through their covenant with God. The prophet, if you will, is the person sent to collect the pledge that the nation freely made with God and itself.

Because of the Exodus event, the group of people who left Egypt consciously realized that they were the "people of God," and that with God they were responsible for carrying out a project of liberation. This awareness was the dynamic force that kept the group journeying on without ever coming to a definitive stop. They were opening a way to the future guaranteed by God's fidelity and power. This fundamental attitude entailed faith, courage, hope, self-giving, and love. It was rooted in their experience and in their unshakable conviction that God was with them, that God was summoning them at every moment, and that they had a mutual commitment with God.

This experiential awareness of friendship with God, also called the "covenant," was structured into certain attitudes and behavior patterns. There was the law, cultic worship, various institutions, feasts, celebrations, and customary practices such as pilgrimages to the Temple. Various traditions kept the past alive and transmitted it to future generations. There were also images and representative items, such as the ark of the covenant and the golden calf. There were institutions like prophecies, the priesthood, and the monarchy, and popular practices such as prayers and wisdom literature. The intense life of the nation coursed through all these, keeping alive in each succeeding generation the awareness that they were the people of God and must remain faithful to God.

All these structures and behavior patterns had arisen out of the Hebrew people's particular faith in God. They were tools designed to keep alive their faith, hope, and generosity. They were means to an end, not ends in themselves, and they were given direction and critical examination on the basis of that end. At some point a given behavior pattern might no longer give real expression to the people's authentic way of life. For one reason or another, it might no longer convey or transmit the value that it had been designed to transmit. At that point the pattern would be criticized and then emended or eliminated. Once again the governing criterion was the original plan God had in mind and for which God had fashioned the people.

These structures and behavior patterns were human creations designed to give expression to the faith of the people. But the great problem with humankind has always been its understandable and inveterate desire for individual and national security. After much searching, people would develop a way of living that expressed their deepest convictions. They would come to regard this as a great achievement and look to it for assurance and security. A phenomenon thus took place among the Hebrew people: The forms of life that had allowed them to express their friendship with God would cease to embody or promote a continuing search for a better future. Instead they would come to embody the inveterate search for security. Losing contact with their original source — an awareness that they were the people of God — the forms would cease to be channels of authentic living. The inner vitality of the nation would diminish considerably, but the external structure or behavior pattern would continue as before as if nothing had changed.

The skeletal framework might look healthy, but there would be no authentic life within.

Some people wanted to cling to those external structures and patterns. They would come to regard them as admission tickets entitling them to intimacy with God and divine assistance. But the structures and patterns would now be nothing more than social conventions, empty shells that let people entertain the illusion that all is well with God when in fact there is no interior life. Fragile by their very nature, these social conventions would be defended by close-minded, violent attacks on anyone who chose to criticize them.

It is here that the prophets went into action. Their mission and activity was almost always prompted by this short-circuit between interior life and externalized behavior. They would denounce the false sense of security behind which the people were hiding — often unwittingly. They would unsettle the people and push them in search of new behavior patterns that would give renewed expression and stimulus to faith and life. They would condemn the external forms that kept the people immobile. The most immediate reaction of the people was a feeling of insecurity. They felt they were being deprived of something that had provided them with peace of mind and a sense of tranquility.

Prophets always act in God's name. They try to show people that their conception of God, as it is embodied in their external structures and behavior patterns, is not a conception of the true God revealed to their ancestors in the desert after they had been liberated from Egypt. The prophets themselves have this clear-cut vision because they are men of God; hence they are in a position to denounce the people's errors. They do not simply teach the people *about* God. They reveal God in their own attitudes, showing the Hebrew people that God is always different from, and greater than, anything they had imagined. God does not permit being domesticated by human beings. No human form, however religious it may be, can contain God. Let us consider briefly what this means in concrete terms.

Prophetic Criticism
of the People's Conception of God

The golden calf. After the Hebrew people had escaped Egypt, they fashioned an image of a golden calf. It was meant to give concrete embodiment to the force with which God had freed them (Ex 32:4). But that image entailed a serious danger. It became possible for the people to equate God with the many other deities who were represented under the likeness of a bull or calf. It was possible to go overboard in visualizing and localizing the power of God, which cannot be confined or limited to any one image or instrument. Much later Jeroboam reintroduced the image of the golden calf (1 Kgs 12:28) to give a religious cast to the political revolution he had accomplished. It became a source of apostasy, condemned in the Bible in the most vehement terms. A golden calf is not suitable for expressing faith in God (1 Kgs 12:31–13:2).

The high places. Once the Hebrew people had entered the promised land, they began to worship God in the "high places," under every spreading tree. They felt that the power of God was concentrated in such places, because God's power managed to raise up huge trees in desert soil. Solomon, for example, went to worship God at Gibeon, "the chief hill-shrine" (1 Kgs 3:4). But there was a danger in this form of worship. Once again God might come to be identified with the many other deities who were worshiped in the same way and in the same places. Once again the action of God might become too localized, and the locale of human encounter with God restricted. When this potential danger became real, the prophets rose up to condemn this form of worship in vehement terms. More than one prophet likened it to prostitution (see Jer 3:1–10; Is 1:21; Hos 2:6–7). Instead of giving expression and impetus to the people's friendship with God, worship in the high places was undermining the life of the people and the nation. It had to be criticized and condemned.

King and monarchy. God had promised that the Hebrews would be God's people and that God would be their God. With the passage of time, this promise was incarnated and individualized in the person of the king: "I will be his father, and he shall be my son" (2 Sm 7:14). Thus the king became the visible sign of God's friendship with the Hebrew people, the instrument that would ensure that God's will prevailed. Gradually, however, the presence of a king in their midst became an excuse for feeling comfortable and oversecure. Since the king was in their midst, the people felt that God was obliged to help them; after all, God had promised that there would always be a king on the throne of David (1 Sm 7:16). Once again the prophets stepped in: the throne of David will become a dilapidated shack (Am 9:11), none of his descendants will occupy the kingly throne (Jer 22:30), and the king of Israel will disappear once and for all (Hos 10:15). The fact of having a king offers no guarantee of safe conduct to anyone.

The Temple. The Hebrew people encountered God in the Temple: "How dear is thy dwelling place, thou Lord of Hosts! I pine, I faint with longing for the courts of the Lord's temple" (Ps 84:1–2). Pilgrimages, processions, psalms, canticles, and prayers — all these were bound up with the Temple, the dwelling place of God. Possessing the Temple, the Hebrew people felt that God was surely with them and committed to their cause. They took good care of the Temple, and this preoccupation gradually caused them to forget the more serious obligation of living the faith in their daily lives. They overlooked the fact that the Temple was merely an embodiment of that faith. Hence Jeremiah launches a direct frontal attack on the Temple (Jer 7:1–15), accusing the people of murder and lying and warning them that the Temple will not keep them safe. The Temple will be totally destroyed — as the shrine of Shiloh had been.

Cultic worship. Worship was the center of the nation's life. It recalled the past and rendered it present, enabling each succeeding generation to commit itself to God's plan and to take cognizance of its rights and duties. But worship gradually hardened into ritual, losing its connection with life. The people no longer lived out the presence of God in their daily actions. Worship became a service rendered for a stipulated period of time in return for God's protection. Great care was given to the ritual ceremonies, but not to one's everyday actions. The prophets called attention to the phoniness, asserting that such ritual was of no use whatsoever: "Your countless sacrifices, what are they to me? says the Lord. I am sated with whole-offerings of rams and the fat of buffaloes.... When you lift your hands outspread in prayer, I will hide my eyes from you. Though you offer countless prayers, I will not listen" (Is 1:11, 15). Worship in itself offers no guarantee of divine protection.

Jerusalem. The city of peace, Jerusalem is praised in numerous Psalms as the symbol of God's power and operative presence in the life of the nation (Pss 122; 137; 147). It was the heart of the nation's life, the "holy mountain." But its glory would be of no real use because it had not inspired the people to practice justice. It would be totally destroyed just as any other city might be (Is 3:8–9). The mere fact that one lived in Jerusalem guaranteed nothing.

The promised land. Abraham set out on a journey toward the land that had been promised to him, but it was not conquered until much later by Joshua. The conquest of the land was a sign that God would fulfill the divine promises. Dwelling in that land, the Hebrew people were able to feel sure that God was with them. They took this certainty too much for granted, however, and lived as if they had reached the final goal of their journey. The prophets then stepped in to unmask this presumptuous attitude for the delusion that it was. The Hebrew people would be torn away from their land, driven into exile, and forced to see their land destroyed (Jer 13:15–19; 4:23–28).

The day of Yahweh. The Hebrews lived in the hope and expectation that some day God would come to manifest divine justice. God would destroy the wicked and exalt the chosen people. It would be a day of light and peace and victory for them. Cherishing this illusion, they neglected everything else they were supposed to do. Then the prophets brought them shocking news about the day of Yahweh: "Fools who long for the day of the Lord, what will the day of the Lord mean to you? It will be darkness, not light. It will be as when a man runs from a lion, and a bear meets him, or turns into a house and leans his hand on the wall, and a snake bites him. The day of the Lord is indeed darkness, not light, a day of gloom with no dawn" (Am 5:18–20).

The chosen people. The Hebrew nation owed its origin to the fact that God had taken them out of Egypt and made a covenant with them. They were God's "chosen people" and this honorable designation was the motivating force behind their great quest. Gradually, however, it led the Hebrews into thinking they were privileged beings. They came to rely more on this privileged status than on the fidelity to God that it demanded of them. But Amos warned them: "Are not you Israelites like Cushites to me? says the Lord. Did I not bring Israel up from Egypt, the Philistines from Caphtor, the Aramaeans from Kir?" (Am 9:7). His point was that in God's eyes the Israelites were no better than other nations, no better in fact than two of their worst enemies, the Philistines and the Aramaeans. The mere fact of membership in God's chosen people did not guarantee security or favoritism.

Children of Abraham. Abraham was the great friend of God whose intercession could save whole towns (Gn 18:16–33). It was an honor to be able to say: "We are Abraham's descendants" (Jn 8:33). But many Hebrews relied on the designation without acting as Abraham had. John the Baptist, the last prophet of the Old Testament, makes it clear that the title alone avails little: "Prove your repentance by the fruits it bears; and do not begin saying to yourselves, 'We have Abraham for our father.' I tell you that God can make children for Abraham out of these stones here" (Mt 3:9). Another prop was pulled out from under the Hebrew people.

The law of God. God gave the people the law. Those who observed it would be safe and secure (Jer 8:8). Hence the people tried to explain the law clearly and to find out exactly what it demanded, so that they could secure salvation for themselves. But somehow the law turned into an instrument for coercing God. St. Paul points out that both the Jews with the law and the Greeks without it are "all under the power of sin" (Rom 3:9). "No human being can be justified in the sight of God for having kept the law" (Rom 3:20).

The prophets undermined all the supports on which the Hebrew people had relied. They swept the floor clean and flashed the light of truth into every nook and cranny. All the supposedly sure lines of contact with God were cut. The prophets opened the ground under their feet and showed the people that there was no easy certainty on which they could rely. It was not that these supports were false in themselves. They were counterfeit because they had ceased to serve as a channel for God's summons in the movement toward the promised future. They were false because they had become tools for compromise and oppression in God's name.

Today a prophet might well say the same about what we regard as sacrosanct and inviolable. And again today the prophet would probably be scorned and rejected in the name of God. Jesus Christ himself was rejected in the name of God and tradition: "This fellow is no man of God; he does not keep the Sabbath" (Jn 9:16). No religious practice or work can *in itself* lay hold of and coerce God. If people cling self-assuredly to attendance at Mass or recitation of the rosary or vigil-light services, then they are relying on a purely personal projection of their own; it is not God but rather a nonexistent, mythical deity. It certainly is not the living and true God whom the prophets intimately knew and worshiped. There is no lever on earth that can move the heavens by itself. The prophets criticized all such ideas. They made it clear that people could not rely blindly on such forms under the delusion that they could thereby coerce God into helping them.

Thus it is easy to see why the prophets met with a great deal of resistance. They meddled with the most important props for ensuring personal security. We can readily appreciate what the author of the letter to the Hebrews has to say about the suffering and persecution of the prophets (Heb 11:32–38).

Seemingly very negative in tone, the criticism made by the prophets stemmed from their view of God. This view was in marked contrast with the structures and behavior patterns of the Hebrew people. The prophets would not permit people to become alienated from life, to flee into a separate religious world of rite, ceremony, and cult. Doing this empties those practices of any real meaning. If they were alive today, those prophets would be the first to say that such religion is truly the "opiate of the people."

One need only read a few pages of their writings to be convinced of that.

Now we must turn to the positive side of the prophetic message and its radical criticism.

The Living and True God of the Prophets

Was everything wrong in the eyes of the prophets? Although the prophets did burn all the bridges that people had mistakenly assumed would lead them to God, they also fashioned a bridge of their own. This bridge was faith. It could establish real contact with God, and it could offer a guarantee of God's presence.

In a deep and thorough way the prophets lived the presence of God. They were men of God. God surpasses everyone and everything. God cannot be grabbed or lassoed; God cannot be turned into a beast of burden and loaded down with the weight of human yearnings and desires. God cannot be tamed or domesticated. Instead of serving God, we want God to serve us; and so we employ ritual and worship as sacralized magic. But in so doing we are turning things upside down.

For the prophets, God was a wholly gratuitous presence offering friendship to whomever chose to accept it. But God wants respect in this relationship of friendship. If someone offers friendship, God wants that person to have confidence in God. God does not want the other party to use devious and spurious tactics in order to guarantee the benefits of that friendship. That would indicate a lack of confidence, and it would be reason enough to withhold one's friendship from the other party in the future. If we approach a friend for help and support, we do not point to the presents and favors our friend has offered us in the past. We simply appeal to the tie of friendship. We tell our friend what we plan to do and ask for that person's help as a friend. Our appeal is based on the tie of friendship and the mutual commitment it entails.

God made a commitment with human beings and offered them friendship. God wants the tie of that friendship to be respected.

God demands faith and confidence as the initial preconditions for any further understanding. God's presence in our midst is a guaranteed certainty because God has said so. At the same time, however, God is strong enough to evade any improper approach to divine friendship where faith and confidence are lacking: e.g., the golden calf, the high places, the monarchy, Jerusalem, the Temple, cultic worship. All these, from ancient ritual to modern-day procession, are relative. They do not have guaranteed purchasing power in themselves. When it reaches the point where we try to use any one of them to buy our way into heaven, they merit critical denunciation and condemnation from the prophets of today.

These various approaches are of no guaranteed value in themselves. They can be good, useful, and even necessary when they are used as tools to express our faith and confidence — which are required conditions for any real contact with God. But the tools are merely signposts pointing us toward God. God remains *far beyond* anything and everything we might imagine, and at the same time *much closer* to us in friendship than any exterior expression. These expressions are like telephone lines. They are a means of communication, yet they do not compel anyone to pick up the receiver at the other end. The party at the other end of the line can take the phone off the hook and leave me talking to myself. But if those instruments are indeed expressions of my faith, then they do make contact with God who does not break off the connection. In the name of divine fidelity and loyalty, God will stay in contact with us, lending aid and support.

On the surface it would seem that the prophets thrust human beings into a state of total insecurity and uncertainty. In reality they lay the basis for the most solid security a human being can possess: the absolute certainty that God is there. God is not far away; God is with us. God's name is Emmanuel, "God with us." And God is loyal, friendly, and powerful. At the same time, however, God transcends us. God is always the Other and cannot be domesticated. God's relationship with us is sovereign and free, so that God can evade any attempt at domination. The attitude of God, who is both close to us and far away, is a challenge and an accusation.

It reminds us that there is at least one who manages to evade our grasping clutches. It also entails a criticism of the domination that one human being exercises over another, awakens the dominated party to the true nature of the relationship, and prompts a desire to have human dignity respected.

Thus the attitude God adopts toward us is one that helps us to adopt the same attitude toward others. The only real and effective means for linking another person to ourselves is faith, trust, and disinterested love. When a human being is wise enough to take a proper stance before God, then God in fact does feel obliged to help that person. As one Psalm puts it: "Because his love is set on me, I will deliver him" (Ps 91:14). God feels obliged to help because such a person takes God seriously. This is not easy, however, because we must leap into the dark, adopt an attitude of faith and confidence in the words of the other party. In sum, it is an attitude that allows the Other to be Other, which allows God to be God.

This is precisely what the prophets have to tell us about God. It is all summed up in God's name: Yahweh, that is, "I will be present." God tells Moses: "I AM; that is who I am" (Ex 3:14). In other words, God will certainly be present to help Moses and his people; but God will decide *when* and *where* and *how* to display this saving presence. We can count on God, but we cannot coerce God. The very name of God is a summons to faith, and God gives proof of the liberating divine presence. The first great proof was the Exodus from Egypt. The last and ultimate proof was the coming of Jesus Christ, who is Emmanuel; and this proof is still in process (Mt 1:23).

God, perceived in these terms and so incorporated into life, is the core and source of all prophetic activity. At the same time God provides us with a new vision of life itself. That is why the prophets never lose hope, even when they are enmeshed in the trials and tribulations that they themselves may have foretold. However much they criticize, the message of the prophets is one of hope. The criticism is necessary when some way of living threatens to narrow and harden life so badly that it will stifle this hope in the people, particularly in the hearts of the poor and lowly.

Today's Prophets

Prophets usually do not use professional titles. They do not print their mission on a business card. Today the prophetic movement in the church and the world is quite strong. Criticism of obsolete structures and behavior patterns is underway, triggered by Vatican II itself. In the days of ancient Israel the prophetic movement was a cultural as well as a faith-inspired movement within the chosen people. The same is true today. Prophecy is a cultural datum that, within the church, takes on a specific faith-inspired dimension. Christians are not the only ones who are criticizing obsolete structures and behavior patterns. They are part of the overall movement, taking their own particular cue from their faith in God.

Today there are people within the church who are trying to overcome the alienation in which many Christians live out their lives, lost in the grip of practices that no longer serve to express friendship with God, but merely the search for human security. The rigid maintenance of the existing situation, both inside the church and in society at large, is not due to the common people alone; it is also due to those in authority. Thus the criticism of the prophets today is also directed against those in power, even as it was in the days of ancient Israel. That is what Jesus Christ himself did. He criticized the Pharisees and other religious leaders. For the common people he had compassion, since he saw them as sheep without a shepherd.

Clearly, then, the mission of the prophet is a hazardous one. When one becomes aware of such a mission, as Amos and Hosea did, the feeling is not a pleasant one. One thinks twice about it. Like Moses (Ex 3:11–4:13) and Jeremiah (Jer 1:6), today's prophet can find good reasons and pretexts for escaping such a difficult task. But prophets will continue to raise their voices today even as they did long ago, however much others may advise them against it: "The lion has roared; who is not terrified? The Lord God has spoken; who will not prophesy?" (Am 3:8).

6

FROM HEZEKIAH TO JOSIAH

The History of a Reform

"The high priest Hilkiah told Shaphan the adjutant-general that he had discovered the book of the law in the house of the Lord..." (2 Kgs 22:8). That piece of information was like a stone dropped into a calm lake. Soon the ripples were spreading out over the whole surface of the nation's life. There are historical situations in which many factors converge suddenly at a given point that could not have been foreseen. The air is heavy with expectation, but no one knows exactly what is going to happen. When it does happen, it is as if some powerful generator has just been switched on and suddenly lights up all the lights of the city in the dark night. The cables were already laid, as though waiting for the light to arrive. Everything changed.

That is precisely what happened when Hilkiah reported his discovery. It was the eighteenth year in the reign of King Josiah, the year 622 B.C.E. (2 Kgs 22:3). We do not know much about the historical circumstances surrounding the discovery of the law in the Temple, nor do we know exactly how the book of the law came to find its way there. But we do know something about the movement that was intertwined with discovery, and that is what interests us here.

Historical movements, like huge trees whose roots are buried in the soil of preceding centuries, are irreversible in their growth pattern. Nothing can stop them. They grow stronger than the individuals involved with them. At the same time, however, individuals can exert an influence on them for good or ill. Because of their influence, it may happen that the power unleashed at a given moment is too great. The result may be that things become worse than they were before. That is exactly what happened with the reform we are considering here.

The Roots of Reform

In 722 B.C.E., a hundred years before the discovery of the law, a great catastrophe befell Israel, the Northern Kingdom of Palestine. Earlier it had split from the Southern Kingdom, now called Judah. In 722 B.C.E. Shalmaneser, the king of Assyria, invaded the Northern Kingdom. Assyria was the great world power of the time, and its army destroyed the capital of the Northern Kingdom (Samaria), devastated the land, deported the native population, and resettled people from other countries in the land of Israel (2 Kgs 17). The smoldering fires of revolt and subversion were thus stamped out, and the history of the Northern Kingdom came to a close (2 Kgs 17:18). But the warfare continued. The Assyrian armies moved southward, skirted the hilly kingdom of Judah, and continued on to meet the armies of Egypt in the Gaza Strip.

The destruction of Samaria was a dire warning to the small kingdom of Judah, which lay isolated in the highlands as the two great powers engaged in battle. The Hebrew people of the Northern Kingdom had ceased to exist as an independent entity because they had abandoned the unifying center of Hebrew national life. They had ceased to be faithful to the covenant and law of God, which was the true constitution of the nation (2 Kgs 17:7–18; 18:21). But the same infidelity, the same cancerous disintegration, existed in Judah (2 Kgs 17:19). Its escape from invasion was due more to luck than to merit. It had been spared because shortly before this, Ahaz, the king of Judah, had gotten on friendly terms with Assyria (2 Kgs 16:5–6; 7–18). He chose not to enter an alliance with the Northern Kingdom against Assyria, and even went so far as to ask Assyria for aid against the Northern Kingdom and to pay tribute to the Assyrian ruler.

What position should Judah take now? Should it side with Assyria? No, because that would negate a whole past effort of struggle and faith. Even when it was helping others, Assyria was really looking out for its own interests. It wanted to ensure its own security and domination of the world. The Assyrian threat from outside continued to grow, while inside Judah's resistance withered away. Ahaz was an impotent leader; he did not know how to tackle the critical situation. The prophet Isaiah had already tried to rekindle the king's faith in the future that God had in mind for the people (Is 7:1–25), but his words found no echo in the mediocre ruler. In his desperation Ahaz had even gone so far as to immolate his own son in order to win the protection of alien deities (2 Kgs 16:3). There was no fight left in him, no feeling of hope, no strength to resist. The people had lost any reason for living, and the inner void widened each day. Isaiah had been right when he said: "Have firm faith, or you will not stand firm" (Is 7:9). But how was such faith to be reenkindled in the people?

Ahaz died. Hezekiah, a youthful but capable political leader, took over the reigns of government at the age of twenty-five and ruled for almost thirty years. He was a man of faith who "put his trust in the Lord" (2 Kgs 18:5). He had confidence in the future that God had in mind, and he tried to communicate this faith to others. Thus he sparked a yearning for reform that he tried to articulate and implement. A breath of new life stirred in the nation and gave new enthusiasm to everyone. Apathy faded away, and the void was filled. A new mentality began to take shape among the people. New ideas arose concerning God, worship, and both the past and future of the nation. So far they were just ideas, but they were forceful and ardent ideas that took wings and began to flutter through people's minds. These new ideas and the reform movement sparked by Hezekiah lay behind the book of the law that Hilkiah would discover in the Temple a hundred years later.

First Steps

The reform movement took shape and began to exert an influence on every sector of the nation's life. The faith was purified, the sources of magic and superstition were rooted out (2 Kgs 18:3–4; 2 Chr 29:3–11). Injustices were eliminated, and the law of God was solemnly reinstated as the true constitution of the nation (2 Chr 30:1–27). Age-old traditions were collected and anthologized (Prv 25:1). Jerusalem was restored, and its defenses were refurbished for any eventuality (2 Chr 32:1–5). Hezekiah made provisions for ensuring a good supply of water in the event of siege. The reservoir and conduit system he engineered still impresses sightseers today (2 Kgs 20:20). He also gained victory over a traditional enemy, the Philistines (2 Kgs 18:8), purified the Temple (2 Chr 19:12–17), and reformed both the priesthood and the cultic worship of the nation (2 Chr 31:1–21).

A new nation was rising out of the ashes of despair and degradation. Hezekiah had somehow managed to touch a vital nerve and restore hope in a dispirited people. The crucial axis of this reform was the spiritual and religious renewal of the people. They made an abrupt turn and went back to the ruling center of their life as a nation: their living covenant with God. Their remembrance of their own past as a nation took on new vitality and vividness (2 Chr 30:5–9, 13–20). New hope and a clear desire to live and fight bravely came into being, grounded in a newfound sense of faith.

Hezekiah managed to reopen the door to the future when it seemed to be on the point of closing for good. He did this primarily through his reform of the liturgy, which embodies the authentic expression of the nation's life. He thus provided access to the vital forces at the heart of the nation's life, so that the Hebrew people were able to rediscover their true identity as the people of God. That was his great merit, and it would go down to his credit in Hebrew history: "There was nobody like him among all the kings of Judah who succeeded him or among those who had gone before him" (2 Kgs 18:5).

His activity was not confined to the internal affairs of his country, however. As a good political leader, he kept his eye on the far horizons of international politics. A tiny nation such as Judah could not close itself off in isolated nationalism. The Egyptian pharaoh had managed to recover from the earlier defeat and consolidate Egypt's position on the international scene. The balance of power, which had been upset by Assyria's victorious advance, was now restored. Once again an anti-Assyrian movement began to take shape, fomented and fed by Egypt. The pro-Egyptian faction grew stronger in the government of Hezekiah, seeking to win him over to its outlook. At the same time the prophet Isaiah, who counseled Hezekiah in religious and political matters, stuck to his previous outlook. He had earlier advised Ahaz not to look to Egypt for support, and he told Hezekiah the same thing. Egypt was not to be trusted (Is 30:1–7; 31:1–3). But Hezekiah did not listen to this advice, choosing instead to take an active part in the international power play (2 Kgs 18:21).

Assyria did not sit on the sidelines long. It soon stepped in and crushed the opposition movement. Judah was invaded, its towns taken one by one (2 Kgs 18:13). The only town that remained free was Jerusalem, whose defensive fortifications had been carefully shored up by Hezekiah over a period of years. We do not really know why, but Jerusalem did hold out and was not taken by the Assyrian forces or even frontally assaulted. Hezekiah came out a winner.

As is always the case in war, each contending party has its own version of what happened. The Hebrew version in the Bible says that Sennacherib laid siege to the city with an army of four hundred thousand men and caused great panic; but then an angel of the Lord stepped in, decimated his army, and forced him to retreat (2 Kgs 18:13–19:37; 2 Chr 32:9–23). The Assyrian version of the same event, found in the city of Nineveh by archaeologists, gives a different reason. Whatever the case may be, the retreat of Sennacherib aroused great euphoria among the inhabitants of Jerusalem, and the event went to Hezekiah's head. He plunged headlong into the international political conspiracy against Assyria (2 Kgs 20:12–19). The people felt greater confidence in themselves and their own strength; they could hardly contain their gratitude (2 Chr 32:23). This event and its outcome helped to advance the internal renewal of the country.

Opposition Forces in Control

The winds of fortune can change direction, however. Hezekiah's successor, his son Manasseh, was a disappointment to the people and a failure as a ruler. An incompetent man, he did nothing to carry through the reform movement that had been started with so much good will and hope. A devotee of political intrigue, he had no time for religion or justice. Everything began to regress, and the backward movement lasted for fifty years or more. Manasseh began to rule around the age of twelve, and he was still in power when he died at the age of sixty-seven (2 Kgs 21:1–18). Nevertheless, the people retained an awareness that change was necessary, and they felt a nostalgic longing for the earlier spirit of reform.

Political intrigue took control of government affairs, and there was little interest in the law of God or the plight of the people (2 Kgs 21:16). Events took a predictable course. Amon, the successor of Manasseh, was assassinated (2 Kgs 21:23) because a group of military leaders and government officials wanted a ruler who would look after their special interests. The murder of the king, however, proved to be the last straw. Despite their disappointment with their recent kings, the common people still identified with the Davidic monarchy, and so they rose up in reaction. An assault on the king was an assault on the Hebrew people, and they rose up against the military men who had killed Amon and deposed them from power. The ringleaders were slain, and the reins of government were transferred to a legitimate descendant of David. He was eight years old at the time, and his name was Josiah (2 Kgs 22:1). From what we know, the running of the government was taken over by a priest named Hilkiah until the boy reached the age when he could govern in his own right. The year was 640 B.C.E.

Renewed Fervor for Reform

This violent turn of events stirred the awareness of the Hebrew people and gave them a new consciousness of their power. It was a new beginning. They reversed the process of decline started with Manasseh. The desire to put through basic, thoroughgoing reforms reappeared in intensified form. And the pervading situation both inside and outside the country helped to foster this desire.

On the international front, Assyria was governed by Assurbanipal. He brought peace to the international scene, but it was the peace of the grave. His cruel policies and murderous aggression silenced those who were his enemies. Thousands were murdered or deported or tortured or struck down in some other way. In the later years of his reign he was able to relax his vigilance somewhat and devote himself to study and pleasure-seeking. He left behind a huge, recently uncovered library and high-relief hunting scenes of astonishing beauty. His reign marked the high point of Assyrian power, and decline would soon set in. Egypt did not yet represent a real threat, but it was again beginning to revolt. Babylon, the third major world power, had not yet grown into a real threat and was viewed sympathetically by the nations that had been oppressed by Assyria. Even Hezekiah had held secret discussions with an envoy from Babylon (2 Kgs 20:12–15).

On the home front in Judah, a nationalist movement began to grow. The elimination of Amon's murderers meant that most people took sides with the new king even though he was still a youth. He was, after all, the ruler whom they had brought to power. Around this time there also appeared two prophets who summoned the people to reform and purification: Jeremiah and Zephaniah. The reform movement widened and took real hold of the country. It had the support of most people, and the international situation made it feasible.

The march forward began, led by the king. But as yet no one knew exactly what road to take. Something was still missing, and eighteen years went by before the reform movement would find the solid roots it needed (2 Kgs 22:3). It does seem, however, that some groping initiatives were taken during that early period (2 Chr 34:3–7). The cable lines, as it were, had been installed, but as yet no electric generator had been found. The nation had to wait until Hilkiah made his great discovery in the Temple. Then the road ahead became clear to everyone, and the whole nation set out optimistically for the future.

History of the Reform Charter

The law found in the Temple was the age-old law of God in a newly revised and augmented edition that corresponded to the new age. The ideas that had been sparked by Hezekiah and then submerged in the reign of Manasseh found concrete and practicable formulation in this new edition of the law. The ideas had not disappeared completely. They had been pondered and formulated and set down in writing by certain idealists who looked toward the future and who would not allow themselves to be discouraged by the political and religious chaos prevalent in the reign of Manasseh. This written revision of the law had found its way into the Temple — how or when or why we do not know exactly. It was discovered by Hilkiah when the Temple was undergoing repairs (2 Kgs 22:3–10).

When the book of the law was taken to the king and read in his presence, it caused great bewilderment and consternation: "Great is the wrath of the Lord . . . that has been kindled against us, because our forefathers did not obey the commands in this book and do all that is laid upon us" (2 Kgs 22:13). It seemed that the clouds had lifted and people could now get a clear look at the horizon. The book pointed out the road that everyone wanted to travel but that no one had been able to locate. It told them *how* to act, giving precise formulation to their vague desires. It offered them a plan of action.

Everyone soon realized the dimensions of the crisis that they faced (2 Kgs 22:14–17). The whole population was convened, the law was read to them, and they pledged themselves to adhere to it (2 Kgs 23:1–3). The reform movement now had its own charter, and the work could begin in earnest. The whole nation pledged that it would implement each and every one of God's demands in the life of the Hebrew people.

In actual fact it was apparent to everyone that drastic reform in the life of the nation was crucial and urgent. Religious practice was riddled with superstition. Pagan elements had infiltrated the cult of Yahweh, and there were many shrines in the countryside where Hebrew cultic worship was indistinguishable from the magical cults of the Canaanites. The prophets had unflinchingly denounced the situation, but to little avail. No sooner had Hezekiah died, for example, than Manasseh reintroduced the whole panoply of pagan worship (2 Kgs 21:3–7). The anxious searching and the void in the life of the people was evident in the fact that many of them resorted to such magical elements. The underlying danger was that slowly but surely their notion of God would be perverted. This would inevitably pervert the life of the nation and its reason for being. That is what had happened to Samaria and the Northern Kingdom in 722 B.C.E. The people had not forgotten, and they were afraid that the same would happen all over again in Judah. The people of the Northern Kingdom had gone to their destruction because they no longer knew who they were or why they were living. Judah desired a preventive medicine. And now they had a document that spelled out how they might live the law of God.

Content of the Reform Charter

Here in brief are the main lines of the reform charter, the new edition of the law, which is now contained in the book of Deuteronomy. The text presents a discourse by Moses to the Hebrew people shortly before they took possession of the promised land. Actually, the discourse is not addressed to the people living in the time of Moses around 1200 B.C.E. It is addressed to the people of Jerusalem and Judah around the seventh century B.C.E. It is addressed to all those who were easy prey to the magical practices and superstitious beliefs that held sway during the reign of Manasseh. Moses speaks to the people in a very direct and personal tone, trying to touch their consciousness and arouse their sense of responsibility. His discourse is meant to help them rediscover their identity as the people of God, their inescapable commitment to God, and the obligations that flow from that commitment. The discourse certainly succeeded with the king, as is evident from his reaction to the reading of it (2 Kgs 22:13).

The line of reasoning in the book of Deuteronomy goes something like this: For the Hebrew people there can be only one God, Yahweh. Yahweh is their one and only Lord and God (Dt 6:4–5). All other so-called gods are empty ciphers, and so they must be rooted out of the country (Dt 6:14–15; 7:25–26). The nation's covenant with Yahweh is not based on what the Hebrew people did for Yahweh but rather on what Yahweh has done for them (Dt 6:20–7:6). It is an obligation of gratitude and love (Dt 7:7–11). Since they have been chosen by Yahweh, all the Hebrews must necessarily observe Yahweh's commands if they are to benefit from the promises made to them. This set of basic ideas is the central preoccupation of the first part of the book of Deuteronomy (Dt 1–11). It is followed by a practical application of those ideas to the life of the nation.

Faith in the one God will find expression in one, and only one, sanctuary. All the other places of worship are to be destroyed (Dt 12:2–3). Yahweh, the God of the Hebrew people, can be worshiped only in the place that Yahweh has chosen (Dt 12:5), and that of course is Jerusalem. It is there that the Hebrews should make their offerings and holocausts (Dt 12:6–7). The proper elements of worship are spelled out in minute detail. Everything is centralized and nothing is left to chance or individual initiative: "You shall not act as we act here today, each of us doing what he pleases" (Dt 12:8). The major concern underlying this approach is to exclude any practice of magic from the liturgy (Dt 12–18).

One of the most important norms was that all Hebrews were to make three pilgrimages to Jerusalem each year to celebrate the three major feasts of the nation (Dt 16:16). This would be an effective way of encouraging a sense of national unity and of giving them instruction about God and the demands of the law.

One must read the book of Deuteronomy itself to get an idea of the vibrant appeal it could make, both then and now, to the consciousness of the people. Its tone is direct, its style highly suggestive. Yet the reader can also perceive the rigid nature of that liturgical reform, which left nothing to chance.

Clerical Security: Obstacle to Reform

Bound up with the problem of liturgical reform was another issue: the livelihood and work of the clergy in the sanctuaries outside Jerusalem. All those sanctuaries, whether dedicated to Yahweh or other deities, had their own priests. For them the sanctuaries represented their only means of making a living. When the Jerusalem clergy decided to eliminate those sanctuaries, they were condemning the rural clergy to hunger and poverty. It seemed to be a vicious circle and an insoluble problem. Hezekiah had attempted to reform the clergy in an earlier day, but to no avail (2 Chr 31:2). Everything took a backward step again during the reign of Manasseh. Without a reasonable solution for the problem of the clergy and their livelihood, other reform solutions would prove fruitless. And no one wants to die of hunger, however lofty the ideas used to support the proposal.

The authors of the book of Deuteronomy confronted the problem and offered their own solution, which Josiah tried to implement. A portion of the rural clergy were transferred to Jerusalem, where they were given second-class employment in the Temple (2 Kgs 23:8; Dt 18:6–8). Others were prohibited from establishing themselves in Jerusalem (2 Kgs 23:9) and commended to the charity of the people (Dt 14:27–29). Thus we get a clear glimpse of the rivalry between the clergy in Jerusalem and those outside the city, and we sense the struggle going on between them to win influence over the people. The clergy in the capital city wanted to be the major influence in the country and to centralize the liturgy in their own hands. They could offer sound reasons for this course of action because there was real danger of worship degenerating into magical practice. And if all the clergy were transferred to Jerusalem, then the original group of clergy in the capital would be reduced to a minority faction.

But now the clergy outside Jerusalem found themselves deprived of their normal means of support. Commended to the charity of the people or confined to second-class employment in the Jerusalem Temple, they did not look with favor on the centralizing initiatives of their confreres in Jerusalem. They hardly appreciated being grouped with "the aliens, orphans, and widows" (Dt 14:29). Social security for the clergy was a problem way back then, critical to the success or failure of the reform that was to be implemented.

It becomes apparent, then, that all the legislation enacted during that period of reform reflected the viewpoint of the central administrators in Jerusalem. They had been thinking through the situation for a long time and had their own clear awareness. But their outlook did not embody the feelings and sentiments of the common people and clergy at the grassroots level. It did not embody their outlook on the overall problem, and therein lay the seeds of its eventual failure.

The Tragic Outcome of the Reform

King Josiah took on the work of reform as a personal mission, doing everything he could to implement it. He traveled through the whole countryside from north to south (2 Kgs 23:4–14), even penetrating the territory of the defunct Northern Kingdom (2 Kgs 23:15–20). He was determined to dismantle all the sanctuaries outside Jerusalem, whether they were dedicated to Yahweh or to other gods, so that the Hebrew religion would be healed from the cancer of superstition and magic. He used violence, killing priests of the false gods and burning their bones on the destroyed altars (2 Kgs 23:20). He did much to reform the clergy (2 Kgs 23:8–9), and he was highly praised: "He did what was right in the eyes of the Lord; he followed closely in the footsteps of his forefather David, swerving neither right nor left" (2 Kgs 22:2).

It is difficult to form a final evaluation of the reform movement implemented by Josiah because his unexpected early death prevented him from carrying out all that he had planned. Incompetent men came after him, and the reforms were never put through completely. Josiah tore down the old structure, but he did not have enough time to complete a new one. Once again it was the international situation that influenced the course of internal affairs and gave them an unexpected turn.

Nabopolassar, the ruler of Babylonia, inherited the spirit of combat and independence from his predecessors. He renewed the struggle against the age-old power of the Assyrians. Through a series of lightning-swift attacks he managed to destroy that power in a relatively short time, overthrowing an empire that had been built up over centuries. Assyria came to the end of the line. In 612 B.C.E., ten years after the revised book of the law had been discovered in the Temple at Jerusalem and the work of reform had been initiated by Josiah, the Assyrian capital of Nineveh was taken by the Babylonians and totally destroyed. The event was something like the dropping of the first atomic bomb; it marked the end of a whole era and the start of a new one. The Assyrians and their surviving forces retreated northward into present-day Syria and made a last-ditch attempt to ward off the inevitable.

As is often the case in international politics, this changed situation brought about realignments in the balance of power. Egypt, the old enemy of Assyria, now sided with Assyria to maintain a favorable balance of power in the area. The pharaoh Necho sent an Egyptian army to reinforce the remnants of the Assyrian force now entrenched in Syria, and this Egyptian army had to pass through the territory of King Josiah. Feeling a bit too cocky, perhaps, Josiah now felt he could make a positive impact on the international scene. Desiring to hasten the total collapse of Assyria, and to undermine the power of Egypt, he decided to do battle with Egyptian forces as they passed through the strategic city of Megiddo. But Josiah had miscalculated. His army was routed in its first encounter with the Egyptians (2 Kgs 23:29), and he himself was mortally wounded. He was carried back to Jerusalem and there he died. The people buried him amid great lamentation, for they saw him as a true friend and hero of the Hebrew nation (2 Chr 35:23–24). It is said that the prophet Jeremiah himself delivered the funeral elegy over the bier of the young king, whose death killed the last vestiges of hope in the Hebrew people (2 Chr 35:25). Josiah was only thirty-nine years old when he died (2 Kgs 22:1).

Twelve years of intense reform work came to a standstill with the unexpected death of Josiah. The year was 609 B.C.E. On his way back from the military campaign in Syria, the pharaoh came through Jerusalem and took control of the government of Judah. He placed his own hand-picked candidate on the throne (2 Chr 36:1–4), and the decline began. Twenty-two years later, in 587 B.C.E., the city of Jerusalem was taken by Nebuchadnezzar, the king of Babylon, who subjected it to total destruction. The independence of the people was destroyed, not to be revived until 1948 C.E. with the creation of the state of Israel. Today the Israelis find themselves fighting similar battles within a similar web of political interplay among the great powers.

Evaluation of the Reform Movement

The reform movement died with the young king who had sponsored it. What was the fatal flaw that doomed it to failure? Was it international politics, the incompetence of Josiah's successors, Josiah himself, or the "reform charter"? If the reform had been put through precisely to avoid the disaster that eventually befell Judah, why was it unable to achieve its goals? Was the movement too weak or too forceful? Was it doomed from the start? There is one curious fact surrounding the reform movement. The prophet Jeremiah, the great religious figure of the day, was present from the very beginning of the movement. He urged conversion of the Hebrew people, and he lamented the death of the young king. Yet in his prophetical pronouncements we do not find him giving wholehearted support to everything that was being done in the name of reform. He did not identify himself with the reform movement that was carried to its logical conclusion by King Josiah. Why?

In those days changes generally took place much more slowly than they do today, yet catastrophe befell Judah in a matter of twenty years after Josiah's death. Did the reform movement hasten the catastrophe or slow it up? It is difficult to form a fully rounded judgment on the question because sufficient data is lacking. The fact does demand some explanation, however, as it is of some relevance to us today: For over thirty years the Catholic Church has been involved in a great effort at reform with a whole host of factors and events involved, both inside and outside the church, both on the national and international level.

With regard to a work of art, we can make all sorts of studies in an attempt to understand fully the message the artist intended to convey. That does not mean that the message deduced by the art critic is the same as the one intended by the artist. But at least the effort of the critic is within the perspective of the artist, since the artist is trying to stimulate the reflection of the viewer and confront him with his own consciousness and awareness. So it is with any attempt to explain the Bible and the facts related in it. The comments of the exegetes are not important, for their presentation is relative. The important thing is that the exegetes, in their capacity as interpreters, be able to let loose the light and power of God's word so that it can operate on the conscience and awareness of other people. Indeed others may arrive at their own conclusions, quite different from those offered by the exegete. That does not matter much. What is important is that people stop and reflect, comparing their lives and deeds with the word of God, that they examine their actions in the light of God's word.

The Fatal Miscalculation

The book of Deuteronomy does indeed present a new approach to living the faith, and it did arise as a response to real needs. Unfortunately, however, it embodied the response of a minority group who chose to impose their solution on everyone in a rather precipitous way. Their solution did not embody the thinking of the whole people, even though most people did want reform. The reform movement plowed ahead at full speed when the light flashed yellow; it should have proceeded with caution. Hence it hastened the catastrophe it was trying to prevent.

When we are trying to get people to change their outlook and their religious practices, we should not rush ahead too rapidly. A bit of patient waiting is advisable if we want to avoid disaster. The Deuteronomic reform was a drastic one, and it closely followed the ground plan laid out by the theologians in Jerusalem. While it certainly left a deep mark on the life of the Hebrew people, it never got beyond the level of theory. In practice it did not work, at least not at that particular time. Only after the exile in Babylon did it become a matter of real praxis.

The Deuteronomic reform remained a reform imposed on the people from above, based on a prefabricated scheme. The common people with their own aspirations did not really have a say in this reform movement, which was undertaken with such intensity. Hence they never really accepted it as their own. The reform died with the king who had been promoting it, and it failed to impress itself on the hearts of the people. The common people were not so readily given to facile reasoning and purely intellectual arguments, however simple and clear-cut those arguments might seem to be. The problem of faith confronting the people at the time was framed in very practical terms through Josiah's reform project; and when theory is applied in a drastic fashion to that sort of situation, it may well fail to provide a sound solution. Theory can have great value over the long run as a potent force for consciousness-raising. But when the real-life situation is not taken into serious consideration, then the direct implementation of drastic theoretical solutions will not work. They are not fully comprehended and accepted by the people, and so they fail.

The fact is that King Josiah did not seem to show much consideration for, or understanding of, the concrete situation of the people and the clergy living outside Jerusalem. He followed the norms of a prefabricated plan without asking himself whether they were really being implemented in a viable way. The success of the reform movement depended on the collaboration of the Hebrew people as a group, but they were not seriously consulted in the process of trying to work out a solution to the problem. It was they who would have to support the clergy, give tithes to the Temple, make the three pilgrimages to Jerusalem each year, and observe all the other prescriptions.

All the public forms of divine worship were centralized in Jerusalem; other forms were prohibited or strictly controlled. Everything was planned down to the most minute details. Although well intentioned, the sudden and brusquely implemented reform deprived the common people of the only prop they could count on in those tumultuous times. However spurious it might have been, their traditional form of worship had helped them to come face to face with themselves and with God. But once the Deuteronomic reform had been effected, they would find themselves outside the law if they continued their traditional religious practices. Now deprived of the way of adoring God that had been theirs for generations and not appreciating the reasoning behind the new forms of worship, the common people could no longer feel at home with themselves or with God. In practice it was impossible for them to get to Jerusalem each year, and in any case the three pilgrimages were not enough to satisfy their intense religious yearnings. At a much later date the establishment of the local synagogue overcame this serious flaw and made it possible for the Hebrew people successfully to implement the reforms spelled out in Deuteronomy.

The end result in the time of Josiah, however, was not a happy one. The Hebrew people found themselves on the sidelines of the nation's official worship. A great void had been created, with nothing to fill it but an abstract idea. The official law of the land reduced the people to a life without God and personal orientation in the midst of religious and political chaos. Thus the reform had a great impact on the people in many respects, but the rigorous application of the new norms lacked grassroots support among the people and hence could not produce solid results. The common people were trodden underfoot and their religious practice was squelched. So the premature death of Josiah opened up the floodgates, and the outlawed pagan practices returned with redoubled force to fill the vacuum created by the reform movement.

It is noteworthy that Jeremiah did not rubber stamp the reform movement. As far as we can tell, he was a man of the people and the great religious leader of his day, but he did not fully and explicitly endorse all the elements of the reform. If ever there was a man who was courageous in criticizing religious abuses, it was Jeremiah. But in a period marked by great confusion, it is not always easy to take a well-defined stand as to what ought to be done. It may be easy enough to say what ought not be done, but it may be unwise to spell out precisely what must be done and officially prohibit any other course of action.

It is not a matter of being faithful *solely* to God. Fidelity to God demands that one be faithful to the people as well. In other words, God's primary concern is the well-being and happiness of human beings. God wants them to grow and attain self-fulfillment. At times people may choose to equate fidelity with a legalistic concern for norms and rules. Such concern, allegedly to purify faith, may be good and proper, but it is not always what God really desires. A father's main concern is not that his son have precise and correct ideas about who his father is but rather that his son be happy and prosperous in life. Insofar as he is happy, thanks to the goodness of his father, he will acquire sound ideas about his father.

Reverence for God is not detached from our happiness and well-being. It is not enough to ask *what* God wants us to do. We must also ask *how* God wants us to carry out the tasks asked of us. The greater errors are usually committed in connection with the second requirement rather than the first. We stay loyal to the abstract doctrine, but we do not adhere to God's outlook in the way we live the doctrine and put it into practice. The law contained in the book of Deuteronomy did and still does contain sound doctrine, for the Bible retains it and we Christians still ponder it today. But the way in which the Deuteronomic reformers implemented it in the time of Josiah precluded any chance of real success. They did not implement it in the right way. They acted in wholehearted obedience and with the best of intentions, but that is not always enough.

Conclusion

In preserving for us this complicated history of a reform movement, the Bible clearly provides us with sound guidelines for orientation and critical thinking. It shows us that the word of God is deeply interwoven with human history and dependent on free human decisions, so much so that it may fail to achieve its objective because of them. Thus the Bible presents us with the great mystery of human history, without explaining it to us. In the Bible we find an unshakable faith that history, given direction and impetus by the word of God, is a victorious history. This certainty led the people of the Bible to make decisions and act upon them. At the same time, however, the human decisions and actions sometimes obscured the presence of God's word and nullified its impact. What happened in the time of Josiah was a prelude to what would happen when the Word-made-flesh arrived. He was eliminated from the human scene, slain on a cross. In his seeming defeat he displayed his invincible power. All of this merely serves to heighten a sense of responsibility in those who truly believe in God.

The Deuteronomic reform started off well and ended up badly because it failed to respect the people. Its complex history indicates that the people of the Bible had a history just like any other nation did. They lived amid an atmosphere of confusion, with fears and hopes of their own. The prophets appeared, scanning the horizon and gropingly trying to detect the signs sent by God. They did not always see their way clearly. But in their company the Hebrew people lived through their ups and downs and reached the goal that God had chosen for them. The people of the Bible did not have a direct telephone connection with God, but they were convinced that God was present amid everything that was happening to them. Their tortured history is an impressive quest for God.

7

JEREMIAH

Running Away Is No Answer

Even though Jeremiah lived in historical circumstances very different from ours, there is something that makes us feel one with him. He alerts us to certain aspects of life in which we do not usually tend to sense or see the summons of God. When we take a close look at Jeremiah, he does not seem to be a figure of the past at all. It is almost as if we might run into him on a street corner.

Jeremiah's Situation

Let us first take a brief look at the historical and social situation of Jeremiah's day. We already considered it in some detail in the previous chapter when we dealt with the reform movement. Here we are concerned mainly with the period that extends from the death of King Josiah (609 B.C.E.) to the exile of the people of Judah into Babylon (587 B.C.E.).

On the international scene, world politics underwent a real change. Assyria and Egypt, which had been the two predominant world powers, lost their imperial control of the area. A third world power, awesome and threatening, had come to dominate. In the year 612 B.C.E., the Babylonians destroyed Nineveh, the capital of Assyria. It was an event that sent shock waves through the Near East, shock waves of delight in many instances (see the book of

Nahum). The people of Judah viewed the changed situation with great pleasure, and they had even attempted to help it along so that they in turn might benefit from the result. As we noted previously, King Josiah led out his army in 609 B.C.E. to prevent the pharaoh of Egypt from going to the aid of the retreating Assyrian army. His army was defeated and he himself was fatally wounded, but the combined forces of Assyria and Egypt were eventually decimated. From 609 B.C.E. on, the road lay open for the advance of Babylon.

The changed international situation had repercussions on the politics of Judah. One faction in Judah favored Babylon, another favored Egypt. Three months after the death of Josiah, who was pro-Babylonian, the Egyptian pharaoh dethroned his pro-Babylonian successor (Jehoahaz) and placed a pro-Egyptian king (Jehoiakim) on the throne of Judah. With the crowning of Jehoiakim (609–598), Babylon became a serious threat to Judah. Once the Babylonian forces had won victory over Pharaoh Necho, Judah became a vassal state of Babylon (in 605 B.C.E.). Pro-Egyptian intrigue in Judah led to a revolt against Babylon that was gradually crushed. From the time of this revolt against Babylon (602 B.C.E.) to the destruction of Jerusalem (587 B.C.E.), confusion reigned in Judah. There developed an almost pathological fear of Babylon, the "disaster from the north" (Jer 1:14–15). The country was marked by intrigue, political maneuvering, and sabotage. No one seemed able to think straight, and ridiculous solutions were proposed to counter the danger that threatened the country.

The national situation was also grave. The sudden early death of King Josiah, the nation's beloved leader, was a heavy blow. It killed the last vestiges of hope in the hearts of many people. The reform movement sparked by his leadership (see chapter 4 and chapter 6) did not move forward. Decay set in, and incompetent kings assumed the throne. Amid this atmosphere of general uncertainty, people looked out for themselves and injustice became a growing cancer.

The nation sought to obtain some measure of security by entering military alliances with Egypt and pretending that there was no danger from Babylon. Some insisted that all was well when in fact nothing was well (Jer 6:14). The nation's happy facade was an attempt to conceal real feelings of terror (Jer 8:11). This false political front was shrouded in the protective mantle of official religion. People felt they would be safe if they were faithful in carrying out the rites and feasts of the liturgical year (Jer 7:10). And it was easy enough to find priests and prophets who would sanction that approach and assure the leaders that their solution was the correct one (Jer 8:10). Religion in Judah truly became the opiate of the people, who believed what the false prophets were telling them: "Prosperity shall be yours.... No disaster shall befall you" (Jer 23:17). But empty rites, lifeless ceremonies, and worthless promises do not provide defense against the enemy. The ultimate disaster moved closer and closer while religion was used to defend selfish group interests.

A Prophetic Vocation

In the small village of Anathoth, about six kilometers north of Jerusalem, there lived a youth named Jeremiah. He came from a priestly family (Jer 1:1) and was probably a descendant of Abiathar, a high priest under David who was later removed from his post by Solomon (1 Kgs 2:26–27). The tradition of the Hebrew people coursed through Jeremiah's veins. He felt the tragic situation of the nation with great personal intensity and recognized the absurdity of the official solutions. They did not go to the roots of the problem.

Insofar as we can judge from Jeremiah's later writings, his faith in God led him to view the situation with a critical eye. He knew what his faith demanded, and he knew that the makeshift solutions of the time would not be effective. His vision was very simple, even simplistic, but it was wide-ranging. The existing situation was clear proof that the Hebrew people had abandoned the pathway of God. Injustice was securely entrenched in power, and it had even reached the king's throne (Jer 22:13–19). This caused Jeremiah to doubt if there was even one person in Jerusalem who was still practicing justice (Jer 5:1). As one oracle puts it: "They run from one sin to another, and for me they care nothing. This is the very word of the Lord" (Jer 9:3).

The simple explanation was that the people had abandoned God (Jer 2:13). Instead of serving the God of the nation, who wanted the people to practice justice (Jer 7:5–6), all were following their own version of God. There were as many gods as there were towns in Judah, as many altars as there were streets in Jerusalem itself (Jer 11:13). And so the nation headed toward total disintegration.

In such a situation the ostrich approach would not help at all. It would do no good to evade responsibility, to seek protection and security in empty-headed religiosity or dubious military alliances. The evil had to be attacked at its roots: "Administer justice betimes, rescue the victim from his oppressor, lest the fire of my fury blaze up and burn unquenched because of your evil doings" (Jer 21:12). All the proposed solutions were equally futile. Instead of warding off "the disaster from the north," they only brought it closer. The people and their leaders were digging their own grave. They did not seem to realize the false solutions would only hasten disaster.

This critical vision of reality aroused Jeremiah to a sense of his own personal responsibility. Something had to be done. God would want that. The problem obsessed Jeremiah until one day in the kitchen he saw a cauldron tipping toward the south: "The Lord came to me a second time: 'What is it that you see?' 'A cauldron,' I said, 'on a fire fanned by the wind; it is tilted away from the north'" (Jer 1:13). Facts and events began to speak a message when they were connected with the problem that so concerned him: "From the north disaster shall flare up against all who live in this land" (Jer 1:14).

That is how Jeremiah's vocation arose. He came to see clearly that God was summoning him to speak out the truth to his people, that this was the mission that had been entrusted to him from his mother's womb (Jer 1:5). He was frightened: "Ah! Lord God, ... I do not know how to speak; I am only a child" (Jer 1:6). But he had to put fear aside because the might of God would be with him: "Fear none of them, for I am with you and will keep you safe" (Jer 1:8). Jeremiah was to be "a fortified city, a pillar of iron, a wall of bronze to stand fast against the whole land" (Jer 1:18). No one will get the better of him because he was on the side of right and truth: "They will make war on you but shall not overcome you, for I am with you and will keep you safe" (Jer 1:19).

So Jeremiah set out on his mission, the mission that had slowly matured in his mind as a personal conviction. He was sure that it came from God, the Lord of his people.

Jeremiah in Action

In an atmosphere of pervasive anxiety Jeremiah remained calm. He forthrightly denounced the falseness of official policy and politics and paid no heed to the pronouncements of opportunists and false prophets (Jer 28:1–17; 23:9–40). He offered no guarantees of protection whatsoever. There was no guarantee in the Temple, for he believed it was a tragic mistake to seek reassurance in the existence of the Temple. God no longer dwelt there, but had become a wandering alien in the land (Jer 14:8). The Temple would be destroyed as if it were just another building (Jer 7:12–14). God no longer wanted to be on familiar terms with the Israelites (Jer 7:15). Circumcision (Jer 9:26), sacrifices (Jer 14:12), fasting (Jer 14:12), and prayer (Jer 11:14): none of these practices on which the people relied for security were of any real use. Not even the great figures of the past, such as Moses and Samuel, could persuade God to have pity on the Hebrew people (Jer 15:1). The law was no longer a source of protection because lying had turned God's law into an instrument of deceit and oppression (Jer 8:8–9). The king, once the apple of God's eye, had become ineffective: "Coniah, son of Jehoiakim, king of Judah, shall be the signet-ring on my right hand no longer. Yes, Coniah, I will pull you off" (Jer 22:24). The king will have no line of successors (Jer 22:30).

The logical conclusion was that God had ceased to dwell in Jerusalem (Jer 8:19). There was no sense in saying that all was well because things were getting worse and worse (Jer 8:11). There was no sense thinking that Egypt might be interested in offering aid (Jer 37:7). "Egypt will fail you as Assyria did; you shall go out from here, each of you with his hands above his head" (Jer 2:36–37). All the proposed solutions were mere evasions, and evasion is never a solution. It hastens the approaching danger instead of warding it off.

At this point one might well challenge Jeremiah himself: "Okay, critic, what solution do you yourself propose?" Jeremiah had no solution to offer. Decay had set in, and the present setup would be swept away: "Can the Nubian change his skin, or the leopard its spots? And you? Can you do good, you who are schooled in evil?" (Jer 13:23). Sin was all-pervasive (Jer 17:1–2). The people could not change their way of life even if they wanted to (Jer 18:11–12). The fact was that fidelity had disappeared (Jer 7:27–28). So God will "shatter this people and this city as one shatters an earthen vessel so that it cannot be mended" (Jer 19:11). Where, then, are the people to go? The Lord's answer is appalling: "Those who are for death shall go to their death, and those for the sword to the sword; those who are for famine to famine, and those for captivity to captivity" (Jer 15:2). The only escape from this fate would be to surrender to the approaching enemy (Jer 27:12; 38:17–18). This was the advice that Jeremiah had to offer to anyone willing to listen to him!

Jeremiah's other counsels about doing good and practicing justice seemed to fall into the void. A man who spoke such alarmist ideas was dangerous and subversive. His words upset the people, demoralized the city dwellers, and sapped the courage of the soldiers who were to defend the city against the advancing Babylonians (Jer 38:4). This man had to be put out of the way because he only spoke words of terror (Jer 20:10). Some plotted his capture. One relatively quiet evening, after a protracted Babylonian siege of Jerusalem, Jeremiah was taken as he was heading out of the city (Jer 37:11–16). He was accused of going over to the other side, but he vigorously denied the charge (Jer 37:14). His explanations were to no avail. He was hurled into prison, and he greatly feared that he would be killed (Jer 37:20).

But the imprisonment of Jeremiah did not solve anything. Whether on the loose or in prison, his kind of person gets under people's skin. Actually, the situation grew worse, because Jeremiah's imprisonment caused further division between the leaders of the nation (Jer 37–38). Both his friends and his enemies were afraid of him, as we can see from the secret meeting between the king and him. The king begged him not to tell anyone about it (Jer 38:24–26).

Jeremiah was a person who did not see "faith in God" as alienated from life. To have faith in God was to live a solid and fruitful human life. He saw the summons of God in happenings around him, in both national and international events. And since his fellow Hebrews all claimed to believe in God, Jeremiah committed himself to the task of showing them what that faith entailed. His message was painful because the people did not want to admit the truth of it. His forthright words and clear-cut actions cut them to the quick. Some wanted to silence him at all costs.

Consequences of Commitment

Looking at the figure of Jeremiah from the safe distance of time, we admire him. Those who saw him close up were bewildered by his violent suffering and unfailing fidelity to his mission. He had not asked for that mission; it had gradually grown inside him as a response to God's summons (Jer 20:7–9). One must suffer a great deal to say what Jeremiah said: "A curse on the day when I was born! Be it forever unblessed, the day when my mother bore me, ... because death did not claim me before birth, and my mother did not become my grave, her womb great with me forever" (Jer 20:14, 17).

He was the victim of plots and attacks (Jer 18:18), "a man doomed to strike, with the whole world against me" (Jer 15:10). He

labored and struggled for twenty-three years without the least success (Jer 25:3). He complains bitterly: "I have forsaken the house of
Israel, I have cast off my own people. I have given my beloved into
the power of her foes. My own people have turned on me like a
lion from the scrub, roaring against me" (Jer 12:7–8). Jeremiah suffers in lonely isolation. Everyone has turned against him. His own
relatives betray him (Jer 12:6), and his fellow citizens of Anathoth
want to kill him (Jer 11:18–21). The nation's priests, the other
prophets, and many of the people want to put him to death (Jer
26:8). Eventually he is hurled into a fetid pit, from which one of his
friends rescues him (Jer 38:1–13). His suffering seems useless and
absurd because he has no results to show for it after twenty-three
years of work.

But in the midst of all this suffering Jeremiah is sustained by a
force that no human being can crush. It makes him a fortified city,
a pillar of iron, and a wall of bronze. For Jeremiah is sure of one
thing: "The Lord is on my side, strong and ruthless" (Jer 20:11). His
lot was harsh and he often fought against it, but at bottom he chose
it and took delight in it. He knew it was the proper road for him.
When his mission brought him suffering, he recalled the moment
when his vocation came to him: "O Lord, thou hast duped me, and
I have been thy dupe; thou hast outwitted me and hast prevailed"
(Jer 20:7).

Without honor in his own lifetime, this man would eventually
become an image of the Messiah to come: a man of sorrows who
would shoulder the sinful guilt of us all (Mt 8:17; Is 53:3–4). It often
happens that a person who seemed to extinguish people's hopes
while alive becomes a symbol of universal hope after his death.

Jeremiah's Contribution to God's Plan

Jeremiah had no human being to confide in during his lifetime, so
he confided in God. He thus contributed to the interiorization of
religion, to its becoming a religion "of the heart": that is, a very

personal force at work in the inner depths of a person and not just relating to external, superficial acts.

Jeremiah did this not so much by his teachings as by his way of living. He had to suffer in order to overcome the obstacles facing his mission, in order to succeed in life. He managed to lead a successful life because in and through his suffering he learned to apply all the collective values of the nation's faith to his own personal life. Suffering led him to interiorize religion and enabled him to grow as a human being.

In his prayer — and there is a great deal of prayer in his writings — Jeremiah did not put on an act. He said what was in his mind and heart, even when it sounded like vengeance and despair. He even came to curse the day that he was born. He grew in the life of faith by living out his personal drama and enduring a life of solitude. (Faithful to his unique vocation, he never married.) All the values of past tradition were assimilated by Jeremiah in his own way.

This becomes clear to anyone who reads the sections known as the "Confessions of Jeremiah" (Jer 11:18–12:6; 15:10–21; 17:14–18; 18:18–23; 20:7–18; 12:7–13). Through his suffering there emerged his own personal and individual conscience over against the collective conscience of the nation. He found himself because he came into contact with the absolute "I" of God. In Jeremiah the Hebrew religion became more adult. He marked the beginning of the reform movement that would be carried forward by the Hasidim, the lowly people of God to which Mary and Elizabeth would later belong.

Clearly reflected in the life and writing of Jeremiah is religion made flesh. Jeremiah was courageous enough to point out God's appeals in real life. For him religion was not an abstract system. It was human beings journeying steadfastly toward the future under the initiative of faith. Jeremiah was even bold enough to point out God's summons in international events. He clearly embodied faith in the fact that the world and its destiny are in God's hands.

In Jeremiah we also find the conviction that the world will be what human beings make of it with their freedom. One cannot appeal to God to justify a situation of decay that is contrary to human well-being.

During his lifetime Jeremiah was a focus of controversy. After his death he became a symbol of hope. When a later author, during the period of exile in Babylon, describes the future Messiah, he probably has the figure of Jeremiah in mind (Is 53).

WISDOM LITERATURE

Yearning for Life and Facing Death

In this chapter we tackle a new section of the Old Testament. We considered certain aspects of the *historical* books in the first four chapters. In chapters 5 and 7 we spoke about the *prophetical* books. Now we shall consider the *sapiential* books.

The title of this chapter focuses on one major theme that runs through the sapiential books. (Another major preoccupation of the sapiential writers is the existence of suffering and evil in the world, but we shall discuss that theme in the next chapter in connection with the book of Job.)

Let us begin our discussion with a brief consideration of how the sapiential books came into being.

Origin of the Sapiential Books

One group of books in the Old Testament is known as the sapiential books. They include: Proverbs, Ecclesiasticus (or Sirach), Ecclesiastes, the Song of Songs, Job, and Wisdom. Some include the book of Psalms in this grouping, but we shall consider the Psalms separately in chapter 10.

There is a big difference between the historical and prophetical books and the sapiential books. The former embody the new thinking that various religious leaders communicated to the people for the improvement of their lives. The latter embody the longstanding thinking of the common people, now expressed in organized fashion so that it might improve the lives of those who read it. Thus we have two different styles of thinking. The former confronts us with reasoned thinking that moves from the outside to the inside, from above to below. In the latter case we are confronted with reasoned thinking that moves from the inside to the outside, from below to above.

We find these two different styles of thinking operative today. Akin to the prophetical writings is the doctrine of the church formulated and embodied in catechetical, conciliar, and papal documents. People read those documents to find guidance in life. Akin to the process evident in the sapiential books is people's quest for a way to improve their lives. In this case people start from the data of life experiences, which have been illuminated by the social disciplines. They study such subjects as anthropology, psychology, sociology, and economics as they relate to life.

Even today it is often the sapiential books that are most favored by average lay people and least studied by the clergy. Perhaps some unconscious class prejudice is responsible for the fact that the educated clergy — and that would include theologians and biblical exegetes — often prefer the historical and prophetical books of the Bible to the sapiential books. This predilection certainly does not help them to gain a solid, well-rounded acquaintance with the whole corpus of divine revelation, for some of that corpus has found expression in the thinking of the common people contained in the sapiential books.

The wisdom thinking contained in the sapiential books is part of a broad cultural phenomenon that typifies the whole ancient Middle East. In addition to the ancient Hebrews, the people of Egypt, Assyria, and Babylonia also had their own sapiential literature. Wisdom thinking does not mean, first and foremost, some sort of abstract intellectual virtue or knowledge. It refers to a basic aptitude for living life well and acting in a sensible way. It is a "philosophy of life." It represents a certain attitude toward life that was typical of those ancient peoples. In itself it had little to do with religion, just as modern thinking about such subjects as anthropology and economics has little to do with the religious convictions of those who work in those subjects. The fact that people are religious believers does not make them better mathematicians or economists. Religious conviction does not play a major role in their thinking as mathematicians or economists, even though it may ultimately affect the way they live their lives as professional persons. It is in the latter sense that faith does in fact have a role to play in our world, even as it did in the world of biblical times. That also explains why wisdom thinking took a different turn in the Bible than it did in other sapiential literature.

The Israelites were in the same basic situation as their neighbors. They pondered life with the same basic principles in mind, and they did not hesitate to borrow passages from the wisdom thinking of other nations. The Hebrews borrowed from the Egyptians (Prv 22:17–23:11), even as sociologists in the Third World today often borrow ideas from sociologists in developed nations.

At the core of wisdom thinking we find the people, who kept reflecting on life and looking for answers to basic questions. How are we to live? What should we do to succeed in life? How should we behave? These are the questions of serious, thoughtful people who want to know how to act meaningfully in life so that they will not be overwhelmed by it. The search for wisdom is a search for the norms and values that rule human existence. People want to find out what these norms and values are so that they can integrate them into their lives and thus make progress in their existential situation.

The search began humbly enough among the common people. Its beginnings can be found in proverbs, which are still passed around today. It took on more complex and scientific form in such writings as the book of Job and the book of Wisdom. The chief concern of wisdom thinking is to confront the evils that beset life, to form the growing younger generation, and thus give direction to human life. The only solutions accepted were those that had proved to be viable in the concrete praxis of life. A typical example of this basic outlook can be found in the book of Ecclesiastes, which is a veritable textbook on the way that wise persons proceed in their exploration. The root source of wisdom thinking, its original milieu, is the realm of family life and family training. Parents tried to help their children open their eyes to reality and look at life objectively. Wisdom thinking was a store of accumulated experiences handed down from parent to child over many generations. The pedagogical approach used was rather interesting. Initially the wise person, the sage, was one who had a special knack for formulating some lesson about life in a pointed saying. This gave rise to popular proverbs, which served as foundation stones for life and embodied the values that had been discovered or worked out by certain individuals in the community. Here are some examples of proverbs from the Bible:

> A merry heart makes a cheerful countenance, but low spirits sap a man's strength. (Prv 17:22)

> To answer a question before you have heard it out is both stupid and insulting. (Prv 18:13)

> The poor man speaks in a tone of entreaty, and the rich man gives a harsh answer. (Prv 18:23)

> Wealth makes many friends, but a man without means loses the friend he has. (Prv 19:4)

> In the life of the downtrodden every day is wretched, but to have a glad heart is a perpetual feast. (Prv 15:15)

> Even a fool, if he holds his peace, is thought wise; keep your mouth shut and show your good sense. (Prv 17:28)

> The sluggard plunges his hand in the dish but will not so much as lift it to his mouth. (Prv 19:24)

> Like a gold ring in a pig's snout is a beautiful woman without good sense. (Prv 11:22)

There are many similar proverbs in the Bible. A proverb expresses some elementary experience in life by way of a *mashal* (i.e., a comparison). Such proverbs forced people to think and helped them discover values in life. They are replete with good sense, learned within the family and in circles of friends. They helped give orientation and direction to the children, not as rote formulas but as illuminators of basic values. They were concerned with the things of immediate interest in life: how to behave, how to deal with other people. There was little philosophic speculation in them, but they possessed a profundity that is typical of popular wisdom all over the world. Examples of the topics treated proverbially in the book of Ecclesiasticus (Sirach) include patience, almsgiving, false security, the unbridled tongue, friendship, fighting, liberty, social relationships, respect for woman, fear of God, table etiquette, value of caution, prudence in the presence of the powerful, the dangers of wine and loose women, making loans, keeping a friend's secret.

The Institutionalization of Wisdom Thinking

Gradually this wisdom thinking grew in scope and content, extending to every sector of life. Moving out from the family circle, it became an object of careful exploration and lost something of its spontaneous character. It became institutionalized, taking its place alongside such institutions as the priesthood and the prophetic office. It would now help to ensure the proper organization of society.

In the hands of the king, this institutionalized wisdom thinking became a tool of government, and it began to be associated with the figure of King Solomon, the sage par excellence (1 Kgs 4:27–34). It would now help the king to govern his people even as it had once helped parents to guide their children.

With this change in status and milieu, wisdom thinking became an object of scholarly meditation and study. Alongside the age-old popular sayings, there arose scholarly tracts on the same basic subjects. The concrete cast of the older proverbs gave way to intellectual probing into the basic philosophy of life that underlay the whole process of wisdom thinking. (We see a similar process at work today with regard to politics, for example. People have practiced politics for countless centuries, but it is only recently that we have seen the rise of schools of political science.)

Thus we can see a gradual evolution in the praxis of wisdom thinking within the Bible itself. The various sapiential books bear witness to different stages in the process. Let us consider each briefly.

Proverbs. This book is a compilation of old and well-loved old proverbs. But the final editors or compilers appended a preface to the whole work, in which they tried to explain the nature and origin of wisdom (Prv 1–9). The first nine chapters were written much later, and so they are more profoundly theoretical than the rest of the book. The proverbs themselves come from the family circle and the daily life of the people, and they deal with the upbringing of children and the concrete problems of life.

The Song of Songs. Everything indicates that we are dealing here with a compilation of popular songs about love. Some sage felt that those songs would help to give concrete expression to God's love for human beings and their love for God. Twelve of the songs were incorporated into this book, which has always been a favorite of commentators.

Ecclesiasticus, or Sirach. This book presents wisdom thinking at the point where it is moving out of the family circle. It contains many small treatises on the most varied matters. The proverbs are now beginning to be organized into various categories. But in this book we see that people have not yet begun to engage in philosophical reflection on the origin and source of wisdom. The practical approach predominates.

Ecclesiastes. This book was put together by one of the official government sages. He expresses his deep frustration with the many different attitudes human beings hold toward life. None of them satisfies him. He has carefully examined them all, and he has reached the conclusion that everything is vanity. Here and there he inserts a proverb on God's activity in life, indicating that he has not completely lost his faith in life and its author, God.

Job. Here we have wisdom thinking in its loftiest literary expression. It tackles one of the problems that most preoccupied the sages: the suffering of the just and upright person. The treatment takes the form of a drama, and the old proverbial approach is left behind. The experience of a human being who has suffered greatly finds expression in this book.

Wisdom. It is the latest of the sapiential books, written sometime in the first century B.C.E. It is also the most profound treatment of the true origin of Wisdom, which it attributes to God. It was written in Egypt, and its style shows marked Greek influence.

The Message of the Sapiential Books

When we read the sapiential books, particularly those written earlier (e.g., Proverbs and Ecclesiasticus), we soon notice that they do not say much about God. They talk about life. We also notice that most of what they say about life could have been discovered by anyone who does a bit of reflecting. They do not seem to contain anything extraordinary. They simply deal with the ordinary affairs of everyday life. So why are these books in the Bible? Why did God take the trouble to inspire such works? We can find similar thoughts, just as profound, in the wisdom literature of Egypt and Babylon. What is the purpose of all this wisdom thinking in the Bible?

The whole atmosphere of wisdom thinking influenced the outlook and thinking habits of people in antiquity much as science influences our mentality today. The seed of God's word was sown in soil that was interlaced with such wisdom thinking. There the tree of divine revelation would take root and grow. It took a long time before the sages perceived the value of divine revelation for their own wisdom thinking. That does not mean they had ceased to be people of faith. It simply means that at first their faith did not exert much influence on their wisdom thinking, on the way they pondered life and sought to find values in it. The same might be true of professional anthropologists today. Even though they might be persons of deep faith and religious conviction, the basic principles of their professional discipline would not be greatly influenced by that fact.

As time went on, however, wisdom thinking became aware of the limited usefulness of the solutions it proposed for human problems. It gradually became more open to the word of divine revelation that had been handed down by priests and prophets and enshrined in other books of the Bible. The sages began to realize that divine revelation had some value for their own explorations into life. They took over the word of God as a useful tool for discovering true wisdom. Thus, without sacrificing its own methodology and patterns of thought, wisdom thinking was deeply influenced by the priests and prophets in the way it approached its reflection on its own origin and orientation. It came to see God as the ultimate origin and goal of all the wisdom thinking that guided human life.

The God in question was not just any deity. This was the God of Abraham, of the one who initiated and gave direction to the history of the Hebrew people. This same God was at the source of the laws and values that ruled their lives. Suddenly everything became clear. God's law, the Mosaic law, was identical with wisdom, as Psalm 119 plainly states. Thus the whole area of investigation was greatly expanded. Now it was not just present-day life and its problems that deserved to be analyzed. All of past history also deserved consideration, because therein God had left traces of divine wisdom.

So we begin to find considerations of past history in the sapiential books (Sir 44–50; Wis 10–19). In this case, history is not seen from the standpoint of priest or prophet but from the standpoint of the common people insofar as they have been imbued with the features of wisdom thinking. This line of thought finds summary expression in the Prologue to John's Gospel, which tells us that the creative divine Word at the source of all life is also the salvific divine Word that gives direction to all history. Both life and history are rooted in God and embodied in Jesus Christ, the Word-made-flesh (Jn 1:1–14). This discovery of God as the origin and end of wisdom placed the age-old proverbs in a new light. They were now considered the first lowly steps on the ladder of life leading up to God. Thus the sapiential books in the Bible bear witness to an optimistic vision of life: for the person who has eyes to see, all reality can serve as a mirror of God. The sapiential books bear perduring witness to the fact that the locus of our encounter with God is the ordinary life of every day, the things that well up from the depths of concrete experience. The great treasure possessed by all of us is the life we are living. The sapiential books urge us to look for God in life itself, not in rites and ceremonies, vigils and pilgrimages. If we live our lives in that awareness, then such events can take on real meaning and importance. The sapiential books are an appeal, urging us never to let ourselves be beaten down by the problems and adversities of life, which are simply stumbling blocks on the road that can lead us to God.

To sum up once again, the wisdom thinking of the Hebrew people was very much like that of other peoples in antiquity. It is the voice of the people that speaks to us in this literature. As time went on, however, they more and more came to see God's revelation as relevant to the issues they were exploring in their wisdom thinking. The issues were intimately bound up with praxis, with God as origin and goal. Hence the sapiential books bear witness to the people's journey toward God — from the ground up, as it were.

This suggests an approach for today. People must think their own thoughts and express their own feelings. They must be allowed to find *their own* path to truth, to God. They must be given direction and guidance so that they may be able to discover God in and through *their own* life experiences. Truth cannot be imposed on people. We should never forget that the final syntheses of salvation history in the Old Testament, contained in the book of Ecclesiasticus and the book of Wisdom, were formulated on the basis of criteria that stemmed from the common people rather than the clergy. And that vision of salvation history crossed the threshold of the New Testament.

No loftier function could be found for the clergy today: instead of using clerical categories, the clergy must try to ground revealed truth in the categories that the people themselves use to give orientation and direction to their lives.

Life and Death

As we have seen so far, the people represented in the sapiential books were characterized by a tendency to reflect on life. The accent was on sound sense and realism. It is not surprising, therefore, that they should be greatly preoccupied with the problems of suffering and death.

They confronted the problem of death with this sense of realism. Initially their ideal in life was to live to a ripe old age and to have numerous progeny. Peaceful death in old age was life's crowning touch, and it caused no great problem in the people's minds. That kind of death was accepted as natural; it was part and parcel of life. The problem was premature death or death by violence, for this cut off a person's life before it had reached full term. It happened frequently enough. Cain killed Abel. Why? In chapter 1 we saw how the author of the Paradise account answered the question. He came from the circle of sages, and he maintained that violent death came into the world because humankind had already parted from God and gone off on its own.

As time went on, however, the fact of death itself became a problem. It called for some explanation. Why should we have to die when we have an indomitable will to live forever? This problem came into view because the people had been reflecting on life over a long period of time and their awareness had been sharpened by this reflection. The sage, schooled in this age-old reflection, began to look at reality more critically. He was no longer so readily willing to accept things as "natural." Moreover, serious reflection on the realities of life made it clear that even a happy death at the end of a long, full life could not be regarded as "natural," as the supreme fulfillment of a human being.

It is the book of Ecclesiastes, in particular, that marks a major step forward in this process of reflection. Looking at the world around him and reviewing all that had been said previously on the subject, even as we might do today, the author found that nothing was worth bothering about. Everything was "emptiness," and life was a farce (Eccl 1:2). To him life was a torment precisely because of the fact of death. Why should we kill ourselves with work if we have to die some day and leave our estate to another who might squander it? (Eccl 2:18–19): "As he came from the womb of mother earth, so must he return, naked as he came; all his toil produces nothing which he can take away with him" (Eccl 5:15).

The author subjects all the old answers to rigorous criticism. Nothing is of much use in life, and everything is worthless after death:

> For man is a creature of chance and the beasts are creatures of chance, and one mischance awaits them all: death comes to both alike. All draw the same breath. Human beings have no advantage over beasts; for everything is emptiness. All go to the same place: All came from the dust, and to the dust all return. Who knows whether the spirit of the person goes upward or whether the spirit of the beast goes downward to the earth? (Eccl 3:19–21)

No one really knows what will happen after life is over.

In his reflection the author had raised dim hopes of some possible future after death. It would be nice if such a thing did exist. But then his bitter irony dashes to the ground any such hope. We yearn to live forever, but a barrier stands over against this yearning. Life has no real meaning, and death takes away all hope.

Here wisdom thinking comes up against an insoluble problem and confronts its own limitations. Insofar as it allows itself to be guided by empirical observation in its conclusions, it cannot help but deduce that everything is ultimately absurd. But the sense of despair produced by the book of Ecclesiastes aroused in people a desire to know more about death and life. It created problems where none had seen any problem before.

Faith in God and Revelation of the Future

Thus people began to develop an even more critical outlook on reality, and certain problems were felt more deeply. What future can we look forward to? Death or life? God's promises to Abraham in the distant past had been framed in very concrete terms. He would be the father of a great people who would settle in a promised land and enjoy a blessed existence (Gn 12:1–3). That is what God had promised, and no one doubted that he would fulfill the promise. But life's realities indicated just the opposite. Instead of obtaining the future promised by God, the just were suffering ever greater oppression (Eccl 4:1–2); meanwhile, those who paid no heed to God were having a high time (Eccl 8:10). The situations of everyday life seemed to deny the justice of God and to speak out against God's fidelity. The author of the book of Ecclesiastes seemed to be right. Why continue to believe in that God?

A conflict arose between faith and experience. It threatened to hurl people into total despair, calling everything into question: life, death, and even God.

The basic problem was that well-being here and now did not exhaust or fulfill our yearning for life and happiness, a yearning that had been stimulated by God's promise. Instead of bringing full life and complete happiness, God's promise brought frustration and ultimate disillusionment. This feeling found vivid expression in the book of Ecclesiastes. Yet this conflict between faith and experience forced people to look for new solutions and ultimately led them to achieve a new vision.

Nostalgic yearning for God and faith in God's fidelity and justice proved to be stronger than the seemingly contradictory nature of life. If God had made a promise, then this promise was somehow capable of being fulfilled. If the here and now seemed to deny that promise by virtue of its contradictory realities and the prospect of death, then God must somehow be stronger than death. In some way God must be able to maintain human life even through death. The bold thinking of faith led the Hebrews to break down the barrier of death that was extinguishing their hopes.

Faith in God's fidelity and strength helped the Hebrews to break out of the closed circle of their own reflections. It alerted them to the broader prospect of a life with God that would endure forever, a life supported by God's power and fidelity. Thus there arose a solid faith in the resurrection of the dead and a life with God after death. The revelation of these new truths did not come about by decree; it came about as a result of poignant reflection over the course of centuries, from the time of Abraham to the centuries just before the coming of Jesus Christ.

The first faint expressions of hope in some sort of life in God's presence after death are to be found in the Psalms (Pss 11:7; 17:15; 23:6; 27:4). But it is Psalm 73 that formulates this dawning realization most clearly:

> When my heart was embittered I felt the pangs of envy, I would not understand, so brutish was I, I was a mere beast in thy sight, O God. Yet I am always with them, thou holdest my right hand; thou dost guide me by thy counsel and afterwards wilt receive me with glory. Whom have I in heaven but thee? And having thee, I desire nothing else on earth. Though heart and body fail, yet God is my possession forever. They who are far from thee are lost; thou dost destroy all who wantonly forsake thee. But my chief good is to be near thee, O God; I have chosen thee, Lord God, to be my refuge. (Ps 73:21–28)

Here we see faith courageously facing reality and not hesitating to affirm something that seems absurd: there is reason to hope because God will resurrect us from the dead. We find this truth clearly expressed in the first five chapters of the book of Wisdom. Here is an explicit passage:

> But the souls of the just are in God's hand, and torment shall not touch them. In the eyes of foolish men they seemed to be dead; their departure was reckoned as defeat, and their going from us as disaster. But they are at peace, for though in the sight of men they may be punished, they have a sure hope of immortality; and after a little chastisement they will receive

great blessings, because God has tested them and found them worthy to be his. (Wis 3:1–5)

This realization represents a great achievement in the attempt to give proper direction to life.

Later, in the New Testament, Christ completed this teaching concerning life after death and the victory of faith and hope. By virtue of faith, this enduring life is already present here and now. The future is already operative, transforming and resurrecting the world and humankind from the disastrous realities of evil and death. To believe in undying life is to believe in the possibility of the world being *renewed,* to wait for the new world to come out of the old world.

Final Considerations

In all this we find a profound human experience that is very much our own. We cannot manage to live wholly on our own. We all have to let our ego depend on someone else. That someone else will to some extent sustain us and make us feel that we are worthwhile and doing something useful. This feeling, in turn, will give impetus to our own energies.

Many depend on the power of friendship and human love. But when they reflect on the matter, they realize that the other person, the friend or lover, will die someday. Thus they will lose their source of support, because human friendship and love are not strong enough to overcome death.

Those who become aware of this limitation on friendship and love look elsewhere for some support that will help them to survive beyond death. (1) They look to their work, to the contribution they can make to the welfare of others. Their contribution will survive their death, and hence they will survive in some way; but their ego will melt into the collective life of the group and disappear. The ancient Egyptians thought like that, and so they invested much energy in constructing pyramids to ensure their survival after death.

It certainly is some form of survival. (2) Others look to reasoned conclusions about life. Life, they say, is absurd and we must accept this absurdity. True human beings will accept the absurdity of life, live as best they can, and then disappear from existence at the moment of death. (3) Still others try to prolong their lives through their progeny. Their name will live on through their children. This, too, is a form of survival; but here again the personal self disappears. This form of survival — i.e., survival through procreation — degenerated into fertility cults among the ancient Canaanites in Palestine.

All these attempts to prolong the life of the self and give meaning to existence failed to give lasting satisfaction. The fact was that the personal self would eventually die and disappear. Biblical thought broke out of this closed circle of reflection concerning survival. A Voice freely chooses to speak to us, a Voice that comes from a realm of life that is not subject to death. It stands outside the closed circle of life and death in which we dwell. This loving Voice establishes a dialogue with us, summoning each of us by name and alerting us to new possibilities. We sense the presence of a force that can now keep us alive and restore us to life after death.

This divine force of love and friendship calls us by name and confers value on us. It will remain operative forever, because love truly lived goes on forever. We have entered into dialogue with God, who summons us to go on living. Our will to live is aroused and given impetus by the love of God; we want to survive death and go on living forever. This new desire is later given confirmation in the resurrection of Jesus Christ. It is this friendship and love that confers eternal value on all human friendship and love. Nothing is lost. Everything is an expression of the faith and hope that enables us to live forever.

9

JOB

The Drama of Us All

The drama is about to begin. The audience in the hall grows silent.
But the curtain stays down, and instead a narrator steps out to in-
troduce the subject at hand. The narrator will acquaint the audience
with the subject that is to be explored and debated in the drama itself. It is a concrete problem dealing with human beings and their
destiny.

The Narrator's Role

The narrator begins: "There lived in the land of Uz a man of blameless and upright life named Job, who feared God and set his face
against wrongdoing" (Jb 1:1). This man Job was upright, wealthy,
well-known, prosperous, and happy (Jb 1:2–5).

Now the narrator takes us behind the scenes to where human
beings and their destiny are discussed and decided. We are allowed
to listen to their conversation that determines what will happen in a
person's life, the kind of conversation that lies beyond the range of
our ordinary human hearing. We are present at a meeting in heaven
where God determines the lot of people. Satan is a participant in
this particular discussion. He is the "devil's advocate" in the testing
of humanity, the prosecutor who lays bare our faults before God.

At this particular meeting God approaches Satan and calls his
attention to the exemplary life of Job: "A man of blameless and up-

right life, who fears God and sets his face against wrongdoing" (Jb 1:8). Satan does not accept that verdict, maintaining that Job's supposed integrity is due to the fact that he is blessed and prosperous: "Has not Job good reason to be God-fearing? Have you not hedged him round on every side with your protection, him and his family and all his possessions? Whatever he does you have blessed" (Jb 1:9–10). Job's goodness is merely a superficial pose, claims Satan: "But stretch out your hand and touch all that he has, and then he will curse you to your face" (Jb 1:11).

God accepts the challenge: "So be it. All that he has is in your hands" (Jb 1:12). Satan is given permission to test Job's honesty and uprightness. He can do whatever he wants to Job, but he cannot touch Job's person. Suddenly, without Job knowing why, one disaster after another falls upon him. He loses everything, including his children; he and his wife are left desolate and alone (Jb 1:13–19).

It is too much to bear! In despair Job rends his garments and cries out: "Naked I came from the womb, naked I shall return whence I came" (Jb 1:21). But even with all that has befallen him, Job will not curse God. He "did not charge God with unreason" (Jb 1:22). Instead he reacts with resignation: "The Lord gives and the Lord takes away; blessed be the name of the Lord" (Jb 1:21).

When the heavenly court meets again, God tries to show Satan that he has erred in his judgment of Job (Jb 2:1–3). Job is virtue incarnate; his piety is not a facade. But Satan is not convinced: "There is nothing the man will grudge to save himself. But stretch out your hand and touch his bone and his flesh, and see if he will not curse you to your face" (Jb 2:4–5). God again accepts the challenge and gives Satan permission to strike Job: "So be it. He is in your hands" (Jb 2:6). The only restriction is that Satan may not kill Job.

Suddenly, without knowing why, Job is stricken with leprosy and becomes a terrible sight. He has only a piece of broken pottery to use for scratching his sores, and he goes to sit on a pile of ashes (Jb 2:7–8). Even his wife wants nothing to do with him because she cannot stand his fetid breath alongside her in bed (Jb 19:17). She even tries to get him to rebel against God, for the Lord has certainly not been kind to Job: "Are you still unshaken in your integrity? Curse God and die!" (Jb 2:9). But Job will not listen to such talk: "You talk as any wicked fool of a woman might talk. If we accept good from God, shall we not accept evil?" (Jb 2:10). He refuses to rebel against God.

So Job has lost everything. His suffering is so great that one can hardly imagine it. What is worse, he himself does not know why he is being subjected to such suffering. He has not been privy to the meetings in heaven at which his fate has been decided. He simply suffers the consequences of the decisions made there. And in the opinion of his contemporaries, there was only one explanation for such terrible suffering: It was a punishment from God! Job must be a terrible sinner!

Three friends hear of the misfortunes that have befallen Job. They come from afar to share his suffering, offer him some consolation, and display their sympathy (Jb 2:11). Job is so changed that they hardly recognize him (Jb 2:12). His plight overwhelms them. Speechless, they sit down to bemoan his plight. For "seven days and seven nights" they did not say a word, for they saw "that his suffering was very great" (Jb 2:13).

The suffering of the just man: Who can explain it? That is the problem that will be discussed in the drama. The narrator has presented the audience with a concrete case, one of countless such cases. The narrator disappears now from the stage, and the curtain slowly rises.

The Question of Suffering

Silence has reigned for seven days and seven nights. As the curtain opens we see Job in his pile of ashes and his friends close by. His silent suffering reaches down through the long centuries into our own hearts. Unable to explain such suffering, we sit silently and wait alongside Job and his three friends.

Suddenly a terrible cry pierces the silence. It is a bitter complaint. The audience shudders, but is pleased at the same time. Job has the guts to voice his complaint, to shout to the four winds. He is willing to give expression to the feelings of the just person who suffers without knowing why:

> Perish the day when I was born and the night which said, "A man is conceived!" May that day turn to darkness; may God above not look for it, nor light of dawn shine on it.... Why was I not still-born, why did I not die when I came out of the womb? Why was I ever laid on my mother's knees or put to suck at her breasts? For then I should be lying in the quiet grave, asleep in death, at rest.... Why should the sufferer be born to see the light? Why is life given to men who find it so bitter?... There is no peace of mind nor quiet for me; I chafe in torment and have no rest. (Jb 3:3–4, 11–13, 20, 26)

Thus Job initiates the debate, laying the problem right on the table. A man has chosen to seek the meaning of life, the reason for his suffering and torment. A problem that confronts us all is laid bare on the stage in the person of Job, the central character in the drama that will unfold before us. We are born without asking to be born, and there are people waiting to receive us. We are brought into life only to suffer and die senselessly, without knowing the reason for either life or suffering or death.

On the stage we also see the various efforts we make to explain the reason for suffering. They are embodied in Job's three friends and in the young man who will show up later (Jb 32–37). None of the characters in the drama knows about the deliberations in heaven or the reason for what has happened to Job. Like the audience, like us, they have brought along their own sufferings and see them vividly imprinted on Job. Like us, they keep trying to find some explanation that will make life more tolerable. Like us, they engage in every sort of rationalization.

Job's three friends are on the side of the audience insofar as they embody the traditional explanations that are offered for the sufferings we encounter in life. But the audience must also admire the courage of Job, who is bold enough to challenge what most regard as sacrosanct. Starting from his own life experience, Job is willing to confront long-held traditions and challenge age-old ways of thinking. Why? Because in their attempt to defend God they tell lies about human life (Jb 13:7–8).

As the drama unfolds, the audience will be able to hear and evaluate the arguments and consoling words offered to Job. We will see to what extent they explain suffering and stand up against the realistic, anguished awareness of a suffering man like Job. His three friends will voice and defend the arguments that people are wont to offer. They will not allow a suffering and disillusioned individual to undermine the solid foundations of traditional piety that had been their source of security in life. Which will win here — tradition or personal conscience?

The dialogue between Job and his friends is one that goes on inside all of us when we are confronted with suffering. It is the dialogue that goes on between the older generation and the younger generation, between those who cling to what has been handed down by tradition and those who find such traditional explanations no answer to the problems and questions raised by their own experiences.

The Existential Problem in the Book of Job

For a long time the cultural situation of the Hebrew people had been tribal and pastoral. Everything belonged to everyone, and all the people shared a common lot. All were well off or all suffered poverty, and hence there was a strong feeling of group solidarity. In that cultural context it seemed quite natural that one person should suffer because of the evil committed by another (Jos 7:1–26). There was even a proverb to that effect: "The fathers have eaten sour grapes, and the children's teeth are set on edge" (Ez 18:2). At this point no one knew anything about the future that lay beyond death. It was felt that all would share the same lot, whether they were good or evil in life (Eccl 9:1–2). All would go down to a shadowy existence in a place called *sheol*.

Living in this cultural context, the people tried to express their faith in a personal God by offering some explanation for suffering. God was just, rewarding the good and punishing the evil. Hence evil was to be regarded as a punishment inflicted by God. If a good person was faced with suffering, then that suffering must be a punishment for sins committed by others. If people were enjoying happiness and prosperity, that must be a reward for their own goodness or the goodness of others. There was no thought at this point of reward or punishment after death. This explanation satisfied the nomadic Hebrew people and resolved the problem of the suffering inflicted on the just person. It fit well into the context of their pastoral culture and gave them a satisfactory idea of God and God's justice.

The transition from pastoral life to a settled agricultural society brought profound changes to the Hebrew people. A sense of personal awareness and individual conscience grew. They now lived in settled towns and cities where people cultivated their own fields or engaged in trade. The older notion of group solidarity in good and evil faded away. It came to be felt that individuals got what they earned, that results were the product of personal work and effort. It was no longer tolerable to think that one person should suffer for the evil committed by another person. The prophet Ezekiel sought to explain God's justice in this new cultural framework (Ez 18:2ff.): one could not maintain that God would punish the children for their parents' sins; each individual would get his or her due from God; otherwise God would be unjust.

But notice what happened at this point. The people attempted to deal with the new cultural data in terms of their old criteria. Evil was a punishment from God. If a person was suffering and if such suffering was not a punishment inflicted on that person because of the sins of others, then only one explanation remained: *The person was suffering because he or she was a sinner!* Wealth and happiness were tokens of God's reward for goodness; the prosperous person must also be a just person. Poverty and unhappiness were tokens of divine punishment for wickedness; *the poor must also be sinners.* In this way Hebrew theology tried to salvage the data of tradition regarding God's justice. Job was right. In trying to defend God, people were telling lies about life (Jb 13:7–8).

That is the backdrop for the existential problem that gave rise to the book of Job and that is discussed in it. It gives vivid expression to the anguish of a suffering human being. Tradition, the whole structure of organized life and its prevailing outlook, and even Job himself insofar as he was a product of that society said that Job must be a terrible sinner rejected by God, that the severity of his sufferings attested to the seriousness of his sin. But on the other hand Job's conscience told him that he was innocent (Jb 6:29). God was cruel and unjust to treat him that way (Jb 30:21). It was a source of keen anguish to find oneself spurned by Someone whom one had tried to love and serve faithfully (Jb 16:17).

God, it seemed, had withdrawn from Job. Job racked his brain and examined his conscience, but he could not find any indication that he had offended God in any way (Jb 27:5–6; 31:1–40). Job could only wonder why "the arrows of the Almighty find their mark in me" (Jb 6:4). Feelings of revolt against God welled up in his heart (Jb 23:2). Yet at the same time Job believed that God was just, more just than human beings. So there must be some reason why God was punishing him this way and treating him as an enemy (Jb 19:11). Tradition said one thing, his conscience another. Which side was right: God, as tradition and Job had always conceived God, or Job's conscience? How could one be loyal to God and to one's own conscience at the same time? This is the root question raised by the book of Job.

The Hebrew people had fallen on evil days. Crises and calamities multiplied day by day. This unfortunate situation came to a head in a personal crisis for the person who wrote the book of Job. The character of Job gives expression to feelings that were stirring in the hearts of all the Hebrew people. Hence the book of Job was a powerful stimulus to consciousness-raising among them.

Invitation to Participation

The way the drama is set up, Job and his friends do not know what the audience knows. They have not been clued in by the narrator. So the audience has a criterion for judging and evaluating the correctness of the arguments that will be put forth by various characters in the drama. In this dramatization, Job represents the new *awareness of personal conscience* that is emerging among the Hebrew people; his friends represent *tradition* and the attempt to defend its inherited arguments and values.

Those in the audience will find themselves on both sides of the fence in the ensuing discussion, because both Job and his friends voice feelings shared by the listeners. Job's friends represent the audience inasmuch as we all have a desire to follow the age-old ways of thinking, thus avoiding new problems and challenges. Job is on the side of the public inasmuch as he is courageous enough to speak out against things we all would like to see criticized. But he is the enemy of the public because he threatens to demolish the supporting framework of tradition and the peace of mind it affords us; he unmasks the false and spurious reasoning behind which we hide. Job's friends are on the side of the audience when they defend tradition. They are enemies of the audience when they seek to dominate personal awareness and impede its solid growth, when they are willing to "assail an orphan" and gang up on a friend in the name of God and tradition (Jb 6:27).

The discussion between Job and his friends proceeds slowly. It reveals humankind as it truly is: fragile yet self-reliant, weak yet proud, ignorant yet knowledgeable, forsaken yet sure-footed.

Job is in torment because tradition suggests that his suffering is the product of personal sinfulness. Yet his own conscience tells him that he has not committed any sin that merits such punishment. In this case the reader of the book of Job, the person watching the unfolding drama, knows that the traditional opinion is not applicable. But Job does not know that, nor do his three friends. To apply the criterion of tradition in a hard and fast way is the height of injustice, the worst lie imaginable.

But how is one to dismantle the arguments of tradition? This is the question tackled by the author in his drama. Operating on the data of his own experience and conscience, Job will attempt to tear down the arguments of tradition. He cannot look to any other person or even to the structure of his society for defense. His only defense is the voice of his own conscience. Yet, despite these odds, personal conscience gains the upper hand as the debate advances. It reduces the arguments of tradition to dust and ashes (Jb 13:12), hot air (Jb 16:3), and treachery (Jb 6:15–18). Job makes his bold challenge: "Tell me plainly, and I will listen in silence; show me where I have erred" (Jb 6:24). He will not be talked down to: "No doubt you are perfect men and absolute wisdom is yours! But I have sense as well as you; in nothing do I fall short of you; what gifts indeed have you that others have not?" (Jb 12:2–3).

An Erroneous Conception of God

The author is not content merely to tear apart the arguments of tradition. The basic problem is a deeper one. It is not enough to say what things are not. Mere refutation of other people's arguments will not provide a way out of the dilemma. Job's real conflict is not with his friends or with tradition. It is with God: "What you know, I also know; in nothing do I fall short of you. But for my part I would speak with the Almighty and am ready to argue with God" (Jb 13:2–3). Job is ready to go all the way:

> You like fools are smearing truth with your falsehoods, stitching a patchwork of lies, one and all. Ah, if you would only be silent and let silence be your wisdom!...Is it on God's behalf that you speak so wickedly, or in his defense that you allege what is false? Must you take God's part, or put his case for him?...Be silent, leave me to speak my mind, and let what may come upon me! I will put my neck in the noose and take my life in my hands. If he would slay me, I should not hesitate; I should still argue my cause to his face. This at least

assures my success, that no godless man may appear before him. (Jb 13:4–5, 7–8, 13–16)

And so Job moves on to argue with God: "Take thy heavy hand clean away from me and let not the fear of thee strike me with dread. Then summon me, and I will answer; or I will speak first, and do thou answer me. How many iniquities and sins are laid to my charge?" (Jb 13:21–23). Before he hurled down this challenge Job had told his friends: "Be sure of this: Once I have stated my case I know that I shall be acquitted" (Jb 13:18).

The drama is a kind of jury trial. God and the human being are brought into court to settle their differences. Job wants to make a case against God, to present his own defense against God's way of dealing with him (Jb 23:4); and he is sure that he will be cleared by his defense (Jb 23:7). But the opinions of Job's three friends, both pro and con, will not do. It is God who must decide between God and humankind (Jb 16:21). In taking this stance, Job detaches himself from his friends, from society, and from everything that had determined his life up to this point. He sets out alone on a bold new path. He simply must find some solution to the problem that now weighs upon him. It is an authentic human problem, a problem concerning God's presence in our lives. God accepts Job's proposal and delivers a long discourse about divine wisdom and its role in the vast universe (Jb 38–41). Job had questioned God and expounded his own problem in life. Now God questions Job: "Brace yourself and stand up like a man; I will ask questions, and you shall answer" (Jb 38:3). God then goes on to describe the marvels of the universe in all their mysteriousness. Job cannot explain or even know them, but they all have meaning in the design of God's wisdom.

At the end of God's discourse, Job sees the whole problem in a new light: "I knew of thee then only by report, but now I see thee with my own eyes. Therefore I melt away; I repent in dust and ashes" (Jb 42:5–6). An old image of God, one transmitted from the past by report, crumbles away. A whole new image of God comes to life in Job's mind, an image based on his own personal experience. A new light has dawned on the horizon of Job's life, and peace and tranquility return to him. The problem in life does not come from God but from the mistaken image of God that traditional report had imprinted on Job's mind. Through his personal encounter with God, Job was able to rid himself of the old image and discover a new vision for himself and others.

The author does not tell us exactly what solution Job found but does offer the reader all the elements and clues we need to go through the same process as Job and arrive at the same conclusion that Job reached. This is the dramatic technique that typifies the sapiential writers. They are not interested in teaching some abstract solution. They want to get the readers to participate in the search for a solution, to discover the truth for themselves. The readers must do their own reflecting to see if they can identify with Job and discover for themselves what Job himself discovered.

Finally the curtain descends. The narrator returns and pronounces the final verdict: Job's friends lost the debate. God's verdict is: "I am angry with you . . . because you have not spoken as you ought about me, as my servant Job has done" (Jb 42:7). In using tired old arguments to defend a no longer defensible viewpoint, they became the people on trial. They are in the wrong and must beg pardon of Job. For he had the courage to confront God, reality, and tradition, relying solely on the testimony of his own conscience (Jb 42:7–9). The narrator ends by saying that prosperity returned to Job, indicating that Job found God and interior peace once again (Jb 42:10–17).

Conclusion

The drama presented in the book of Job represents the actual experience of some Hebrew. He shares with his readers his own itinerary, his own way of confronting the mystery of suffering. Perhaps the readers would find this useful as well. Hoary outlooks inherited from tradition must be discarded when they can no longer account for reality. A new sense of awareness must be developed.

Job and his friends represent humanity journeying the road of life, arguing about the sufferings that bow them down. Thus we have perennial conflict between revelation and reality, between the thoughts enshrined in an age-old culture and the happenings that confront individuals in their own lifetimes. Today the human conscience is again on the stage, sitting on a pile of ashes, alienated in a thousand different ways, forced into debate with traditional views. The general public is privy to the drama through the news media and the television set. The debate proceeds slowly with many twists and turns, but human awareness and personal conscience are getting the upper hand.

In the last analysis, it was not Job's three friends but Job himself who defended and preserved the authentic value of tradition. It was he who broke ground for a new encounter with God, who got beyond the barrier erected by his three friends and their traditional schemas. The book of Job brought down a whole theology and cleared the ground for something new. It did not solve the problem once and for all, but that was not its intention. It simply wanted to clear away an obstacle that was preventing further progress, and it succeeded admirably. Job's three friends were left with the shell of tradition after Job himself managed to dig out the real meat.

The book of Job shows us that the people of God must engage in criticism and challenging confrontation. Job was not afraid to raise questions when he realized that his conscience could not accept the traditional position. To rule out the possibility of critical questioning is to dig a grave for the very position we are trying to defend against criticism. When the human conscience is not permitted to express itself, then it cannot help but speak out bluntly: "Be silent, leave me to speak my mind. What you know I also know" (Jb 13:13, 2). Job's three friends, and their descendants living today, must remember that God acquitted Job. He had spoken rightly of God though they thought he was in error.

The book of Job represents a most significant and truly human breakthrough. The author, a member of the chosen people, uses the figure of a legendary character known as Job to describe an experience with God. This legendary character was an internationally known figure, not a member of the Hebrew nation. It is as if a modern Christian were to describe his personal experience with Christ in terms of a figure like Gandhi, who is already legendary.

The book of Job typifies the attitude of the sapiential writers toward life. Their point of departure is our conscious awareness, our yearning not to be ground under by life. Life and its problems are their chief concern. Their approach is not to impose some solution on the readers but to get them thinking, to have them discover their own way. The distinguishing mark of these writers is realism, and their discussions take place in the intimate circle of close friends. On stage, in this particular case, we find Job, his three friends, and later a young man named Elihu. It is a meeting of wise men to discuss the problems of life, and such meetings are commonplace around the world.

The book of Job is hard to understand because its literary idiom is complex and alien to us. But the problem under discussion was never more pertinent. Despite the problems of communication on the literary level, the discussion and its message come across loud and clear.

10

THE PSALMS

A Summary of the Old Testament

The Psalms are almost a summary of the entire Old Testament, not in the sense that they contain a little bit of everything but in the sense that they present the most basic attitude of the Old Testament in every conceivable form. When people are disposed to live their lives as a response to God's summons, then their lives should be characterized by a particular attitude or outlook. They must be ready to move ahead to hold the reins of history with a sense of certainty and of history in their hands.

Difficulties in Praying the Psalms

The Psalms portray God as Someone who makes the divine presence known at any given moment. God is in direct communication with human beings, intervening at critical moments in life, helping the Hebrews to win battles, curing illness, guiding people's events in order to carry out the divine plan. But today God does not seem to be around. God's activity is not within the bounds of empirical observation. For people today, and particularly for city dwellers, God is no longer a natural fact of life. Instead God has become an unnecessary hypothesis. Atheism is a practical attitude that more and more people accept without question. The world of the Old Testament and the world of today are very different ones.

It seems impossible to recite the Psalms and then go out and live life earnestly in today's world.

Praying itself is a difficult project. It is not easy to have recourse to Someone who remains invisible. Contact with other human beings is difficult enough. It takes real effort to open up to another person, to exclude other stimuli and focus our attention on the person to whom we are talking. Most of our conversations are superficial chatter rather than dialogue. How much more difficult it is to talk to Someone who is invisible.

Moreover, the Psalms come to us as ancient prayers from a very different cultural milieu. Their idiom is alien to us, their symbols and imagery quite different from those we are used to today. We are unfamiliar with the historical events to which they allude, with the life situation of those who formulated them. Thus it is not easy for us to identify with the Psalms, to recognize our own selves and our historical circumstances in them.

Finally, some of the Psalms seem far from perfect as prayers. Some express desires for violent and hate-filled revenge. How indeed can we recite such imperfect prayers today?

The Psalms as Representative Prayers

The Psalms should not be regarded as the most perfect form or expression of prayer. There are excellent Psalms and imperfect ones, Psalms that are literary masterpieces and Psalms that are little more than plagiarisms.

Nor should the Psalms be viewed as a monolithic block that dropped from heaven one day. The book of Psalms was not composed in a day. It was fashioned over a long period of time. Composition probably began in the time of King David (around 1000 B.C.E.) and was completed around 300 B.C.E. Even after the book of Psalms was completed, the original wellspring of such prayers did not dry up. Several facts reveal this to be true. First, in the Greek translation of the Old Testament (called the Septuagint), we find fourteen Psalms or "odes" that are not in the original Hebrew text. Second, in the Dead Sea Scrolls, which were discovered between 1947 and 1956 but date back to somewhere around 100 B.C.E., we find a large number of Psalms that are not contained in the biblical book of Psalms. Third, in many other sections of the Bible, including the historical, the sapiential, and the prophetical writings, we find prayers and psalms that are not recorded in the book of Psalms itself.

Thus the book of Psalms contains only some of the prayers that were recited by the Hebrew people. It is a limited anthology, a sample of the way people prayed and sang to God. It is part of a centuries-old movement of prayer, and it does not claim to hold a monopoly over the nation's prayer life. It does not rule out other prayers. Instead it is intended to stimulate prayer and carry on a long tradition. Most important is not the Psalms themselves but the longstanding prayer movement from which they arose and to which they try to give further impetus.

The Psalms are a reflection of humankind's slow ascent toward God over the centuries, and our progressive liberation through this contact with God. They preserve both the perfections and the imperfections connected with that ascent.

The imperfections (the sentiments of hatred, self-sufficiency, and vengeance, for example) tend to diminish over the course of time. They are more evident in the older Psalms. The Psalms bear witness to humankind's earnest effort to be loyal to God and itself. They are prayers of people like ourselves, people journeying toward the goal established for us by God.

The imperfections show us that God is willing to accept the prayers of which we are capable. Otherwise God would not have inspired them. The important thing is that the prayer be sincere.

The Origin of the Book of Psalms

The book of Psalms is an artificial collection of 150 Psalms, brought together in one book for liturgical purposes. Its Hebrew title is *sefer tehillim,* which means "Book of Hymns." Yet the explanatory titles for the individual Psalms, which are not translated in all English versions, indicate that only one Psalm is a *tehila,* a "hymn": Psalm 145. The more frequent title for the collection is the "Book of Psalms." The word "psalm" (*mismor* in Hebrew) indicates a particular way of singing or chanting. Today we talk about ballads, blues, country and western, and rock songs. The ancient Hebrews talked about hymns (*tehillim*), psalms (*mismor*), canticles (*shirim*), and so forth.

If you are reading an English translation with the Hebrew titles included, you will notice a certain element of confusion. One title may indicate that the Psalm in question is a "hymn"; another title may indicate that the Psalm in question is a "Psalm." But the fact is that the book of Psalms contains all sorts of chants and prayers: hymns, psalms, canticles, lamentations. Evidently the Hebrews did not find it easy to classify the content of the materials in the book of Psalms, since those materials were quite diverse in their origin. It is always difficult to classify the complicated features of life under a neat title.

There is nothing sacred or exhaustive about the number of Psalms in our present book of Psalms. There we find 150 Psalms, which was a nice round number for the anthology.

Various collections of chants and prayers were in existence before the book of Psalms was put together, just as we have various collections of hymns today. The Hebrews had songs to be sung on pilgrimages, and we note that some Psalms are called "songs of ascent" (Pss 120–34). Others were meant to be sung during the paschal meal, and they are referred to as *hallel* or "Alleluia" songs (Pss 105–7, 111–18, 135–36, 146–50). The Hebrews also had collections by various authors, just as we have records and song books by different entertainers today. At the end of Psalm 72 we find this notation: "Here end the prayers of David, Son of Jesse." Other Psalms are attributed to Moses, Solomon, and the sons of Korah.

Eventually an attempt was made to put together a definitive or standard anthology of the songs and chants on the market. They were culled from every available source, which explains why we find some repetition: compare Psalm 14 and Psalm 53, Psalm 40:13–17 and Psalm 70. Some Psalms existed in more than one collection with slight textual variations, and others were added without too much organization in mind. The biblical text says that the prayers of David end with Psalm 72, but in fact some subsequent Psalms are also attributed to him.

The composer of the final edition divided the Psalms into five basic collections or divisions. Each division ends with a similar refrain: "Blessed be the Lord the God of Israel from everlasting to everlasting; and let all the people say 'Amen'" (Ps 106:48; also see the end verse of Psalms 41, 72, and 89). Psalm 150, the final one, is an elaboration of this basic proclamation.

Thus the background and history of the psalter reveals its roots in the life of the Hebrew people. The Psalms focus and channel the living concerns of God's people, and hence they were much publicized and widely known.

Singing the Psalms

If we want to appreciate the place that the Psalms held in the life of the Hebrew people, we must also know something of the way they were recited or sung. Here again their approach was very much like ours today.

Many Psalms have brief explanatory titles that indicate their origin and the way in which they were to be sung. Many had instrumental accompaniment. Psalm 150 mentions some of these instruments. They were obviously instruments used for popular music, just as we use the guitar, banjo, and fiddle for our folk music. The people often joined in with a simple phrase or verse such as "Amen" or "Alleluia." "Amen" is equivalent to "So be it" or "That's right!" "Alleluia" means "praise to Yahweh." Some of the Psalms are equivalent to our litanies. Instead of saying "Pray for us" the Hebrews responded *ci ad olam hesdo,* which means "his love endures forever" (Ps 136). At times the people would simply join in with a short rhythmic chant — reiterating the name Yahweh, for example (1 Chr 29:20).

The Hebrews often adopted the melody of some popular song for a given Psalm, just as we adapt old melodies to new lyrics today. Thus Psalm 22 is to be sung to the tune of "The Hind of the Dawn." The melody of another tune, "Do Not Destroy," is to be used for Psalms 57, 58, and 59 (see also the explanatory titles for Pss 18, 45, 46, 53, 56, 60, 69, 75, 80, 81, and 84).

Some of the titles also give directions to the chorus or choir. Certain Psalms are to be started by "the leader" (Pss 14, 21, 31). Psalm 88 is to be sung "as a lament." Psalm 7 is to be sung "as a plaintive song."

All these little pieces of information in the book of Psalms attest to the popular origin of the Psalms themselves.

The Author of the Psalms

According to the Hebrew text of the Psalms, seventy-three were composed by David, twelve by Asaph, eleven by the sons of Korah, one by Heman, one by Ethan, one by Moses, a few by Solomon, and thirty-five by anonymous authors. The Greek translation attributes eighty-five Psalms to David.

The frequent attribution of individual Psalms to David and the attribution of the whole book of Psalms to him is more a theological datum than a historical one. There is no reason to deny that David composed many Psalms, but he certainly did not compose all of them. But just as Moses stands at the origin of Hebrew legislation and Solomon at the origin of Hebrew wisdom thinking, so David stands at the origin of the Hebrew prayer movement. He was a striking personage whose sincere piety gave great impetus to the people's prayer life. To attribute the authorship of a Psalm to David was to give it official status in the liturgical life of the nation and to underline its value for the people's prayer life.

Modern Interpretation of the Psalms

The Psalms have been recited throughout the history of the church, and many have tried to explain them and interpret them for the Christian people. One of the most famous of these commentators was St. Augustine. His concern was to interpret the Psalms in such a way that the people of his own day (fourth century C.E.) could see them as a reflection of their own faith and life circumstances. He took the needs of his contemporaries as his point of departure and tried to offer a solid response to them.

As time went on, however, there developed a separation between the existential situation and the life of faith. The Psalms were relegated to the sidelines of life; they were to nourish a faith that often was out of touch with experience. Scriptural exegesis then sought new approaches to address this problem and reestablish a link between faith, prayer life, and everyday living. Most of the time, however, the Psalms were treated and presented as a monolithic block of homogeneous material.

Then a German exegete entered the picture. Herman Gunkel applied the critical notion of "literary genres" to discover the place of the Psalms in the life of the Hebrew people. He managed to pinpoint the varied strands in the Psalms and trace them back to the diverse aspects of the nation's life. Using the notion of literary genres, he divided the Psalms up into different types of prayer: hymns, laments, petitions, meditated history, and so forth. Each type presupposed some specific milieu in which it grew.

Gunkel's work marked an important step forward, for now the Psalms could be seen as reflections of the people's life and its various aspects. But important and valuable as such research is, we simply cannot stop there. We must untangle the various threads, but that in itself does not get us back to the ultimate source. One seemingly curious thing, for example, is the fact that exegetes and commentators often disagree in their classifications of a given Psalm. Why? In my opinion, it is because life itself does not respect our neat divisions and classifications. We must therefore go beyond the literary genres if we wish to find the wellspring of the Psalms.

That source is closer to us than we might think. It is our own lives as human beings, illuminated by the summons of a God who calls out to us. As we probe the Psalms we discover life, the same life that we are living today. In the Psalms we discover something of ourselves and our life; they thus become authentic expressions of what is going on in our own minds and hearts. Viewed from this perspective, the Psalms present us with life in all its rawness, with life as it wells up from inside us. Life forces us to ask questions, to experience its joys and sorrows and anxieties, to consciously feel disquiet and uneasiness. We are forced to echo the words of St. Augustine: "You have made us for yourself, O God, and our hearts will not rest until they rest in you."

In this way the Psalms can achieve the purpose for which they were inspired. They can help us to discover who we are and what our true responsibility is. Shaking us out of our comfortable ease, they can give us new hope and keep us moving in the direction God wants us to go. They are a faithful mirror of life, a critical reflection of our true identity.

Difficulty in Interpreting the Psalms

At the root of the difficulties mentioned earlier it the most serious problem that faces us in trying to recite the Psalms. For reasons already mentioned, the Psalms lie outside the bounds of our own interests. They seem to have nothing to say of our lives. Everything is different: the problems, the language, the culture, the historical situation. Since there is no common bond of shared experience, all the various interpretations and explanations of the Psalms seem to fall into a void. They just do not seem to have any real value for us. They leave us in the dark about ourselves because they do not really speak to us; and hence they also leave us in the dark about God, who supposedly is speaking to us through them.

This difficulty, however, is based on a mistake we ourselves make. First, we do not probe deeply enough into our own lives; hence we cannot detect the pulse that throbs through the Psalms. Second, we do not try hard enough to deepen our knowledge of the Psalms; hence we do not come to see human life itself as the true source of all those prayers. If we probed deeply enough into our own lives and into the Psalms, we would soon discover that the two realities are interconnected and go back to the same source: people seeking meaning in life, people confronted with the problem of the Absolute as it is reflected in the many and varied problems of everyday life.

We cannot get at the root of the Psalms and pray them as our own unless and until we arrive at the realization that we have the same root deep inside ourselves. Strange as they may seem to us, the Psalms grew out of the same kind of situations and experiences that we are confronted with today. We share the same feelings: joy, gratitude, sadness, despair, anguish, and frustration. We must face the same problems: war, betrayal, lack of understanding, pain, and suffering. We, too, experience the seeming contradictions of life and its lack of meaning. If people have not faced up to such situations in their own lives, then they will find it very difficult to pray the Psalms as their own.

Hence if we are to interpret and pray the Psalms correctly, we must face up to one major task. We must live our own lives here and now in all the scope and depth that true living entails. We must face the problems and feelings of life openly and completely. This is what will unite us across the distance of time and space with the authors of the Psalms. Only then will the Psalms become an authentic expression of our own lives, regaining their full force as a human discourse directed to God. Only then will they be able to stimulate us to create new prayers of our own. Only then will we be able to pick up and continue the human search for God that finds such eloquent expression in the Psalms: "All the time that I dwelt among men who hated peace, I sought peace" (Ps 120:6–7).

Our Search for God

Today it seems to many people that God has become superfluous. They still believe that God exists, but they cannot determine God's relevance to human life. Of what use is God? What value or meaning does God have in terms of concrete living?

We find the same problem expressed in the Bible. The Hebrew people believed in God's existence, but the divine presence was hard to discover: "How long, O Lord, wilt thou quite forget me? How long wilt thou hide thy face from me?" (Ps 13:1). The Hebrews felt abandoned: "But now thou hast rejected and humbled us.... Thou hast sold thy people for next to nothing and had no profit from the sale" (Ps 44:9, 12). The state of abandonment to which they were reduced at times seemed to prove that God was absent. It gave rise to terrible crises of faith: "I will say to God my rock, 'Why hast thou forgotten me?' Why must I go like a mourner?...My enemies taunt me, jeering at my misfortunes; 'Where is your God?' they ask me all day long" (Ps 42:9–10). Like many people today, the ancient Hebrews often felt that they did not know what to tell their children about God.

Where is your God? (Pss 42:3, 10; 79:10; 115:2). That was an ever recurring question, and the Hebrews, like us, often found it hard to answer. To have a God and yet not be able to point God out is a disturbing situation. It prompts a person to rebel. After all, what sort of a God is that?

The Bible is nothing else but a vivid response to that question, a question that is still ours today. Leaving aside the theoretical problem, many people today focus on the practical issue of God's significance in their own lives The traditional God concept does not seem to offer any substantive content for everyday life. God is considered irrelevant, an opiate preventing people from making progress and alienating them from the world. God is dead! Long live humankind!

If we read the Psalms, however, we soon realize that this is an old problem. Even then people had the same thoughts: "What does God know? The Most High neither knows nor cares" (Ps 73:11).

Many come to the conclusion that "there is no God" (Ps 14:1). And so they conspire against God and God's people: "Let us break their fetters, . . . let us throw off their chains" (Ps 2:3). They become cocksure: "Our tongue can win the day. Words are our ally; who can master us?" (Ps 12:4). People look out for themselves and get along the best they can (Ps 11:1–2).

Indeed life does seem easier without God. We are freed from useless anxiety and are more capable of unhindered progress and growth. People say God neither knows nor cares, "yet still they prosper, and rogues amass great wealth" (Ps 73:12). It is those who try to believe in God that seem to suffer most, and they are sorely tempted to rid themselves of the burden: "So it was all in vain that I kept my heart pure and washed my hands in innocence. For all day long I suffer torment and am punished every morning" (Ps 73:13–14). Yet something tells the faithful believers that this line of thinking will not solve anything, that it is mere evasion: "Yet had I let myself talk on in this fashion, I should have betrayed the family of God" (Ps 73:15). They choose to take on the contradictory burden of God, to reject the easy way out that has been taken by many people.

Why? The reason is that this God who seems so alien does indeed have something to do with human life. Without God life would have no further meaning: "They who are far from thee are lost; thou dost destroy all who wantonly forsake thee. But my chief good is to be near thee, O God; I have chosen thee, Lord God, to be my refuge" (Ps 73:27–28). Every human being looks for security in life, and the author of the Psalm has found a source of security so solid that he seems to be able to live tranquilly in the midst of life's turmoil: "Though heart and body fail, yet God is my possession for ever" (Ps 73:26).

God is the *foundation* and *future* of the psalmist's life. Hence the psalmist possesses a rare brand of independence, solidity, freedom, and security that is the ideal yearned for by all people. Such a God really does have something to do with life.

True humanity, realism, and concern for everyday life pervade the Psalms. So it seems quite clear that *this* God, the God of the psalmist, is not a product of autosuggestion but rather a gratuitous reality benefiting humankind. Believing in this God makes a person more truly human, and great human qualities develop as a result of contact with God. Here we might enumerate a few of them:

1. The courage to live: "The Lord is the refuge of my life; of whom then should I go in dread? ... If an army should encamp against me, my heart would feel no fear; if armed men should fall upon me, even then I should be undismayed" (Ps 27:1, 3). It is the attitude of mature people who know what they want, who have found their security in God.

2. A pervading sense of tranquillity: "Yet in my heart thou hast put more happiness than they enjoyed when there was corn and wine in plenty. Now I will lie down in peace, and sleep; for thou alone, O Lord, makest me live unafraid" (Ps 4:7–8).

3. Clear perception of what justice demands: "Who may go up the mountain of the Lord? And who may stand in his holy place? He who has clean hands and a pure heart, who has not set his mind on falsehood, and has not committed perjury. He shall receive a blessing from the Lord" (Ps 24:3–5). "O Lord, who may lodge in thy tabernacle? Who may dwell on thy holy mountain? The man of blameless life, who does what is right and speaks the truth from his heart; who has no malice on his tongue, who never wrongs a friend and tells no tales against his neighbor; the man who shows his scorn for the worthless and honors all who fear the Lord; who swears to his own hurt and does not retract; who does not put his money out to usury and takes no bribe against an innocent man. He who does these things shall never be brought low" (Ps 15).

4. Courage to denounce the injustices committed by those in power: "Answer, you rulers: Are your judgments just? Do you decide impartially between man and man? Never! Your hearts devise all kinds of wickedness and survey the violence that you have done on earth" (Ps 58:1–2).

5. Clear awareness of God's justice, which makes one sure of the ultimate fate of the unjust: "The righteous shall rejoice that he has seen vengeance done, and shall wash his feet in the blood of the wicked, and men shall say, 'There is after all a reward for the

righteous; after all, there is a God that judges on earth'" (Ps 58:10–11).

6. Rejection of any religion based solely on empty words or rites: "God's word to the wicked man is this: What right have you to recite my laws and make so free with the words of my covenant, you who hate correction and turn your back when I am speaking?" (Ps 50:16–17).

To know this God and share one's life with this God is the most precious gift we can receive: "Thy true love is better than life" (Ps 63:3). Contact with this God awakens us to the true values in our own life. We are brought back to life and new hope. From some deep source within us there well up prayers of praise, thanksgiving, and supplication. We begin to understand the psalmist's feelings: "Whom have I in heaven but thee? And having thee, I desire nothing else on earth" (Ps 73:25). His real life is a continuing journey toward God: "But my chief good is to be near thee, O God; I have chosen thee, Lord God, to be my refuge" (Ps 73:28).

All the actions of this person are a response to a summons in the inner depths of his being: "'Come!' my heart has said, 'seek his face.' I will seek thy face, O Lord; do not hide it from me" (Ps 27:8–9). Listening to this inner voice will lead a person into the unpredictable and the unknown, for God is full of surprises. The immediate result of God's approach is obscurity, and only those who are wiling to accept God into their lives wholeheartedly can make true progress. We must have firm confidence in this God, knowing that God's strength can get us through any crisis: "I wait for the Lord with all my soul, I hope for the fulfillment of his word" (Ps 130:5); "Well I know that I shall see the goodness of the Lord in the land of the living" (Ps 27:13).

When everything else fails, our only support is God. Though invisible, God is indeed with us: "I cry to thee, O Lord, and say, 'Thou art my refuge; thou art all I have in the land of the living'" (Ps 142:5). Treasuring this certainty, faithful people keep moving forward and waiting to hear the friendly voice of God again some day. In the midst of continuing crises, their attitude is: "I humbly follow thee with all my heart, and thy right hand is my support" (Ps

63:8). This kind of person knows the true law that governs existence: "Those who sow in tears shall reap with songs of joy. A man may go out weeping, carrying his bag of seed; but he will come back with songs of joy, carrying home his sheaves" (Ps 126:5–6).

If we do not keep moving forward, we will not perceive anything. We must keep moving forward with confidence and take the reins of history in our hands. Only then will we be able to put things in their proper perspective, thanks to God's enlightenment. Only then will we be able to give up false supports and fallacious certainties. Only then will we be able to awaken to the authentic values in life, to look to God as the *foundation* and *future* of our lives. To discover this foundation and future is to find true peace: "O Lord, my heart is not proud, nor are my eyes haughty. I do not busy myself with great matters or things too marvelous for me. No, I submit myself, I account myself lowly, as a weaned child clinging to its mother, O Israel, look for the Lord now and evermore" (Ps 131).

That is what the Psalms tell us about God and ourselves. They go to the core of the human problem. When they are well translated, they can be taken over as an authentic expression of our own experiences and hopes. They can then alert us to certain features of life to which we do not pay sufficient attention.

The Raw Material for Prayer

Where are we to find the raw material for prayer? There is only one answer, and it can be put in one word. We find the raw material for prayer in *life,* in the life we are living. The affairs of life were like an alarm clock to the psalmist. Observing life, he was awakened to something else — or rather, to Someone else. Everything now reminded him of God: the happiness and sadness of life, nature with all its beauty and its dangers, history with all its twists and turns. Everything became transparent, revealing the God who was summoning and inspiring humankind. Almost without realizing it, he began to use the happenings of life as the raw material for conversation with God. Thus the Psalms welled up from *life with God*.

If we do not make this link with life, then all our talk about the Psalms will be in vain. It would be like buying a fine new television set and failing to plug it into the electric current. The television set might serve as a decorative piece of furniture, but it was not made for that purpose. The Psalms can serve to document the prayer life of people who lived long ago, but they were not meant to be historical archives. They were inspired to be recited; they were meant to awaken us to prayer here and now.

PART TWO

The New Testament

11

THE ORIGIN OF
THE FOUR GOSPELS

Dictionaries reflect popular ideas when they list the following meanings for the word "gospel":

1. the teaching of Christ;

2. one of the four main books of the New Testament;

3. passages from these books read during the celebration of a liturgy;

4. something held to be true; and

5. a set of principles normative for a sect.

Which of the five meanings is right? As well as these, we very often identify "gospel" with the life of Jesus, and in this case "gospel" starts to mean the same as history, because it gives us information about Jesus, and the things he did and said.

Why this great range of meanings? Does the cause lie in the Gospels or in our way of looking at them? Did the first Christians think the same, or was there the same confusion among them as among us?

After all, it makes a lot of difference to the way you lead your life if you think of the Gospels as just books or mere history, or as a moral standard, a rule of truth, or a set of teachings, or again

Chapters 11–17 and the Epilogue were translated by Francis McDonagh. Biblical citations are from the *New Revised Standard Version*.

just as a text prescribed to be read during worship. Or is there, perhaps, something else that is, as it were, the root from which all these different aspects spring?

For all these reasons, it is very useful to investigate briefly how the Gospels came into being, their origin. Studying this may help us to acquire a more accurate view of them. We miss many things written in the Gospels because we don't have the right glasses. If we know better how the Gospels came into being, we will be able to discover and correct our failing. This could enrich our lives today.

Questions That Unearth Differences

Here is a set of questions with answers found in the Gospels. The result of the investigation will be surprising: none of the questions has a correct answer. It is rare to find complete agreement among the four Gospels on the same subject.

1. How many years did Jesus' apostolic life last after his baptism by John the Baptist?

2. To whom did Jesus appear first after his resurrection, and where?

3. What were the exact words used for the consecration of the wine at the Last Supper?

4. What were the words of the centurion at the foot of the cross after Jesus' death?

5. What was Jesus' route in his journeys through Palestine?

6. How many Beatitudes did Jesus pronounce at the beginning of the Sermon on the Mount?

7. How many days did Jesus spend on earth after the resurrection before ascending into heaven?

You should look for the answers simultaneously in the four Gospels. Anyone who takes the trouble to do this will find that, depending on the evangelist, Jesus's apostolic life lasted less than one year, more than two years, or as long as three years. They will find that Matthew says one thing and Mark another, that Luke says this and John says that. They will notice that on some points only one or two of the four have any information. The result is uncertainty about the most important things: the words at the Last Supper, the Lord's Prayer, the length of Jesus' life, the route of the journeys, the appearances, the discourses, deeds, and miracles.

All this gives the impression that the evangelists weren't interested in the same things as we are. It seems that they were not interested in descriptions that were exact in every detail; if they were, there would not be such great differences on such important matters. When they wrote about the events of Jesus' life, they had a different attitude from the one we usually have when we read the Gospels. This can mean that we do not discover the whole message they put in the text, since we don't place ourselves in the same position as they did to view the content of the Gospels.

Another Dimension of the Four Gospels

The Gospels were written long after Paul's letters. In order to understand a piece of writing properly we need to know something about the world in which it was written. The world in which the four Gospels were composed was the one Paul's letters tell us about, that is, it was made up of the fervent Christian communities living in Palestine, Asia Minor, Greece, or Italy. It's a bit like popular music: to understand a particular song we have to know the period and the region in which it was written. This is what I want to talk about here. The accompanying diagram tries to set up a comparison between Paul's letters and the four Gospels. There is a clear development.

Paul's letters focus mainly on the "paschal mystery," that is, the events of the passion, death, and resurrection of Jesus. They talk about Jesus and the gospel on almost every page. On the other hand, they say little about the things that happened to Jesus before his passion, death, and resurrection. They talk about Jesus as

Someone among the faithful, Someone who is alive. This living and active presence of Christ in the community is what Paul means by "gospel," the great "Good News." The basis of this presence is the passion, death, and resurrection.

Mark's Gospel starts to be interested in the things that happened to Jesus before the passion, because Mark begins his narrative with Jesus' baptism by John the Baptist, that is, the beginning of Jesus' apostolic life.

The Gospels of Matthew and Luke, which were given their basic shape after Mark's, begin to widen their interest, and begin with the infancy and birth of Jesus.

John's Gospel, the last, goes back to the beginning of the world and begins with the sentence: "In the beginning was the word..." (Jn 1:1). This Word of God is Jesus Christ, who became flesh (Jn 1:14).

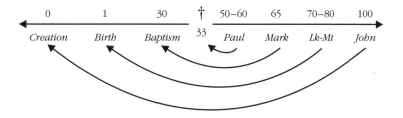

Thus, as we move on in time, the interest in Jesus Christ recedes further and further into the past. All this suggests the following conclusion: the root of the evangelists' interest is not teaching or history, truth or morality, not books or ceremonies. It is the person of the risen Jesus alive among them. In the minds of the first Christians, Christ was not someone who died, rose, and then went off to heaven. The first Christians, when they talked about Christ, did not have their eyes on the past. For them, Christ was there with them in life, alive like them, and they were alive because of him. The primary interest stopped there, in this friendly presence of Christ in life: "To me, living is Christ" (Phil 1:21). If subsequently the written Gospels tried to give information about things, facts, and discourses that took place or were done in the past, it was in order to use this information to provide a deeper knowledge of Christ alive among them.

It's like when a person strikes up a friendship with another person. The focus of interest is concentrated on the other person. As the friendship deepens, there comes a desire to know the friend better. And this process takes place, very naturally, through contact with the friend's family, with the parents, trying to find out what the friend did before, at school and college, as a child. All this has only one purpose: to gain a deeper knowledge of the friend, his or her demands and aspirations, and to deepen the friendship with that person *now.*

In the same way Paul's letters and the Acts of the Apostles, which describe for us the attitude of the earliest Christians to Christ, show how they went no further than Christ and his living presence in their midst. For them this living and friendly presence that took over their hearts was enough. This was the Good News, the gospel. But as this life of faith in Christ deepened, they began to want to know more about him and began to investigate his past and the things he said, did, and taught. The difficulties of the Christian life pushed them to do this, because the encounter with Christ gave life a new direction, transformed everything, provoked a "conversion." They needed to know how to behave in this new life and so began to go back into Christ's past, not for the sake of the past in itself, but for the sake of the present, in which they were living with their difficulties, in a life shared with Christ. They wanted to know better what this Christ wanted, who he was, where he came from, what he promised them. This going back into the past reached its high point in the Gospel of John, which went back even before the creation of the world (Jn 1:1) and so explained the meaning of Jesus alive among them, not just for Christians, but also for all human beings and for the whole universe.

Therefore anyone who reads the Gospels just to find history, teaching, truths, morality, or material for ceremonies is not reading the Gospels with the same eyes with which they were written.

Reading the Gospels presupposes something in the person who reads them, namely, an assurance of friendship with Christ alive today, at the end of the twentieth century. It is to get to know this Christ, and to discover what he is asking of me, that I have to read the Gospels.

The gospel, the "Good News," is not in the first place teaching, it is not ceremony, it is not a book, it is not morality, it is not history, it is not truths. It is *someone,* Jesus Christ: "To me, living is Christ." This is the root; all else is branches and flowers. Without the root the rest dries up and rots. But there is also no such thing as a root without branches and flowers.

Teaching makes sense only when it is related to the person it came from. Otherwise it becomes an abstract set of truths to be learned by heart without our knowing what they are for.

Christian morality makes sense and is Christian only when it is related to this friend alive and present in our lives. If it is not, it can become a set of burdensome rules. It is because they are committed to Christ that Christians do the things they have to do.

The history provokes interest only because it speaks of this person who is a friend. Who, for example, is interested in teaching the whole world the history of Julius Caesar?

Ceremony makes sense only when there is friendship with the person at the center of it. We don't celebrate the birthdays of people we don't know, but when it's a friend's birthday, everyone comes.

The book has meaning only when it talks about the person. We don't keep photographs of people we don't know.

Finally, the truth makes sense only because it gives me information about my friend. It is an expression of the conviction that binds us together.

The root and the trunk from which everything grows is the person of Jesus Christ. It is he who arouses the interest. It is his person that is able to bring about conversion and transformation, not mere teaching. The gospel, before it is a written book, is a living, personal reality. The books written by Matthew, Mark, Luke, and John are only trying to explain this living gospel. If this living gospel does not exist in real life, the four Gospels are not much use. They would be like the strings of the violin without the soundbox, like a map that shows the outline of a region that doesn't exist. It would be a fiction.

Maybe this is one of the causes of the present crisis: our contact with the root is weak; we insist too much on the branches without seeing very clearly their connection with the root. "News" becomes "good" when it corresponds to an expectation within us. People who have everything, who feel no need of anything, who live lives of total contentment, can never receive good news, because they have nothing to look forward to. There is nothing in such persons that can be touched by anything. In the same way, perhaps, the fact that we live peaceful and comfortable lives, following a religion we like, thinking everything's fine, is the reason why the "news" of Christ alive, among us, has stopped being "Good News" for us. It has even become uncomfortable, because it awakens our attention to the failings and limits of our personal and social life that we would like to ignore. In such a case, this Good News turns against us and becomes a judgment, as it was for the Pharisees (Jn 3:19–21).

Comparing the Four Gospels

There is another curious aspect in the four Gospels that is worth paying attention to and that may help us to understand better their purpose in relation to our lives. Many of Jesus' sayings, discourses, deeds, and miracles are described in all four Gospels, or at least in the three so-called synoptic Gospels: Matthew, Mark, and Luke. If we compare these descriptions carefully, we see differences, as we mentioned before. Here are some examples:

The Lord's Prayer. Matthew has this as part of the Sermon on the Mount (Mt 6:9–13), while Luke puts it on another occasion (Lk 11:1–4). Who is right? Matthew is concerned with catechesis. He writes, we could say, to help religion teachers. For that reason, he made things easy and combined in a single discourse everything Jesus said about prayer (Mt 6:5–15).

The Parable of the Lost Sheep is presented by Matthew as an image of apostolic zeal (Mt 18:12–14) and by Luke as an image of the merciful love of God, who goes in search of sinners (Lk 15:3–7).

The transfiguration. Matthew talks of Jesus' face shining like the sun and of a bright cloud (Mt 17:2, 5). This recalls Moses when, on Mount Sinai, wrapped in a bright cloud, his face shone as he gave the old law to the people. In this way Matthew wants to present Jesus as the new Moses, who gives the new law to human beings. The law is Jesus himself, presented by the Father, who says: "This is my Son, the Beloved; listen to him" (Mt 17:5). Luke, however, in describing the transfiguration, says that Elijah and Moses were talking to Jesus about his passion and death (Lk 9:31) and mentions the apostles' weariness (Lk 9:32). He is think-ing of the agony in the garden, when Jesus faced his passion while the apostles fell asleep (Lk 22:40–46). The passion of Christ began at the moment when he decided to suffer, on the occasion of the transfiguration.

The list of examples is endless. The important thing to under-stand is this: The evangelists are not interested in transmitting Jesus' words literally. They are primarily interested in the readers who will read Jesus' words. These readers have to be touched in their lives, and that is why each evangelist presents things in the way that will make the greatest impact on his readers. This implies that we can-not read the Gospels as though they had nothing to do with our lives. We cannot limit ourselves to explaining the texts and going no further than the texts. We have to make the connection with the life we live.

There are people who think that fidelity consists in preserving literal truth, without changing anything. This means that they keep repeating things. Whether the truth corresponds to the demands of life or not is secondary. What concerns them is the presence or not of the orthodox truth. They get lost in discussions that of-ten have no point. But all this is of little use unless there is a reflection of truth in life. The evangelists thought that having the true faith meant being ready to change one's life in accordance with Jesus' demands. Fidelity was not limited to the content of the creed professed. This is why the evangelists are not so worried about copying exactly, in the same words, the sayings and deeds of Jesus' life, but they present them in such a way that the reader can understand that this deed or that saying has something to do with life.

Anyone who reads the Gospels just to learn and not for living is missing the point of the Gospels. The evangelists' first concern was to insert Christ's message into their readers' lives. Since readers in Asia were different from readers in Italy or Palestine, each evangelist presented the story of Jesus' life in a different way. Their concern was not history or the past, but Christians' lives here and now. They don't seem to have had many scruples about changing the wording of Jesus' sayings a little as long as the message was understood by the readers.

Just as they constantly made the connection between the "situation of the reader" and the "message of the Gospel," so the person who reads the Gospels today must have the same concern: to make the link between the "situation of the reader" and "the message contained in the Gospels." If we do not do this, we shall be like the person who "hears these words but does not act on them" (Mt 7:26).

From the Gospel to the Four Gospels

After everything we have seen so far it is easier for us to describe the origin of the Gospels. We shouldn't imagine that one day the Holy Spirit came down and called in these four men to write down what the Spirit was going to dictate. It's the reverse. Jesus did not order anything to be written down, but ordered the Good News of his death and resurrection to be preached and proclaimed. The Good News is that he became a human being like us, a friend to all, in order to lead us all into the path of life and show everyone the true meaning of the human life we live. We are certain of this because he rose and lives in those who believe in him. This is the Good News; this is the gospel.

This was what the apostles preached and proclaimed to everyone: Christ is alive among us to help us discover a meaning for our lives. This preaching began on the day of Pentecost. We need only read a little of the Acts of the Apostles to get an idea of what it was like. Many people accepted this message, accepted the person of Jesus Christ, who gave them a new outlook on life. This showed itself practically in a life of love and charity. In this way fervent communities of people sprang up, and the members were called "Christians" (Acts 11:26) because they believed in Christ.

These "Christians" made a total change in the way they looked at life. This created a whole range of questions: How can we communicate this faith to others (because if you find a good thing you want to share it with others)? How can we defend the faith against the accusations of others, Jews and pagans? Can we go on keeping the old law? How do we settle the community's internal problems? Can we use the civil courts? How do we organize our worship? How do we celebrate together these things that inspire us and are now what brings joy to our lives? What should relationships within our Christian community be like? Above all, after accepting Christ they developed a great love for him and a desire to get to know him better and to understand the place he occupied in God's plan.

They wanted answers to all these very specific questions about everyday life. They turned to the apostles, and the apostles remembered the things Jesus had said and done. In this way dozens of stories about Jesus began to circulate in the community of the Christians: pieces of discourses, accounts of miracles, descriptions of facts of his life, and stray phrases he had said on different occasions.

By means of these stories obtained from the apostles as answers to their questions, the Christians tried to find their way in this new life. Little by little, as always happens, some started to make collections of sayings of Jesus, to make them easier to memorize and preserve. Others collected stories of miracles, others tried to record the arguments between Jesus and the Pharisees (because they helped to settle the arguments they themselves had with the Jews).

Finally, when the disciples began to disappear, as one after another died, a desire grew up among the Christians to fix in writing everything that had been passing from mouth to mouth about Jesus' life, having been passed on to them by the apostles. So, finally, four people, in different places and at different times, Matthew, Mark, Luke, and John, decided, each on his own initiative, to collect into one book everything they could collect or remember about Jesus (Lk 1:1–4). In all this work our faith recognizes the action of the Holy Spirit, to the extent of treating the words of the Gospels as the Word of God.

All this shows that the Gospels do not just describe the events of Jesus' life, but equally reflect the first Christians' anxiety to find answers for their everyday problems of living the faith. If the first Christians had not had this interest in putting the faith into practice in their lives, the Gospels would never have been written.

Why Investigate the Origin of the Gospels?

So are the entries in the dictionary right or not? How do we define the gospel? As teaching, a book, a ceremony, morality, truth, or history? The answer has already been given and can be summed up as follows. The gospel is first and foremost a new *life,* generated in a human being by acceptance of Jesus Christ. This is the great *truth,* which provokes a conversion, which has as a result a new *moral* behavior. Reflection on this situation gives rise to a *teaching;* when this is set down in writing we get a *book,* and the community's celebration of this life produces the liturgy with its *ceremonies.* The foundation of all this is the *history* of Jesus of Nazareth, who was born and lived for about thirty-three years, died by assassination, and rose again. He now continues to be present and active in those who open themselves to him by faith. History is the foundation, but not just the history of Jesus, also our history today. This history must display the veracity of the gospel in which we believe. It's no good doing a lot of talking if nothing of this shows in our lives, if we do not rise to a new life, there for all to see.

12

THE SERMON ON THE MOUNT
Counsel, Law, or Ideal?

The so-called Sermon on the Mount is found in chapters 5–7 of Matthew's Gospel. It is called the Sermon on the *Mount* because, according to Matthew, Jesus used a nearby hill as a pulpit. According to the Gospel, "When Jesus saw the crowds, he went up the mountain; and after he sat down, his disciples came to him. Then he began to speak, and taught them, saying..." (Mt 5:1–2). In these few words the evangelist prepares the canvas that will shortly glow with the revolutionary words of the Sermon on the Mount, for all to read, hear, and ponder.

The Sermon on the Mount is the first of the five great discourses of Jesus in Matthew's Gospel. Here Matthew brings together everything to do with entry to the reign of God: who can enter God's reign, what the conditions are, what sort of behavior is required within God's reign. The other discourses are about the extension of the God's reign through the apostles' preaching (Mt 10), the "mystery" of God's reign, presented in parables (Mt 13), how to live together in this reign (Mt 18), and the final establishment of the reign of God (Mt 24–25).

The Sermon on the Mount divides into three parts: (1) the Beatitudes (Mt 5:1–12), which indicate who are the members of the reign of God; (2) the attitudes to be adopted by those who belong to God's reign (Mt 5:13–7:12); (3) and concluding remarks (Mt 7:13–27), in which Jesus insists forcefully on action as opposed to mere attitude or intention.

The attitudes described in the second part are presented in groups: (1) the function of the members of God's reign in the world is to be the salt of the earth and light of the world (Mt 5:13–16); (2) the spirit that inspires them must be different from the spirit that inspires the Pharisees (Mt 5:17–20); (3) through six contrasts, Jesus defines the Christian's attitude to the Old Testament (Mt 5:21–48); (4) Jesus defines the spirit that should inspire the three great practices of piety: almsgiving, prayer, and fasting (Mt 6:1–18); (5) he explains the proper attitude to this world's goods (Mt 6:19–34); (6) he describes how people should relate to others (Mt 7:1–5), to "dogs" and "swine" (Mt 7:6), and to God (7:7–11). The sermon ends with the so-called golden rule (Mt 7:12).

Three Difficulties for Readers of the Sermon on the Mount

The Sermon on the Mount presents various difficulties:

1. It gives the impression that Jesus is turning everything upside down: for him, happiness is among the poor, with the sad, the lowly, and the persecuted (Mt 5:3–12). He says he has come to fulfil the law, but he lays down rules that seem impossible to keep (Mt 5:22, 48).

2. If the Sermon on the Mount really sets out the road that leads to happiness, then we might as well just give up. Never get angry with others (Mt 5:22), never insult another person (5:22), never take part in the Eucharist if someone has a complaint against us, but be reconciled first (5:23–24), never look at a woman with lustful feelings (5:28), never swear, never lie, always tell the truth (5:37), do not resist evildoers and if a person hits you on the right cheek, offer the left (5:39), give your shirt to the person that wants to take your suit (5:40), love your enemies (5:44), always forgive (6:12), never do anything in order to be seen by others (6:1); have such great trust in God that praying in words becomes unnecessary (6:5–8); don't save money (6:19), choose between God and money (6:24), don't worry about food, drink, or clothes and live like a bird, un-

concerned about anything (6:25–31), never judge anyone (7:1–2), treat others as you would have them treat you (7:12), in short, be perfect as our heavenly Father is perfect (5:48). Is it possible to keep all this? Is it possible for someone to get to the point of saying, "I've done all this! I am perfect as God the Father is perfect"?

3. Luke gives an account of the same discourse, but it is very different from the one in Matthew's Gospel. It is in Luke 6:20–49. The main differences are the following: (1) It is not on the mount but on a plain (Lk 6:17); (2) there are only four Beatitudes and not eight as in Matthew (6:20–22); in addition, there are four curses absent in Matthew (6:24–26); (4) Luke omits many things that are in Matthew; for example, he does not record the Lord's Prayer, does not give any of the contrasts between old and new, says nothing about the salt of the earth and the light of the world (he has these in another place). Is it really the same discourse? And if it is, which of the two evangelists has the correct version?

Solutions Suggested in the Past

The first difficulty was: "Jesus turns everything upside down." This is true not just of the Sermon on the Mount, but of many other things Jesus said: the first shall be last and the last first (Mk 10:31); the least among all of you is the greatest (Lk 9:48); to be the greatest it is necessary to be the servant of all (Mt 23:11); you must lose your life to save it, but if you try to save it you lose it (Mt 16:25); sinners, tax collectors, and prostitutes will enter God's reign before the Pharisees and the righteous (Mt 21:31).

We are so used to these words that we've stopped noticing the danger they contain for our security, which is based on things and ideas that we ourselves have made or accumulated. We've heard them so many times, and there are so few people who seem to take them seriously. It seems as though they're not really serious after all. We preserve the words of Jesus the way swords and cannon are preserved in some museums: attractive to look at and study, but no longer dangerous in any way. They have been neutralized.

It is like the crucifix. In Catholic countries it is everywhere: houses, bars, shops, government offices, gas stations, parliament, places where justice is done and where injustice is done. It's automatic, just as coffee after lunch and dinner is automatic. We've stopped even noticing that it has to do with a man who was tortured and legally murdered because of an ideal he refused to abandon. In the same way, the words of the Sermon on the Mount are, as it were, placed in a very beautiful frame and preserved in cotton. The word of God, this two-edged sword (Heb 4:12), doesn't cut any more. Its action has been controlled and neutralized. Our consciences have stopped feeling uncomfortable with it. We do with Christ's words what the press does every day with new ideas that appear: it seizes them and turns them into headlines. From that moment the new idea has stopped being uncomfortable because it has begun to serve the interests of those who don't want it to make them uncomfortable. This solution, frequent and easy, reduces Christ's words to the scale of our own.

The second difficulty was this: "Is it possible to live by the Sermon on the Mount?" This is not the first time that Christians are seeing this problem and looking for a solution. Here are some of the solutions suggested from times past until today.

1. *The Sermon on the Mount is only for a tiny elite*. There are people who take the following view: "What Jesus commands in the Sermon on the Mount cannot be for everyone. It's impossible." As a result, they think that the Sermon on the Mount has to be understood, not as a universal law, valid for all, but as a counsel, intended for the most determined, who feel a vocation for it. This tiny elite may be made up of bishops, priests, and religious or of the occasional lay person in Catholic Action. For ordinary mortals the Ten Commandments will do, and they're already quite something. You couldn't ask all lay people to do what Jesus lays down in this discourse. This opinion is very common among Catholics, not as an official theory, but in practice.

2. *The Sermon on the Mount must be explained and kept like any law*. Jesus is a doctor of the law. This means he has come to codify in a new way the commandments of God's law. Didn't he

say himself that he came, not to abolish the law, but to fulfill it (Mt 5:17)? So the Sermon on the Mount is a law and must be explained like any other law.

When we're faced with a law it's no good to complain and say, "This law is too difficult for me." Before the court excuses like "I didn't know about this law," or "I didn't obey this law because I think it is an impossible law for me to keep" have no force. All citizens have to behave in such a way that they are always within the law and that the law is on their side. That way the courts can do nothing against them, and they keep on the right side of the courts.

In the same way obeying the Sermon on the Mount came to be, for many people, a way of protecting themselves against God the lawgiver. They began to produce weighty studies to discover how Christians had to act in order not to feel condemned by what is written in this discourse and what had to be done to ensure that its contents were fully observed. They wanted to ensure that Christians could always have clear consciences about being within the law and always having the law on their side. Extreme forms of this position led many people to slip into what is called legalism and casuistry. The Sermon on the Mount then becomes like the TV games where the winners are told, "The car is yours! Drive it away!" or "The reign of God is yours! The winners — the poor!" (see Mt 5:3). But in both cases the conditions are so difficult that neither the car nor the reign of God will ever leave the showroom. Promises, promises.

3. *The Sermon on the Mount is meant to bring us to repentance.* Luther tried to obey the Sermon on the Mount as though it were a law. But he was unable to, and he asked himself, "In the end, what did Christ come for?" To make salvation easier or to make it more difficult? To give us hope or to plunge us into despair? Luther saw that no human being would ever be capable of doing what Christ commands in this discourse, however hard he or she tried.

So why did Christ preach the Sermon on the Mount? Luther offered the following reply: through the Sermon on the Mount, Jesus sought to convince human beings, once and for all, that we, by ourselves, would never succeed in doing what God has a right to demand of us. If God were really to demand everything, we might as well give up and buy a one-way ticket to hell right now. To ensure that this was firmly imprinted on our minds, Christ set out this ideal in the Sermon on the Mount. It describes what we ought to be but are not and cannot be. Deliberately, Jesus asked the impossible. The purpose of the Sermon on the Mount, said Luther, is to break human pride before God. It has two aims: First, faced with such demands, human beings must despair of being able to attain salvation by their own efforts; they must recognize their weakness and their radical inability to ascend the stairway to heaven alone. Second, the Sermon on the Mount must lead human beings to throw themselves into the arms of God's mercy and say with the tax collector: "God, be merciful to me, a sinner" (Lk 18:13). Human beings must place their hopes of salvation solely in God and not in their own efforts. God *promised* salvation and pledged support of the promise. God does not fail. As a result, do not trust in your own strength, because it won't get you anywhere. The function of the Sermon on the Mount is merely to lead us to Christ and make us recognize him as our only Savior.

4. *Jesus did not give a law, but taught an attitude.* This is an opinion that is being accepted today by many people. It says that, through very vivid teaching, with lots of examples and illustrations, Jesus is teaching a new attitude. For example, the statement: "If you are angry with a brother or sister, you will be liable to judgment" (Mt 5:22), in this understanding, is not a prohibition, not even a law, but just a vivid way of telling us that if we believe in Jesus we should have an attitude such that the slightest fault in charity becomes impossible.

It makes a big difference if I consider the Sermon on the Mount a law, a counsel, an attitude, or a real but impossible demand. This range of opinions in itself shows that this is not a problem that is easy to resolve. Later on we shall see what to make of all this. These opinions have had a great influence on the lives of Christians, and even today influence the lives of many.

"It's a law!" they said. The result was that mass of rules and observances, all imposed in the name of Christ, that left so many people anguished and angry, rightly, all their lives, without knowing anything of God's love or the meaning of life. For these people, the gospel — which means "Happy News" — was and still is left with the name as the only happy thing about it. Instead of peace and tranquillity, it caused and still causes agony and despair of conscience and has left many people wanting nothing more to do with religion.

"It's a counsel!" they said. The result was that very common approach of teaching most people only the morality of the Ten Commandments. Ordinary people were left knowing little or nothing about the ideal of the reign of God. They didn't feel attracted by the gospel promise. They acted more out of self-interest and fear. They didn't want to lose the chance of heaven after death.

"It's a way of producing repentance!" they said. The result was that attitude of Christians who can't see the ground in front of them and only look up to heaven, waiting for everything to happen without any effort from them. God had to do everything, human action was worthless, and God became the answer to all problems. Many Christians didn't even see the connection between the gospel and working to make the world a better place. For them, the world is useless, no good for anything, not even for earning a place in heaven.

"It's just fine words!" Nobody said this, but many people thought it. The result was that religion and faith became just a beautiful frame around life. They stayed on the sidelines, without really troubling people's consciences. Faith and life became separated from each other.

"It's a state of mind!" they said. The result was a vague attitude with no specifics. We all can follow our own impulses with total freedom. The need for structures and rules is denied as having nothing to do with the gospel.

It's not easy to find the standpoint from which to appreciate and understand the full profundity of the message contained in the Sermon on the Mount.

As for the third difficulty — "Why does Luke give such a different discourse?" — the answer has already been given, in part, in the last chapter. Here all we need are a few additional remarks.

Matthew was writing for Jewish converts, and so he collected remarks and statements of Jesus' that would produce a synthesis of Jesus' message that would be accessible to them. This explains the continual comparison between the Old and New Testaments in chapter 5: this mattered to the Jewish converts. Luke is writing for converted pagans. They were less interested in the comparison between the morality Jesus brought and the morality of the Old Testament, and so Luke omits it completely and simply keeps what is useful to his readers. He does the same as Matthew: he summarizes Jesus' thinking, not for Jewish converts but for pagan converts. Both groups are trying to be faithful to the gospel: the gospel wants to "convert," bring about a change of life. Therefore fidelity to the gospel implies that Christ's message should be presented so that it touches people in their real situations. The situations of converts from paganism and converts from Judaism were very different. As a result, fidelity required Jesus' words to be presented in different ways to these two groups of people. In addition, as we noted, Matthew was interested in "religion teachers." Religion teachers in general don't have the time or opportunity to produce summaries of their subject. They're always looking for a textbook that collects together everything to do with a particular topic. Matthew took on this task and presented in the form of a discourse everything to do with the behavior required for a person to belong to the reign of God.

People's Lives Give Meaning to Their Words

In the midst of so many different opinions, it is not easy to work out exactly what Jesus' thinking was. Exegetes always run the risk of presenting their own ideas as those of Jesus. However, it is necessary to obtain some criteria to help us to see clearly how to lead our lives. To make sure that the explanation that follows is not just my ideas, but corresponds to what the gospel tells us about Jesus,

I think it is necessary to situate the Sermon on the Mount within the general context of Jesus' life and see how he himself lived and practiced what he taught and commanded. It is his life that will give us the key to open the door into the Sermon on the Mount.

For example, Jesus said we must not get angry (Mt 5:22), but he got angry, several times (Mk 3:5). Once he got so angry that he made a whip and drove the traders out of the Temple (Jn 2:15). He said that we should never insult others, but he insulted people in very strong terms: "hypocrites" (Mt 23:13, 15, 23, 25, 27, 29), "white-washed tombs" (Mt 23:27), "descendants of those who murdered the prophets" (Mt 23:31), "snakes, brood of vipers" (Mt 23:33).

He said we should offer the right cheek when someone strikes us on the left (Mt 5:39). But when he received a blow, during the judgment before Annas, he did not offer the other cheek. On the contrary, he protested vigorously and stood his ground: "If I have spoken wrongly, testify to the wrong. But if I have spoken rightly, why do you strike me?" (Jn 18:22–23). He said we should not be worried about food, drink, and clothes, but he had the group of the twelve apostles who took care of this (Mt 16:7), and there was a group of women "who provided for them out of their resources" (Lk 8:3). He said we should not judge others (Mt 7:1), but he judged others, as when he made this comment about the Pharisees: "Do whatever they teach you and follow it; but do not do as they do, for they do not practice what they teach" (Mt 23:3).

Now we cannot ignore these facts of Jesus' life when we want to explain the words he spoke. It is his life that will be able to explain the true meaning of the words. A life lived and words spoken are like the soundbox of the violin and its strings: they are an inseparable unity, the unity of the violin that transmits the music and message of the Sermon on the Mount to us.

In addition, the same thing happens to the Sermon on the Mount today as happened with the person of Jesus Christ: there are many opinions, totally different, but none of them seems to capture the reality. Everyone gives an opinion, but no one gets it right: it isn't a law, it isn't only for an elite, it isn't to throw us into despair, it isn't just a model, it isn't just an attitude of mind.... But what is it then?

The same thing happened with Jesus Christ himself. Everyone knew him, had heard him speak, and had an opinion about him. Some of the opinions were even very complimentary, but they were like colored soap bubbles: they burst when touched. Once Jesus gathered his disciples together to make a survey of people's views about him: "Who do people say that I am?" (Mk 8:27). The result was disappointing: no one had gotten it right. Some said he was John the Baptist or Elijah; others believed he was a prophet (Mk 8:28).

If we collect the opinions scattered through the Gospels, we see the great variety of judgments expressed about Jesus and his message: "come from God" (Jn 3:2), a subversive agitator (Lk 23:2), "Jeremiah or one of the prophets" (Mt 16:14), "the prophet who is to come" (Jn 6:14), a threat to the safety of the people (Jn 11:47–50), a destroyer of sacred traditions (Mt 26:61), "a man who is not from God, for he does not observe the Sabbath" (Jn 9:16), "foolishness and a stumbling block" (1 Cor 1:18, 23), "a glutton and a drunkard, a friend of tax collectors and sinners" (Mt 11:19), "the Messiah" (Mk 8:29). Essentially people all judge Jesus in terms of what they know, are, and want. They reduce him to the scale of their own ideas, and Christ doesn't fit. He doesn't fit into the parameters we design. Sooner or later he shatters them all, he is so new.

So we see that the same thing happened to Jesus as is happening to the Sermon on the Mount. Why did no one understand it? An everyday example may help to explain the problem. A man from a remote village went to the city and there saw, for the first time, an airplane, "an iron box with wings that lifted off the ground by itself and flew." When he got back to his village, where no one had ever seen a plane or even heard of one, he tried to explain to the others what a plane was. Then everyone asked a question, to see if they had understood. "Does it fly?" "Yes, but it doesn't beat its wings." "Does it make a noise?" "Yes, a lot, but the noise doesn't come from its mouth." "It has a mouth?" "Yes, but it doesn't open." "Does it eat and drink?" "It drinks something called gasoline, but it has no stomach?" "Does it digest?" "It seems to, because everything it drinks disappears from its inside, but it has no intestines." "It rises by itself?" "Yes, but it's not alive." "But how can that be, old John?"

No one was able to imagine the airplane. John tried to compare it to things his community knew, but the plane was something so new that it didn't match any of their ideas, and it was impossible to reduce it to their familiar categories. It was only by seeing the plane at close quarters and touching it that they would be able to understand what this thing might be that John talked about with so much enthusiasm.

This is what happened with Jesus and still happens today with the Sermon on the Mount. What appeared on earth, in person, in the life and words of Jesus was so new and so different that there was no room for it in the heads of the people of that time, and there isn't in ours either. They tried, and we try, to compare it with things and people we are familiar with: John the Baptist, a prophet, a man from God, a law, a reason for despair, counsel, attitude, model. But our ideas and concepts aren't capable of getting to the root from which Jesus Christ thinks, acts, and speaks. There's no way of understanding who Christ is and what the meaning of the Sermon on the Mount is if we just use the ideas that come from inside us. We give our opinions and we get it wrong.

The reason is that before Jesus God never succeeded in coming down so far, coming so close, becoming so human, so hidden in life. This was so new that it was only by seeing and touching Christ himself at close quarters, living with him, that the flash would take place in people's heads that enabled them to understand who he was and what the meaning of the Sermon on the Mount was. This was and still is the key to understanding the Sermon on the Mount. So what might this be, this new thing revealed in Jesus' life?

The New Element in Jesus' Life and Message

I now want to analyze three aspects that can give us an idea of the background against which we need to read the Sermon on the Mount.

1. *Jesus' arrival: the transforming force of love.* With Jesus' arrival among human beings, something changed. Something new was happening. Jesus comes like an owner: drives out the usurpers (Lk 11:22), sweeps the house (Lk 11:25), weeds the garden (Mt 3:12). The human family rediscovers peace and well-being: the blind begin to see, the lame begin to walk, lepers are cured and the deaf hear (Mt 11:5), smiles of happiness begin to return to the faces of the poor (Lk 6:20–21), the excluded — prostitutes, sinners, and tax collectors — are readmitted to human society (Mk 2:16). Diseases are cured (Mt 8:16–17; Mk 6:56), nature ceases to be a threat (Mt 8:23–27) and returns to the service of human beings (Lk 5:4–7), hunger is overcome (Mk 6:30–44) and the hungry eat their fill (Lk 6:21). Dead people rise and the sadness of mourning is dispelled (Lk 7:11–17; Mk 5:41–43), sins are condemned (Mt 23:13–31; Jn 16:8–9) and pardoned (Mk 2:5; Lk 7:48), the weak are welcomed without condemnation (Jn 8:1–11), justice is affirmed (Mt 5:10–20; 6:33), sincerity is proclaimed (Mt 6:1–6; Mk 7:17–23), truth is announced (Jn 8:46), barriers fall, people unite, a warm breath of love blows through life (Jn 13:34–35; Mt 11:28–30) and makes the dry bones rise (Ezek 37:1–14).

As the dry lands come back to life under the rain, the human race is renewed under the beneficent action of Jesus Christ. Something has changed, changed radically: sin and error have been removed from the world (Jn 1:29), cut off at the root as guilt is recognized (Mk 1:4–5) and forgiven. The power of evil is broken and writhes in mortal agony as the demon is driven out (Lk 11:20; Jn 12:31; Acts 10:38, etc.). Human beings are freed from all forms of oppression (Lk 4:18), are born again into goodness, whose victory is already coming into view (Jn 16:33). Jesus' coming really was a joy for the whole people (Lk 2:10). All this began to exist among human beings with Jesus' arrival. It was the green light, awaited for centuries. It was the proof that the reign of God had come (Lk 11:20; 17:21; Mk 1:15).

2. *Jesus' coming: a dazzling and provoking light.* Along with good and love come evil and hate. Jesus comes and divides human beings (Jn 7:43; 10:19). Everyone feels affected by him and takes

up a position. No one remains neutral (Lk 11:23). His coming is like
a judgment (Jn 3:19–21): those who look at life without prejudices
and selfish interests, those who love truth come out in support
and recognize in him the voice of God (Jn 8:32; 18:37; Mt 11:25).
However, in those who lack this love of truth, Christ's voice encounters resistance (Jn 8:43, 44), is silenced (Jn 11:57), excluded
(Jn 9:22), and finally choked in the blood of a victim whose murder
is officially sanctioned by law (Jn 19:7).

Confronted with Jesus, human beings define themselves. Jesus
does nothing to provoke resistance: he is simply a humble but firm
presence of love and truth (Jn 8:39–40) and lets this light shine
into all the corners where people hide. In this way he reveals all
weaknesses and failings and above all condemns lack of authenticity and sincerity (Jn 8:45–47; 3:19–21; 12:46–50). He awakens in
human beings the voice of conscience, lulled to sleep beneath so
many human rules and regulations. Those who are afraid of their
consciences react and try to silence Christ's voice. Those who are
sincere accept Christ's judgment and join him (Jn 3:21; 6:68). The
waters gradually clear to allow a sharper division between good
and bad. The judgment is under way (Lk 22:51; Mt 10:35). And despite the resistance to Jesus, he is not affected or conquered by the
attacks of his enemies who bring him to death. That is the degree
of his freedom (Jn 10:18).

3. *Jesus' coming: demand for a radical change of life.* Jesus provokes a reaction because he does not ask permission to act and
speak, but acts and speaks with a disorienting freedom. He really
presents himself as a person who is master of the situation. He
makes demands that no other human being ever had the courage
to make of others. He presents himself as the standard, criterion
and end of all human action. He alone has the key of life that leads
to happiness.

He not only has it, but he even claims to be that key. We need
only analyze his statements: "I am the door" (Jn 10:9): there is no
other door that gives us entry to salvation. "I am the light of the
world" (Jn 8:12): outside him there is only darkness. "I am the
truth" (Jn 14:6): the rest is lies (Jn 8:44). "I am life" (Jn 14:6):

there is no other way to avoid death (Jn 11:25–26). "I am the way" (Jn 14:6): without him we get lost (Lk 11:23). "I am the bread of life" (Jn 6:35): without him we go hungry (Jn 6:35). He is the spring from which water flows (Jn 7:37–38): without him we never manage to slake our thirst (Jn 4:13–14).

For love of him, human beings must deny everything (Lk 14:33), otherwise it is impossible to be his disciple. For love of him, human beings must lose their lives (Mk 8:35), otherwise they cannot possess life. Whoever follows him must carry the cross every day (Lk 9:23). He places himself above parents and brothers and sisters and does not allow anyone to put family before him (Lk 14:26). He says that he knows only one thing about God (Mt 11:27) and that no one can get to God without going through him (Jn 14:6). And the greatest sin is not being willing to believe in what he says (Jn 16:9). In making these demands he neither explains nor justifies himself. When he is asked for an explanation, he doesn't answer (Mk 8:11–12). He speaks with authority (Mk 1:27), without being authoritarian, because he is always "gentle and lowly in heart" (Mt 11:29).

The Sermon on the Mount in Jesus' Life

Anyone who tries to explain the Sermon on the Mount, but doesn't take into account everything that we find in the life of Jesus, won't be able to understand anything. In the examples we've just seen, we find that in Jesus something totally new appeared among human beings, something radically new. It was so new that the Jews, with all the Old Testament, were unable to understand it.

Jesus defined this new element by saying that it is the kingdom, or reign, of God: "The time is fulfilled, and the kingdom of God has come near; repent, and believe in the good news" (Mk 1:15). This Good News, this gospel, does not just consist of words, even the words of the Sermon on the Mount, beautiful though they are. This Good News is, first and foremost, Jesus himself. The reign of God is in him, or, in him God rules. In him we see what happens in human beings when they open up to God and allow God to be God in their lives. Then everything changes, changes radically for the better.

This is what Jesus did. Through his life he showed that human beings can only be human, fully human, when they let God be God in their lives, when they open up to the reign of God: only then will a person be what he or she ought to be, according to the intention of the one who created them. Only God knows what there is in men and women, and only God can make them function to their highest potential. God did this through Jesus Christ. That is why Jesus is Good News for all human beings, because he corresponds exactly to what human beings want.

If we see and hear this we find a spontaneous desire springing up in us: "I'd like to be part of that. What do I have to do?" The answer to that question is given in the Sermon on the Mount, where Matthew collected together all Jesus' specific instructions about the life and behavior of those who decide to let God be God in their lives and really decide to be part of the reign of God. The Sermon on the Mount is the working out of that demand for radical change that Jesus brings. The Sermon on the Mount shows how far human beings can go when the power of love begins really to transform their lives. The Sermon on the Mount is the expression of that light that dazzles and challenges by forcing human beings to face their consciences and enables them to see the root of their problems. That is why it produces such contrasting opinions.

The Sermon on the Mount is the expression of the new thing that begins to exist in human life when we open up to God. It is the detailed description of the conversion that takes place in those who join Jesus. None of us can carry out the Sermon on the Mount with our own power, just as none of us can get in touch with God by our own power.

So what use is it to give me an impossible goal that I cannot attain? A comparison will sort this out. Our life is like a car we buy that has a sign on it: MAXIMUM SPEED 125 MPH. The purchaser gets into the car and tries to get up to 125, but can't, even on a straight downhill slope, pushing the accelerator into the floor. The driver can't get up to the maximum specified on the car. It's made to do 125 miles an hour, but the driver has to struggle to get 80 out of it. Life is the same.

The Sermon on the Mount gives us life's top speed: "Be perfect as your heavenly Father is perfect" (Mt 5:48). However, trying our hardest, giving the car all the gas, in fourth gear, on a wide, straight downhill slope, we can barely get it to do 80 miles an hour. We've convinced ourselves that it's impossible to get up to the 125 miles an hour indicated in the Sermon on the Mount. Well then, what was the point of putting the sign on the car of life saying MAXIMUM SPEED 125 MPH?

The point is that God has gotten into human life, and when we open up to God and come into contact with Jesus Christ, by joining him, we discover, so to say, that our car has a fifth gear that allows it to go faster than before and one day get up to 125 miles an hour. Within us human beings there are dormant possibilities and strengths that we don't even know ourselves. God, who knows us, can come into our lives and stretch our human capacity to the maximum of its potential. What seemed impossible, humanly speaking — and really was totally impossible — now becomes a real possibility.

Similar things happen every day. An ordinary friendship can make us discover in ourselves strengths and possibilities we knew nothing about, which we would never have discovered had not that friendship turned up in our lives. In the same way, in contact with Christ, entering the reign of God, we break through the rocky floor of our consciousness and discover other deposits of oil within us that produce new and unknown energy. Life takes off and acquires a new meaning. A new environment is created. The Sermon on the Mount belongs to this new life-environment. It can be read, explained, and understood in this environment because it is only within it that it can be observed. Those who live outside this environment understand nothing and hold wrong opinions, just as the Jews were wrong about Jesus.

That is why it seems to me absurd to require people to follow the Sermon on the Mount if they don't know who Jesus Christ is, if they think Jesus Christ and St. Anthony are the same thing, if Jesus is just an idea for them. The only person who is capable of following the Sermon on the Mount, and succeeds, is the person who has come to know Jesus Christ and followed him, in other words, the person who really has faith. And just as a friendship is something dynamic, so too the transformation it brings into our lives, the new discoveries it makes possible, and the new strengths it awakens, all are part of an unfolding process. The Sermon on the Mount is not something we can observe overnight. It is a program for life. It is the sign, growing steadily brighter and clearer, of an inner personal acceptance of Jesus Christ. By following Jesus Christ a person opens a door for God to come in, and through the power of God life is gradually transformed in accordance with what is written in the Sermon on the Mount.

Discussion about Opinions

The Sermon on the Mount, understood in this way and seen in the overall context of Jesus' life, *is not a law*. In the case of a law, we find out about it, try to study it, explain it, and obey it. In this sense, the Sermon on the Mount is not a law. There's no point in studying it and explaining it because it can't be obeyed in the way we obey ordinary laws. Legal expertise and legal scholarship, legalism and casuistry, so highly valued by the Pharisees, are all useless. They tend to empty the Sermon on the Mount of its content and reduce it to a human law to be obeyed by ordinary human effort. If we do this, the whole force of what is new, that is, the reign of God, which is at its heart, disappears. Not only that, but the Sermon on the Mount then becomes an intolerable burden, which is impossible, since Christ himself says: "My yoke is easy and my burden is light" (Mt 11:30).

Jesus condemned the Pharisees who explained God's law as if it were an ordinary human law (Mt 23:4). If that was so, so much the worse for the poor and ignorant who do not know the law and can't explain it. Jesus, however, called the poor "happy" or "blessed," and said that they would possess the reign of God (Mt 5:3). Jesus said "Come to me, all you that are weary and carrying heavy burdens, and I will give you rest; for I am gentle and humble in heart, and you will find rest for your souls" (Mt 11:28–29). It is impossible that the person who said that could have given human beings a law that, instead of rest, brought only worry, anguish, and scruples. Worry, anguish, and scruples come when the Sermon on the Mount is detached from the person of Christ and his friendship and is explained and obeyed like any other law, simply with a legal attitude. Despite this, however, Christ did not make life easier. On the contrary, he was able to touch us in the way we want to be touched in life, to open a new horizon and awaken in response love, courage, perseverance, hope, initiative, and creativity.

The Sermon on the Mount _is not intended to provoke despair_ and cast us into the arms of God's mercy, as Luther thought. It is true that the Sermon on the Mount makes us very clearly aware of our limitations and weaknesses. It shows that, on our own, we are unable to do what God asks of us. But in the general context of Jesus' life, Christians, behind the Sermon the Mount and at its root, see and encounter the person of Jesus Christ, feel his love and friendship, and discover that, if they accept him, they become able to do what the Sermon on the Mount commands.

At this point there are no human criteria to judge by, just as there are no human criteria to explain Jesus' life, as we saw above. God has different, confusing criteria. Anyway, if that really was the purpose of the Sermon on the Mount, Christ could have expressed it a bit more clearly, because nothing of this comes across in the text. At no point are we told that the discourse is intended to plunge us into despair and cast us into the arms of God's mercy, disbelieving in our own power. Does Christ treat us like the employer who sent his workers along a very difficult, almost impassable, road and left them to give up in despair, at which point he said, "You see you can't do it on your own! Get in. My car will take you to the end"?

The Sermon on the Mount _is not for a tiny elite_ of priests and sisters and a few particularly zealous lay people. It is for everyone. Jesus didn't speak just to the apostles, but to "the crowds" (Mt 5:1–2). Jesus never thought in terms of an elite religion.

To the extent that we all leave our Old Testament behind and start to meet Christ, all of us will cross the threshold of the Sermon on the Mount. The real question is whether we are all able here and now to enter the New Testament. It isn't a matter of saying: "Let's make things easy for the ordinary people and just give them the Ten Commandments to obey." We don't have the right or the power to do that. What we have to do is to help people to get on to the road that leads from the Ten Commandments to the Sermon on the Mount, through following Christ. From this point of view, we all still have one foot in our Old Testament and are trying to get out of it to allow that new plant to grow in us that no one can explain because it comes from God, but that at bottom we all want. We are all marching toward perfection: "Be perfect, as your heavenly Father is perfect" (Mt 5:48).

The Sermon on the Mount *is not intended simply to inspire a new attitude.* Christianity is not made up of ideas and attitudes. It is "conversion," that is, practical action. Especially at the end of the Sermon on the Mount, Jesus insists heavily on the need for action. Instead of talking about a new attitude, maybe we should talk about "a new power." The gospel is like the drills oil companies use to look for new oil deposits. When it reaches a deposit, the oil shoots up on its own and immediately heats homes and makes cars and machines run. In the same way, the gospel breaks through the ground of our personality and reveals, deep down, new reserves of incalculable power. They shoot up and change our lives and make the car of society run better. This drilling takes place through "conscientization." In this case conscientization is the realization of our own value that takes place when we discover God's call within us. God's call is like the roots of tall trees: they disappear into endless threads inside the earth, capillary vessels of great fragility, but together they produce the trunk that withstands the strongest storms. God's call comes, quite simply, in the ordinary events of every day.

Hints for Interpreting
the Sermon on the Mount

With all that has been said so far, we can begin to draw some conclusions about how best to understand the Sermon on the Mount.

The Sermon on the Mount is the judgment Jesus makes on
human life: human life, lived well, should be like this. It is the ideal
he puts forward. An ideal is not obeyed. An ideal is something we
work toward, try to attain. I shall be judged, not by whether or
not I attained the ideal, but by whether or not I worked toward it,
faithfully.

The comparison with the Old Testament (Mt 5:21–48) shows the
following: the Old Testament law, the Ten Commandments, are the
first steps on a road that, if we continue along it, will lead to the
type of life described in the Sermon on the Mount and, in the end,
to God.

For those still in the Old Testament, God's demand applies just
as strongly. The difference between the Old and New Testaments,
however, is in the awareness of the scope of this demand in our
lives. In the Old Testament, the divine demand was presented as:
"You shall not murder" (Mt 5:21). If we are faithful and follow the
road signposted "You shall not murder," God will come closer and
will be revealed more clearly to us, and we, because we understand more clearly God's friendship with us, will understand better
the demands of "You shall not murder" on our human lives. Finally
we will recognize that God is laying on us, with equal force, the
demand "Do not get angry." In other words, we will realize that
the only way of completely obeying the command "You shall not
murder" is to pull out of our hearts the root of murder, which is
anger. This is the meaning of the difficult sayings in Mt 5:21–23 and
the others that follow. In Jesus God came so close to human beings
that the full demand of God's commands for human life became totally clear. The Ten Commandments are ten paths opened in human
life intended to educate human beings for love and self-giving
(Mt 7:12).

The Beatitudes (Mt 5:1–12), which seem to turn everything upside down, show that the criteria God uses are different. They overturn and transform this world of ours that is so well organized by our criteria of individual and collective security, our criteria in part stemming from a basic distrust of one person for another, one nation for another. That is why the happy, the rich, the important people, all those who derive advantage from the earthly organization of this world, in God's eyes do not have the same value as they have for the world.

When the *new thing* appears, everything will change. That is why we can say, "Blessed are those who mourn, for they will be comforted; blessed are those who suffer injustice, for they will possess the kingdom; blessed are the meek, for they will inherit the earth; blessed are the pure in heart, for they will see God." The Beatitudes are the greatest threat ever uttered against humanity closed in on itself, concerned about its own security. The main product of the present world is exclusion. It is none other than those who are excluded by society who are declared blessed. It is a sign that when the reign of God comes, injustice, which excludes so many people today, will be over.

In the Sermon on the Mount, our relationship with God is placed on a different foundation. It is no longer based on what we do for God, but on what God does for us: therefore, in almsgiving, prayer, and fasting a totally different attitude is required (Mt 6:1–18). If we think that everything depends on us, we will concentrate on saying more and more prayers, thinking that words and actions have power to move God. But if we realize that we are being freely upheld by God, we will do everything to show our gratitude and will rely, not so much on the things we do, but on God's own inherent commitment to uphold us through to eternal life. We will hold God to the commitment God has made, and God will never refuse. That is why our prayers will always be heard (Mt 7:7–11).

This new relationship with God brings with it a new relationship to material goods (Mt 6:19–21, 24). It is a matter of the vision or the glasses with which we look at life and the world (Mt 6:22–23). This vision, or these glasses, are now different since, in God's light, human beings have now understood better the meaning of their lives. They can put in their proper place worries about food, drink, and clothing. These are absolutely necessary concerns for life, but they are no longer the most important thing (Mt 6:25–34).

Jesus did not come to repair this or that wall of the house, he did not come to cut off the odd rotten or dried up branch of the tree. He came to heal the root of the tree, to improve the foundations of the house. If these are fixed, everything else is fixed. In the same way, the Sermon on the Mount is concerned with the roots of human actions: it demands radical sincerity with God, with our own consciences, and with others. Its radical sincerity is possible only to the extent that we discover who we are. There is such a heavy facade covering our identity that we do not even know ourselves. That is why the process of conversion or transformation that the Sermon on the Mount demands, toward radical sincerity, is a painful process that meets with great resistance, both within ourselves and within society. It is given all sorts of names, which are no more than a form of individual or collective self-defense.

13

THE PARABLES

Revealing Divine Meaning in Human Affairs

One of the greatest difficulties comes from the sermons of some parish priests. When the Sunday gospel contains a parable, we find that Jesus was talking about the twentieth-century world with mathematical precision. The weeds (Mt 13:25) are the modern world; the enemy who sows the weeds is the people who do the opposite of what the church commands; the one sheep lost and found out of the flock of a hundred is a famous recent convert (Lk 15:4); the Good Samaritan (Lk 10:33) is the well-known Christian active in good works. And so on. How do they know? That's the question we want to ask when we hear these explanations. Is it right or wrong to explain the parables like that?

A parable that is very difficult to explain is the one about the Dishonest Manager (Lk 16:1–8). This man carried out a series of frauds (vv. 5–7) and Jesus holds him up as a model: "Make friends for yourselves by means of dishonest wealth" (v. 9). How could Jesus praise such behavior? How are we supposed to imitate it?

Jesus used the parables as a way of teaching the people, but almost never explained them. The people seemed not to understand them, since even the apostles used to ask what they meant (Mk 4:10). They felt the problem and brought it into the open: "Why do you speak to the people in parables?" Jesus replied: "The reason I speak to them in parables is that 'seeing they do not perceive and hearing they do not listen, nor do they understand'"

(Mt 13:13). So did Jesus speak in parables to trick the people (Mk 4:11–12)?

And what about the meaning of all the parables that Jesus doesn't explain? What do they mean?

Two Real-life Examples

A parable is a sort of comparison or image taken from ordinary life to explain something of a different order, something connected with the reign of God. There are two ways of using comparisons and images to explain something obscure to others. Both ways occur in the Gospels. But before talking about the comparisons used in the Gospels, it may be useful to illustrate the problem with two real-life examples.

Example 1. Someone asked, "How's it going, Jim?" The other replied: "We keep going flat out, but she never does more than fifty. On the straight it's fine, no problems. Going uphill things get rough, but the worst is corners."

For anyone who understands life today, this answer, while enigmatic, is clear. It implies that the subject is a car, but the speaker is really talking about life. Trying to do a hundred but only managing fifty is a way of saying that things are not what they should be. "The straight" is the easy days in life when everything goes smoothly. "Uphill" means the setbacks; the "corners" are the crises of life. If we are alert to the issues, there is no problem.

In this real-life example, the speaker *talks* about driving a car, but is *thinking* about something else: the *talk* is about the car, but the *meaning* has to do with the way life is going. In the same way, Jesus uses some comparisons in which he talks about the sower, the seed that falls on the road, on stones, among briars, and on good soil. But he is *thinking* about the evangelist or preacher (sower), the word of God (seed), the fickle heart (the stones), the forgetful heart (the road), the heart seduced by the pleasures of life (briars), and the heart that is open, ready, and sincere (the good soil, Mt 13:3–8).

In this type of comparison or parable, I can ask about each element of the comparison, "What does it mean?"

Example 2. Someone addressing a group of married men used this example: "A man, who was married, used to get up early, fix breakfast for the other members of the family, leave the house tidy, and go out to work in the fields. He would work all day, take little rest, put in a lot of effort in the heat, and push himself until late at night. He used to come home, happy and at ease with himself because he had spent another day devoted to his family."

In this example or comparison, we can't ask, "What does 'get up early' mean? What is meant by fixing breakfast for the other members of the family, leaving the house tidy, and going out to work in the fields? What does it mean that he gets back home happy and at peace?" These questions — we can all see — don't make sense here because the various elements of the comparison don't mean anything; that is, they don't have their own independent meaning. It is the comparison as a whole that has a single meaning: to stress the industry and devotion of the man to his family in order to encourage the married men listening to adopt the same attitude.

In the first example, each element had its own meaning, connected with the particular situation in life. In the second example, each element contributes to explaining the overall meaning of the comparison. In the same way Jesus uses many comparisons or parables about which we can't ask "What does this part or the other part mean?" We cannot ask "Who does he mean by the lost sheep?" "Who does the Good Samaritan represent?" "What could the weeds be?" or "What does Jesus mean by the mustard seed?" "Who is the man who sleeps while the seed grows?" (Mk 4:27). "The crumbs that fall from the table, who are they?" (Lk 16:21). In most of the comparisons Jesus uses it is the whole image that has a single meaning. It's no use trying to find out the meaning of each of the elements, because they don't have a meaning on their own.

Specific Applications: The Dishonest Manager and the Abandoned Vineyard

The parable that causes most difficulties is that of the Dishonest Manager (Lk 16:1–8). It causes difficulties precisely because we try to find an independent meaning in each element of the comparison when there is only a single meaning for the whole image. What causes most difficulty is the sentence in which Jesus holds the manager up as a model because he acted cleverly. What are we to make of this?

On another occasion Jesus said, "Be wise as serpents and innocent as doves" (Mt 10:16). Paul says: "The day of the Lord will come like a thief in the night" (1 Thess 5:2; cf. Mt 24:43–44; 2 Pet 3:10). No one concludes that the Lord is a thief, even though he has been compared with a thief. No one concludes: I have to be a dove and a serpent. In these three cases the comparison is obviously between a quality characteristic of the action of the thief and a distinctive feature of the behavior of doves and serpents. Thieves do not advertise their arrival, but come unexpectedly: that is what the Lord's coming at the end of time will be like. Simplicity and cunning are the two qualities that should be imitated in the example of the dove and serpent. The same is true of the image of the dishonest manager.

The only difference is that, in the case of the dishonest manager, the comparison does not hinge on a single word (as in the case of the thief, the serpent, and the dove), but is a whole story invented by Jesus to stress a *single* quality in the dishonest manager. This should be imitated (just as the day of the Lord imitates the quality of the thief who comes unexpectedly in the middle of the night). What is this aspect in the dishonest manager's conduct that Jesus is stressing?

To discover this, we have to make a detailed examination of the comparison and see what the focus of Jesus' interest is. In an artist's painting, all the elements serve a single point that the artist wants to put across. In the same way, the parables are like small pictures that sum up a situation in a few quick brushstrokes. If we analyze the parable of the dishonest manager, we find the following: Suddenly this man gets a shock because his employer has discovered the fraud he has been carrying out. He will have to submit to an audit and afterward will be dismissed from his post. He will lose his job. The future is in danger and will change radically. However, the manager doesn't lose his calm, isn't overwhelmed by events, but starts to think. He examines the situation and weighs it up coolly. He makes a list of his options: "I am not strong enough to dig, and I'd be ashamed to beg. Ah, I know what I'll do so that, when I'm dismissed as manager, I'll have some friends to rely on" (cf. Lk 16:3–4). He has the accounts of his employer's debtors altered. That way, he'll be sure that he can turn to these debtors when he's been dismissed. They will not be able to refuse him because he could denounce them and have them charged with fraud. In this way he guaranteed his future.

This is the point that the parable seeks to stress: *the man was clever enough to act efficiently, wasn't overwhelmed by events, but guaranteed his future in a clever and well-thought out way.* This is the quality Jesus is interested in and the one sketched out in deft strokes in this story. Jesus' point is: "Why don't you do the same? Why don't you, in your field, act with the same shrewdness and efficiency?" And it is true that, with the coming of Jesus Christ into someone's life, the future of that life will have to change radically. The person will not be able to carry on living in the same way as before. Jesus wants us not to be vague, but to take a hard look at life in the light of faith, to think things through and act with efficiency and shrewdness in order to secure the new future of God that opens up to any one to whom Jesus Christ introduces himself. He is not encouraging us to be dishonest, but prodding us to be efficient in what we do in the area of faith. .

We should not ask: "What does management mean in this parable?" "What is the meaning of the hundred barrels of oil or the hundred containers of wheat?" All this doesn't mean anything. Its only point is to stress, like the details in the story of the man who got up early and fixed breakfast, the quality of efficiency and shrewdness in the face of a threatened future. It is part of the picture, in the same way that the tree in blossom at the side of the house is part of the picture and contributes to the atmosphere of happiness that the artist wishes to communicate through the picture.

The parable of the Abandoned Vineyard (Lk 20:9–19) is of the other type, sometimes called an allegory. When vineyards were mentioned, the Jews would remember the prophet Isaiah's poem about the vineyard (Is 5:1–7). They would know that, although Jesus was *talking* about a vineyard, he was *thinking* about the people of God, for whom God had so much love. Jesus *talks* about "leasing the vineyard," but is thinking about the people's responsibility to bear fruit. He *talks* about the slaves and employees that the owner of the vineyard sends, but he is *thinking* about the prophets whom God sent in the Old Testament: they were rejected, beaten, sent back empty-handed (Lk 20:10–12). He *talks* about the beloved son whom the owner sent, thinking that they would respect him more than the other employees, but is *thinking* about himself, God's last messenger to the people, described as the beloved son by the prophets. He *talks* about the murder of the vineyard owner's son, but he is *thinking* about his own death.

Jesus ends the comparison with the question: "What will the owner of the vineyard do to them?" and answers immediately: "He will come and destroy those tenants and give the vineyard to others" (Lk 10:15–16). The Jews understood very well the meaning of the answer and said, "Heaven forbid!" or "Never!" They understood the meaning of the image: Jesus was threatening them with the transfer of the reign of God to the pagans.

The parable or allegory of the Abandoned Vineyard is one of the few of which we can examine each element and detail and ask: "What is the meaning?" Two others of the same type are the parable of the Good Shepherd (Jn 10:1–18) and the True Vine (Jn 15:1–8). In the other parables, however, we have to look for the one meaning Jesus is concentrating on. There are various ways to discover this.

In some parables, drawn from everyday life, strange things happen that never happen in everyday life: for example, it is rare to find a shepherd who abandons a hundred sheep in the desert, just to go and look for the one that strayed (Lk 15:3–6). It is rare to find a father who waits for the ungrateful son who leaves home without any explanation and who then goes out to meet him and prepares a great feast (the Prodigal Son), and it is rare to find a woman who loses a coin, sweeps the house, and after finding the coin calls all her neighbors to tell them the story (Lk 15:8–10). The person who hears these stories is surprised because, although they are taken from life, they are things that don't usually happen. This is exactly the purpose of these parables: to call attention to the strange thing that is happening here. That is where the one meaning that Jesus wants to communicate is hidden. That is what all the other elements of the comparison lead up to.

Sometimes, however, there is a mixture of the two types of comparison. For example, when Jesus in his parables talks about a king, judge, or father, he is always *thinking* about God. When he *talks* about the king's sons or servants, about the flock or the vineyard, he is *thinking* about the prophets or the people of God. When he *talks* about audits, harvests, or fishing, he is *thinking* about God's judgment on human beings. When he *talks* about feasts or marriages, he is *thinking* about the happiness of the reign of God.

How do we know this? Because Jesus did what everyone else did at that time. The method of using parables was a very common teaching method. Other teachers of religion also knew about it and used it. And, according to the rules of the method, known from the studies done of it in recent years, the meaning of these symbols had already been generally agreed upon. In his teaching, Jesus used the language of the people.

The Advantages of Teaching in Parables

All the parables are images taken from the ordinary life that everyone knows, situations that make us laugh or weep, things we deal with from morning to night. In using everyday examples as illustrations of the mysteries of God's reign, Jesus showed himself to be a great teacher.

I can say: "The renewal of the church is like the trees on the avenue. Their branches had grown very long and they were cut back to let the trees grow and to prevent a mass of leaves from sucking up all the sap and killing the tree." If you heard this, next time you went down the avenue and saw the trees you would remember the comparison and the trees would begin to speak and convince you that it was true. Life begins to speak of God and the reign of God.

If we bring together all the elements of Jesus' parables, we get a curious mosaic of the most diverse situations and aspects of life: seed, plow, light, salt, birds, flowers, pigs, weeds, lilies, grass, doves, serpents, feasts, weddings, bread, wine, yeast, business, management, barbecue, war, building, tower, house, road, briars, good soil, fisherfolk, net, children, house-cleaning, lost jewels, found pearls, talents, wine, sheep, shepherd, inheritance, education, wages, robbers, rich and poor, ungrateful children. They can be found on almost every page of the Gospels. All this has great meaning.

Jesus almost never explains the comparisons he uses. Sometimes he ends the example with these words: "Let anyone with ears listen!" (Mt 13:9). The meaning of this saying is: "There you are. You've heard it. Now, try to understand it!" He leaves the people to discover the message. It is a vote of confidence by Jesus in human beings. He thinks that we have sufficient intelligence to discover, from the things of life, the meaning of the things of the reign of God. He doesn't spoon-feed us. Instead of solving problems and supplying answers, he puts problems and questions in the heads of others and forces them to think. They themselves, afterward, by thinking, living, and reflecting, will discover the solutions to the problems Jesus has put in their heads.

All these diverse aspects and situations of life mentioned in the parables begin to speak and question us. Plowing the field and cutting the furrow, the plower will remember the saying: "No one who puts a hand to the plow and looks back is fit for the kingdom of God" (Lk 9:62). Jesus makes life transparent. He gives the events of life a new meaning. The parables are valuable, not just for the teaching that each of them contains, but also and especially for the new vision they give us of everyday life: everything has to do with the reign of God and speaks of it.

Jesus comes, partly, to create problems for us. When we live with no worries at all, it's a sign that something in our lives is not working. Jesus came to present us with problems and to elicit answers, through the parables, not to torment us but to put us on the right track, the one that leads to God and happiness.

Finally, an image or a comparison is much richer, has much more communicative and evocative force than a mere theoretical argument. It may be vaguer and less precise, but it is much more profound and conveys much more meaning.

In choosing the method of the parables, Jesus did not invent something new. He adopted the existing teaching method and renewed it from within. He placed himself more in the line of the teachers of wisdom than in that of the prophets, at least in his teaching to the people. To the Pharisees his preaching has more of the character of prophetic denunciation.

The Parables and the Kingdom of God

In the chapter on the Sermon on the Mount, we saw what the reign of God might be. This reign was present and active in Jesus, in his person and in his work. When he introduces parables with the words, "With what can we compare the kingdom of God, or what parable will we use for it?" (Mk 4:30), he is trying to illustrate for the people the meaning of his own presence among them. Each of the parables seeks to explain one or another aspect of this mystery. In other parables again, especially those told at the end of his life, Jesus is thinking of the reign that will be established through his death and resurrection and that will go on growing, slowly, through human history, until the end of time.

This invisible reality that is the reign of God is explained by means of the visible things of every day. This presents a difficulty, which was mentioned earlier. How could Jesus say, "I speak in parables so that they may listen but not hear and look but not see" (Mk 4:11–13; Mt 13:11–15)? He gives the impression that, far from being chosen to explain, parables were intended to conceal and to prevent understanding.

The answer to this difficulty seems to be as follows. I can talk about life and use the following comparisons. "We have to open up and widen our horizons." "We have to open up a clearing in that dense forest." "We have to tune in to the correct frequency." "We have to take the bends out of the road." "We have to re-fasten the buoy to the anchor." "We have to keep going till the mist lifts." These are images that everyone knows, but not everyone understands the meaning. For example, someone who thinks life is fine, straightforward, and simple won't understand why I'm talking about "taking the bends out of the road," "widening our horizons," "opening up a clearing in the dense forest," "tuning in to the correct frequency." These images indicate that life is not straightforward, and they also disclose a conception of life.

This is what Jesus did. He used images that everyone knows, because they come from ordinary life. But not everyone succeeds in understanding that new, unknown vision of life that he wants to communicate by using these images that are accessible to every-one. They lack the key to understanding. This key is Jesus himself. As long as the people do not understand who Jesus is, they will not be able to understand the total meaning of the images he uses. To the apostles it was "given to know the secrets of the kingdom" (Mt 13:11) because they were opening up to Jesus Christ. They were not doing what the Pharisees and the people were doing, wanting Jesus to be the way they liked, but were trying to be as Jesus wanted them to be. They accepted Jesus without advance conditions.

This attitude to Christ was a light that could reveal to them the ultimate and true meaning of the parables. For the others, in con-trast, the parables were just "questions in the head." They made people think, in order to break the mold they carried inside them and into which they wanted to fit Jesus. A parable is like a lamp we put into someone's hands. The person begins to examine it and see how it works, only to find that to give light it must be connected to an electric circuit. The parable reveals its full meaning and really begins to give light only when it is connected to the person of Christ, through a sincere conversion to him. Then the person begins to see clearly what the road is like. But the parable, even before a person connects it to Christ, is able to bring people to try to find out for themselves how it works and how it can begin to light up and give light to the road. This ability comes from the inherent power of the image or comparison.

Dealing with Difficulties

Many applications of parables in sermons or books come more from the fertile imagination of the preacher than from the text. Imagination, when used properly, is an important instrument for explaining the images used in the parables. However, the person listening has to have common sense and judge what is said with care. We have to do what Jesus wants us to do: think and search until we ourselves discover the meaning of things.

The parable of the Dishonest Manager has already been explained. It also shows that Jesus was more human than us and understood more about life than we do. He is not afraid to use an example that depends on bad things that happen every day. In everything that happens, however bad it is, there is always something good that we can make use of.

14

JESUS' MIRACLES

A Free Sample of Our Future

When he went up to heaven, Jesus left the promise of miracles to those who would believe in his name (Mk 16:17–18). The Acts of the Apostles describes many miracles in the church of the first Christians. Where today are these miracles Jesus promised? At Lourdes? At the shrines of the great pilgrimage centers? Where?

Statistics show a fall in the number of miracles at Lourdes. As scientific investigation increases, miracles decline. Science today can explain what couldn't be explained before. These things are no longer miracles. But then who do miracles depend on? On us, on science, or on God? Who can tell me if something is a miracle? Was everything that Jesus did a miracle? If we applied all the criteria of science, what would be left?

The New Testament, two thousand years ago, said this:

A large crowd kept following him, because they saw the signs that he was doing for the sick. (Jn 6:2)

They carried out the sick into the streets, and laid them on cots and mats, in order that Peter's shadow might fall on some of them as he came by. A great number of people would also gather from the towns around Jerusalem, bringing the sick. (Acts 5:15–16)

Is there a difference in the attitude of the people who went after Jesus and the apostles and those today who seek healing through their faith?

The general impression we are left with is this: Modern, enlightened Christians don't seem to believe much in miracles. Others, non-Christians or traditional Catholics or fundamentalists, seem to believe strongly in them. How do we explain this? Do modern Christians not believe in miracles any more? What is a miracle?

Thoughts about Miracles

Our usual concept of a miracle is this: it is something that doesn't have a natural explanation, conflicts with the normal process of the laws of nature, and is scientifically inexplicable. People think that a miracle is something different and out of the ordinary that doesn't normally happen, something we can't bring about because it is beyond our powers. They think that miracles happen when we have exhausted all our resources: "It's in God's hands now." This assumes that God is absent when we can cope and don't need God to solve our problems! It assumes that God has nothing to do with what is common, natural, ordinary, human, what has nothing extraordinary about it. If that were true, we would have to agree with those who say: "One day science will be able to explain everything and will do away with miracles."

In addition, miracles are generally seen as a *favor* done by God for the person who receives it. It's a sort of personal present, which doesn't lead us to ask: "What conversion is God asking of me?" It's a purely personal favor, unconnected with the church, unconnected with God's plan for human beings, unconnected with anything.

Finally, the commonest reaction of people today to a miracle is "Is it genuine?" or "Lucky me!"

The word "miracle" comes from the Latin word *miraculum,* something that causes wonder. The Bible talks a lot about the "wonderful things" God did for the people. But a miracle isn't just any wonderful thing. For example, a three-year-old child who can jump fifteen feet is a wonderful thing, but it wouldn't be described as a miracle. A miracle is a wonderful fact, event, or situation in which we see God revealed.

An ordinary example will illustrate what the Bible means by a miracle. One day, Maria, Francisco's wife, put a pretty colored flower in the window. She wanted Francisco to see it, be pleased, and know that Maria loved him. It was a gesture of affection. When Francisco came back from work, he saw the flower and immediately understood. He went to Maria and said: "Thank you, Maria. You're the best!" Other people passed by the window, saw the flower, and didn't notice anything. Nor did they need to notice. The flower was for Francisco. Francisco noticed it, and that was enough. The flower became a sign of love, affection, friendship, presence, faithfulness. The flower achieved the objective that Maria had given it. Anyway, it wouldn't have been good for everyone to notice; it would have broken the secret between the two of them. For other people the flower wasn't a sign; it was no more than an ordinary flower, just like any other. For Francisco and Maria the flower meant a whole world.

In the same way, God puts many flowers in the windows of our lives. Some flowers are noticed by everyone, because they are for everyone to see. Others, smaller, but sometimes much prettier, are just for you. Life is full of these flowers, these signs from God, signs that reveal love, affection, friendship, presence, fidelity, power, strength: signs that provoke wonder and remind us of our friend. The flower made Francisco stop and think. He was ecstatic, because he saw it as the expression of Maria's love for him. A miracle is, as I said, anything that makes us stop and think because it reveals God's love and God's call.

So in the Bible a miracle can be the commonest thing in the world or the most unusual thing. It can be a storm, a sunset, the beauty of nature or the charm of a child, the manna in the desert or the plagues in Egypt. It can be the resurrection of a dead person, the curing of someone paralyzed, the multiplication of loaves. In all these things a loving heart sees the hand of a friend, just as Francisco saw Maria's hand in the flower in the window. This *wonderful thing* doesn't depend just on God, but also on us, on what we are looking for. Where this eye of friendship is absent, not even God can achieve anything. That is why Jesus couldn't do any miracles in

Nazareth, because of the lack of this vision, because of the lack of faith in the people (Mk 6:5–6). In modern discussions about miracles people often forget that in order to understand the message of the flower, to be able to see the miracle, we have to have this eye of faith, love, and friendship.

How the Bible Describes Miracles

The words most used in the Bible to describe what we today call a miracle are "sign," "power," "wonder." The fundamental characteristic of a miracle in the Bible is that it reveals the active presence of God, power that acts and that produces a *wonder* and attracts attention and so becomes a *sign of God*. It is not essential to a miracle that it be against the laws of nature or have no scientific explanation. What is essential for a miracle to be a miracle is that it should be *a sign of God's active presence in life.*

In the Bible, a miracle is like a *word* that God speaks to human beings, to tell them something and make a call to them. In this way, the Bible recognizes "miracles," "signs," "wonders," and "demonstrations of power" in creation, that is, in things that for us have nothing miraculous about them: God sends the rain (Jer 5:24), God sets the sun to give light to the day and the moon to give light at night (Jer 31:35). It is God who controls the sequence of days and nights (Jer 33:20, 25).

> The heavens are telling the glory of God,
>   and the firmament proclaims his handiwork.
> Day to day pours forth speech,
>   and night to night declares knowledge.
> There is no speech, nor are there words;
>   their voice has not heard;
> yet their voice goes out through all the earth,
>   and their words to the end of the world.
>
>   (Ps 19:1–4)

How many are your wonders!
I would like to count them,
  but they are as many as the sand on the seashore.
And even if I could count them,
  in the end I would be confronting the Greatest Mystery, you.
                    (Ps 139:17–18, author's translation).

Nature was the great book in which the features of God's face were revealed. Of course the idea of nature at the time was limited and pre-scientific. Nothing was known of the laws of nature that we know today with increasing detail. Nonetheless, this does not mean that scientific progress can declare the Bible's vision of nature superseded or deny the traces of God that it sees in nature. These do not depend on scientific instruments of observation, but on a vision based on faith. If science says, "That sunset, the storm, rain, drought, all that is the most natural thing in the world, and has nothing extraordinary about it," that verdict is true and correct. Science is right. But even so there is nothing to stop my eye from seeing in them a reflection of my friend God and pausing in wonder or, as the Bible says, from seeing in them a *miracle,* a sign from God for us. With the same outlook, the Bible sees the signs of God in everyday life, in the most ordinary aspects of life, and in the history of the past. We need only read the books of Proverbs and Exodus. God's hand is visible in everything, filling life with a friendship so often lacking.

In the Bible, we could say, a miracle has two sides: on one side it presupposes action by God, while on the other it presupposes that human beings have an eye of faith capable of detecting the meaning of what God does. Without this it would be like a silent film. No one understands it and it has no meaning. This wouldn't be a "miracle" in the biblical sense of the term. In the Bible the question prompted by a miracle is not, "Is it genuine?," but "What does God mean by this?" "What is God's message?" "What does God want of me or of us?"

There can be "false" miracles and "true" miracles. There are criteria for distinguishing between them: true miracles must be within the overall plan of God and in accord with the rest of revelation (Dt 13:1–18). It is not enough for something strange or wonderful to appear for us to say immediately, "It's God." Jesus himself says that people will come and do great miracles and warns, "Beware of them" (Mt 24:25). He also says that at the end there will be people who say, " 'Lord, Lord, did we not prophesy in your name and cast out demons in your name and do many deeds of power in your name?' Then I will declare to them, 'I never knew you; go away from me, you evildoers' " (Mt 7:22–23).

A miracle says nothing to a person without faith. It may make a person ask about God. If we have faith we see the hand of God in a miracle because we are tuned to the wavelength on which God is transmitting a divine message.

These criteria may help us to form an opinion about the "miracles" that are happening in many places today.

The Historicity of Jesus' Miracles

There have been people who denied the historicity of Jesus' miracles. Some of the reasons included: They were inventions by Christians to "canonize" Jesus. There were miracle-working gods among the pagans, and Jesus had to be able to compete with them. There were also human miracle-workers, like Apollonius of Tyana, who worked real miracles. There were also miracle-workers among the Jews. Jesus was just an ordinary miracle-worker.

Today this view is no longer accepted. The arguments don't stand up. Generally the miracles are denied, not so much because of the arguments, but because, in advance of any argument, these people reject the possibility of miracles.

The arguments used do not stand up for the following reasons. It is not possible to dismiss out of hand the massive testimony of the Gospels. In addition, in Jesus' miracles, there is none of the magic so characteristic of the other miracle-workers of the time. If we compare the accounts of the other miracle-workers with those of the Gospels, we see a great difference: sobriety, with no exploitation of the miraculous aspect. Jesus works miracles on his own authority; he does not have to ask for them, like the Jews.

The so-called apocryphal books, written mostly after the beginning of the second century, contain reports about sensational miracles performed by Jesus as a child that lack any historical basis. They are more an expression of a search for security. When children realize that their parents are not at home, they do everything they can to reassure themselves. In the same way, when real contact with God through faith and trust has atrophied or been lost, people look for security in rituals and miracles. Miracles then are not important for their meaning, but in their own right. In this case, the greater the element of the sensational or wonderful, the better. But the Bible doesn't have this view.

It may be that, after applying all the criteria of modern science, we have to conclude that one or another fact of Jesus' life was not a miracle by our criteria. But this doesn't make it stop being a miracle (sign, power, wonderful event) in the biblical sense of the word: a sign of the active presence of God among human beings.

Jesus' Miracles as Signs

As we saw in chapter 13, with the coming of Jesus something changed, changed radically. As a result of his word and action, everything was "redirected" and "reintegrated." A radically new situation sprouts and springs up from Christ as though from its root: a new human race, a new world. The miracles are part of this more general renewal and are a sign of it. The miracles make visible the "power" that is bringing into being this "new world."

If we look at the whole range of Jesus' miracles, we find that his miraculous activity touches all sectors of life: diseases, hunger, blindness, nature, death, sin, demons, will, sadness. It is a direct attack on all the evils that afflict human beings. First, Jesus drives out the demons that are behind the evils. Then he forgives the sins that produce the evils. He takes control over weak human wills and strengthens them; it is enough for him to say, "Follow me," and a man like Levi immediately leaves his job as a money-lender with all its profit in order to follow Christ (Mt 9:9). Jesus also takes control of nature where it represents a threat to human beings: he calms the storm, walks on the water, and brings about the miraculous catch of fish. He abolishes hunger by multiplying the loaves. He cures all sorts of diseases: of the lame, the blind, the mad, the dumb, the deaf, lepers. Jesus is more powerful than the power of death and raises three dead people: Lazarus, the son of the widow at Naim, and Jairus's daughter. Jesus' presence was a cause of great joy and hope for the people.

Jesus' way of working miracles recalls God's action in creation: a word is enough to cure diseases, banish demons, calm the sea, and raise the dead (Gen 1:3). There's no magic. A new creation is under way with the arrival of Jesus.

Jesus doesn't work miracles just for the sake of it. He doesn't work them to satisfy human curiosity or for self-promotion. He refuses Herod when Herod wants to see miracles (Lk 23:8–9). He refuses to work miracles in the desert at the demon's request (Lk 4:3–12). He refuses to work them for himself when he is on the cross and others are saying: "Let him come down from the cross now, and we will believe in him" (Mt 27:42). He never worked miracles as a joke, as the apocryphal gospels suggest. His miracles are signs. Signs of what? On various occasion, Jesus indicates the meaning of the miracles.

1. When John the Baptist sent his disciples to Jesus to ask, "Are you the one who is to come, or are we to wait for another?" (Mt 11:3), Jesus replied: "Go and tell John what you hear and see: the blind receive their sight, the lame walk, the lepers are cleansed, the deaf hear, the dead are raised, and the poor have good news brought to them" (Mt 11:4–5). The miracles listed here are the same ones proclaimed by the prophet Isaiah as signs of the messianic age (Is 35:5ff). In other words, Jesus worked these miracles and referred to them so that others could see that the messianic age had arrived.

2. The Pharisees were doubtful about Jesus' exorcisms. He replied: "If it is by the finger of God that I cast out demons, then

the kingdom of God has come to you" (Lk 11:20). Jesus cast out demons as a sign that the reign of God had arrived.

3. On another occasion, Jesus cured a paralytic to prove that he had power to forgive sins (Mk 2:10–12). The miracle here is a sign of the power Jesus possessed to cut off the root of problems, which is sin.

4. The miracle of the calmed storm prompted the question: "Who is this, that even the wind and sea obey him?" (Mk 4:40). The miracle was not an act for its own sake, but turned the spotlight on Jesus; miracles were designed to reveal an aspect of his personality.

5. He cured the man with the withered hand to show that he was greater than the Sabbath (Mk 3:1–5; 2:27–28).

6. The miracles were worked to convince others of the words and the message he addressed to them (Jn 12:37; Lk 10:13–14).

7. The miracles are signs to show that Jesus is in the Father and the Father in him (Jn 10:38; 14:11).

The miracles, therefore, are not significant for their own sake, independent of anything else. They have a purpose, to reveal to human beings something about Jesus. Through them, Jesus introduces himself with the mission he has received from the Father.

Jesus does not allow the people to remain content with the miracles, or the "favors," without going on to ask about the message that God is trying to send them through the miracles. He lets the people look for the cause of the miracles. We only need to read the Gospels to see this. He tries to get the people to go beyond the miracles and look for their meaning. For example, the people were trying to find him because of the miracles (Jn 6:2) and stayed with him so long that their food ran out. Jesus multiplied the loaves (Jn 6:11–12). Later the people came looking for him again, and Jesus said: "You are looking for me, not because you saw signs, but because you ate your fill of the loaves" (Jn 6:26). They were only thinking of the "favor" and weren't interested in the "sign," that is, they weren't interested in discovering the meaning and the message. Jesus then spoke very sharply (Jn 6:60–71), distancing himself from the people, who remained trapped in their immediate interests without wanting to open up to a deeper meaning in things (Jn 6:66).

The miracles exist and happen in order to help the people to open up to God's message, to be prepared to follow Christ in faith, and to recognize him as the Messiah and Son of God. Where this faith-openness is missing, not even a miracle can do anything. So, for example, Jesus was unable to work miracles in Nazareth because of the people's lack of faith (Mk 6:5–6). The Pharisees saw all the miracles, but did not believe (Jn 12:37) because they lacked this sincerity and openness to the truth (Jn 18:37; 8:39–47). Without this openness, miracles achieve nothing.

Jesus' Miracles: "Free Samples" of the Future

As well as being signs of the coming of the reign of God, the miracles are also the beginning of the establishment of the reign, "free samples" of what God's power and fidelity will achieve for and through those who believe. As a result, the miracles, as well as being mere signs, also inspire hope because they show the beginning of the future. They inspire faith because they show the power that guarantees the future. They inspire generosity and the strength to struggle and resist, because they guarantee that dedication to the cause of God's reign is worthwhile and will not be frustrated.

In Jesus' hands, the future takes definite shape, and paradise, where all is order, peace, and harmony, begins to exist among human beings. It comes into being because a new power, the Spirit of God, is active in Jesus. This Spirit, who was active at the creation (Gen 1:2), who breathed life into human beings (Gen 2:7; Job 33:4), who brought about the great miracles of the past (Ex 15:10; Is 63:11–14), who fills the vast spaces of the earth (Wis 1:7), who was promised for the future as the great gift of God (Joel 2:28–32 [3:1–5 in the Hebrew text]), this creative Spirit (Ps 104:30), Jesus possesses in fullness (Is 11:2; Lk 4:18) and communicates it to all who believe in him (Jn 16:12–15) and to all who try to live a proper human life (Gal 5:22).

But we need the eye of faith to see the Spirit at work. Sometimes this power that produces the order that will result in paradise finds a greater response and acts in a more concentrated and dramatic form in particular people: St. Francis, Pope John XXIII, the saints in general. In all of us, everywhere, however, the Spirit is the fight against evil, the struggle for liberation from everything that oppresses human beings, the attempt to establish order, peace, and harmony.

The first purpose of miracles is to produce *conversion* and *change* as a step toward the establishment of the reign of God in the lives of individuals and society. "The kingdom of God has come. Change your lives!" (Mk 1:15). To sit waiting for miracles, or to imagine that miracles by themselves are a sign of God's protection that make action on our part unnecessary, is self-deception. Where a miracle does not achieve this aim of conversion, it has the opposite effect and becomes a ground for judgment and condemnation (Lk 10:13–14; Jn 15:24). This is still true today: to stay at the stage of miracles and be satisfied with them can have the opposite effect to the one expected. Miracles are like the word of God, a two-edged sword (Heb 4:12).

Jesus, the Great Sign or Great Miracle

Miracles are like windows opened by God on the meaning of life. Miracles exist, above all, to point us to Jesus Christ. John's Gospel teaches this very clearly.

In John's Gospel there are relatively few miracles, only one of each type. For John, miracles are not just favors for particular individuals but also the revelation of particular aspects of the salvation that Christ brought to human beings: he turns water into wine to show the superiority of the New Testament to the Old (Jn 2:1–11). He cures the royal official's son to show that human faith triggers the power of God (Jn 4:46–54); he cures the paralytic on the Sabbath, not only to bring happiness to this particular unfortunate person, but also to reveal that he has no fixed working hours, since he is like God, who acts everywhere and at every moment for the good of human beings (Jn 5:1–17). He multiplies loaves, not simply to relieve the hunger of one group of people, but also to reveal that he is the bread of life (Jn 6:1–59); he cures the man born blind and restores light to his eyes, not just to help this man, but to show that he is the light of the world (Jn 9:1–7). He raises Lazarus, not only to help a friend and relieve the grief of Mary and Martha, but also to show that he himself is the "resurrection and the life" (Jn 11:1–44).

All the miracles, however, are simply an anticipation of the great and definitive miracle of the resurrection, which revealed who Jesus was and what the future was that he sought to bring about. The power of the resurrection was already active in Jesus and is still active in those who believe in him (Eph 1:17–21), bringing about through them conversion and change of life and of the structures that prevent the establishment of paradise.

Miracle or Law of Nature?

The contrast between miracles and the law of nature is false. There can be a "sign of the active presence of God" in the sight of a sunset, in everyday events, in the beauty of a child, in a cure produced by a drug. Science may be able to explain all this, but it will never get to the point where it can forbid me to say: "Thank you, Lord. What do you want of me?"

We all have our own experience of friendship with God and perceive the signs of God's presence in our own way. We might say that we all have our own miracles in our lives. The criteria should be: Is it in accordance with the gospel? Does it produce a change of life? Does it take us beyond the miracle to look for the call of God revealed in it? Does it support faith and not encourage a taste for the magic aspects that obscure the gracious presence of God and tie God's power to material things that are incapable of having such power?

The day may come when science is able to explain everything

that happens in places such as Lourdes. This won't mean that it can conclude that God was not present there. This depends on a different measuring instrument, faith. If Francisco had not had his faith and love, he would have seen nothing in the flower that Maria placed in the window. He would have seen in the flower, and in the clothes and the food, something that Maria, as his lawful wife, had to supply him with. In that case the flower would have had the effect of increasing in him the sense that he was the husband whom his wife had to obey. There would have been no growth of love in him. Quite the opposite, his love would have decreased and he would have slid into even greater selfishness.

In the same way, many people regard miracles as something that God *has* to do, because God is God, because God is the boss. The boss, they think, has an obligation to give charity to the employees. Employers give it as and when they see fit. We can and should ask for it. The more charity an employer gives, the better the employer, so people think. The more miracles God works, the better God plays the role of God. But this would mean that we employees, poor humans, would stay forever in the position of employees and slaves. We would never be able to become children of the master from whom we asked and received charity. But a miracle is not a boss's charity. A miracle is a sign of love that a parent performs for children. Until we have developed in ourselves the attitude of children, we shall not have the vision to appreciate the true meaning of miracles.

Miracles Today

The great miracle — so big that we can't see it because it's right before our eyes — is life being renewed through faith in Christ, life that keeps finding new courage and never gives up, life that endures persecution, that may even die, but always rises again, life that renews others by its mere presence, life that dazzles with its enormous richness, despite the poverty all around it. This is the great miracle, walking around among us all the time, the result of the action of the Spirit present in human lives. Where sensitivity to this power of life and of the Spirit weakens, that is when we find a hunger for miracles to get us through life. Where people lose the sense of the active presence of God in their midst, a presence guaranteed by the Word of God, then they look for other means of guaranteeing that presence, and that is when "miracles" appear.

It is difficult to pass judgment on the "miracles" that take place all over the world today and fill the miracle rooms of major shrines. Many people shake their heads and say, "Poor fools!" But we should remember the sentence in the Gospel: "A large crowd kept following him, because they saw the signs that he was doing for the sick" (Jn 6:2). And Jesus welcomed those people, "had compassion for them, because they were like sheep without a shepherd" (Mk 6:34). He even allowed a woman who had had a hemorrhage for twelve years to touch him to be cured (Mk 5:25–34). It was a magical and superstitious attitude, but Jesus did not condemn it. To condemn the people's attitude is relatively easy, but to find the inner void that makes people look for miracles is much more difficult. Instead of dismissively passing judgment on people's attitudes, perhaps it would be more honest to carry out a serious examination of our own attitudes.

Are we offering people hope, something that opens a door for them to a better future that's worth fighting for? Should we not see in this growing search for miracles a sign of increasing despair among people who have stopped believing in official solutions, whether from government or church? Is not the right attitude "to have compassion for them, because they are like sheep without a shepherd," and to offer them, in all its fullness, the "Good News" of the reign of God?

This is not true just of poor and backward people. Horoscopes are fashionable today even in religious newspapers. Esoteric religions are gaining followers everywhere, even among educated people who have full lives. Somehow their lives are not what they want them to be. They too are wandering along the road of life like sheep without a shepherd, in need of a vision of the future to awaken a hope, a faith, a great love.

15

JESUS' TRANSFIGURATION
The Meaning of Life's Crises

Generally, when we hear about the transfiguration, we think of a particular event in Jesus' life. We don't place it within the general context of his life. In fact, the transfiguration is a landmark in Jesus' life. It begins a new and different phase of his activity. The main purpose of this chapter is to illustrate, through a study of the transfiguration, this aspect of Jesus' life and attitude, which will show us more clearly the human side of his personality.

In general, when we read the Gospels, we only think about the things written in them and don't think about the people who wrote them or the people for whom they were written. That is, we don't think about the evangelists or about the real situation of the first Christians. The account of the transfiguration is a typical example of the way the evangelists talk about three things at once: about Jesus, about the lives of the first Christians, and about the intentions of the evangelists who described it. A second aim of this chapter is to explain this threefold dimension of the Gospels: Jesus, the first Christians, and the evangelists. A third aim is to explain the meaning of the suffering and passion, because the transfiguration marks the point at which the passion appears on the horizon of Jesus' life and he starts to talk to his disciples about the need for him to suffer.

In this way this chapter may help to pull away the veil from one aspect of Jesus' life, and Christian life in general, that is generally kept under wraps. It seeks to show how God's plan is gradually realized through the ups and downs of everyday life that depend on human decisions. It also shows how the crises of life are opportunities, given by God, for us to grow and for God's will to come to pass in our lives.

The Differences between the Two Phases of Jesus' Activity

Once, shortly before the transfiguration, Jesus gathered his disciples together and asked them: "Who do people say that I am?" (Mk 8:27; Mt 16:13; Lk 9:18) From that moment, the direction of events changed, and we find profound differences in Jesus' activity.

The miracles become less frequent. In the first phase of his activity among the people, Jesus worked many miracles. In the second phase, miracles are almost an exception. Mark mentions only two, as opposed to dozens in the previous phase. Matthew, again, reports the same two miracles, plus one more (Mt 17:14–21; 20:29–34; 17:24–27). Luke knows of only five miracles, that is, two known by Matthew and Mark and three more. That's all. Why so many miracles in the first phase and so few in the second?

The passion starts to be mentioned constantly. In the first phase, the passion is mentioned only occasionally as a future possibility. Now, in the second phase, the passion is a certainty and mentioned repeatedly. Jesus even makes prophecies of the passion (Mk 8:31–32; 9:30–32; 10:32–34).

Jesus changes his attitude toward the people. Previously Jesus' great concern was the people. Now, in this second phase, his great concern is his disciples and their instruction. He is often alone with them, teaching them (Mk 9:28, 30, 35; 8:27, 31; 10:10, 23–27, 28–31; 9:38–41). He even makes a journey abroad with the disciples, to Tyre and Sidon, to be alone with them. For the first time he talks about a church (Mt 16:18).

Jesus starts to talk about the necessity for the disciples to undergo the cross. He talks not only about his own passion, but also about the need for us to suffer with him. He insists on the demanding conditions required for anyone to be his disciple (Mt 16:24–28; Mk

8:34–38; Lk 9:23–27; 14:27; 17:33; 12:9; Mk 10:28–31, etc.). Previously, in the first phase, there was no such insistence on the need to suffer with him.

The perspective of the parables is different. In the first phase, Jesus used many parables to illustrate the mystery of the reign of God. Now, this is to be established in the future, through his passion and death.

The Pharisees' opposition becomes clear. In the first phase, there was concealed opposition to Jesus on the part of the leaders of the people. Now, in the second phase, this opposition becomes clear, open, and irreversible.

These are the main differences revealed by a careful reading of the Gospels between the first and second phases of Jesus' activity. These differences require an explanation. What happened to make Jesus' activity take a different direction?

Change of Course in Jesus' Life

Jesus had left Palestine and gone to the region of Tyre and Sidon. Returning from there with his disciples and approaching Caesarea Philippi, he stopped and made a sober assessment of the situation: "Who do people say that I am?" The disciples gave the people's views, which were very varied: "They say you are John the Baptist, Elijah, Jeremiah or one of the ancient prophets" (Mt 16:14; Lk 9:19; Mk 8:28). A questionable result! No one got it right. Everyone was wrong. They had failed to discover who Jesus was.

Then Jesus asked the apostles, "What about you? Who do you say I am?" Peter replied in the name of all of them and confessed that Jesus was the Christ, that is, the Messiah, the savior promised by God (Mk 8:29). Matthew adds: "the Son of the living God" (Mt 16:16). They had got it right. In their case, Jesus' activity had not been useless. Now, that Jesus had done this survey of the results of his work among the people, what was his reaction going to be to the findings?

Jesus was always obedient to the Father. Obedience was the

dominant feature of his life. Paul says he was obedient to death (Phil 2:8) and that he came into the world for no other reason than to do the Father's will (Heb 10:9). And Jesus himself stressed this on various occasions: "I do nothing on my own, but I speak these things as the Father instructed me. . . . I always do what is pleasing to him" (Jn 8:28–29).

However, we should not think of this obedience as meaning that Jesus did not need to analyze situations and events, as though everything was clear to him. He read the Father's will in things that happened, in the Bible, in the real situation. To do this, he used to withdraw and pray to the Father, in solitude, for whole nights (Lk 6:12; 9:18; 5:16). On a number of occasions the situation made him change his behavior. The Letter to the Hebrews goes so far as to say that Jesus "*learned* obedience through what he suffered" (Heb 5:8). In this respect Jesus was really human, "like his brothers and sisters in every respect . . . yet without sin" (Heb 2:17–18; 4:15). He not only tried to discover God's will, but also carried it out to the letter.

God has a profound respect for our freedom. In the first phase of his activity, Jesus announced the arrival of the reign of God (Mk 1:15). He gave all the signals necessary for the people to understand that he was the promised Messiah. But the people had such a different idea of the Messiah that they were unable to see in Jesus the Messiah they were waiting for. Jesus, in this first phase, did not use the term "Messiah" for himself because it was a politically suspect term. Jesus didn't want to increase the misunderstandings that already existed. He brought the content of the promise without giving it its label. The people themselves would have to discover it and change their way of thinking about the reign of God. This didn't happen. The great opportunity of "the year of the Lord's favor" (Lk 4:19) was proclaimed and offered, but was not recognized or accepted. God left it to human beings to decide how salvation would take place.

All this was confirmed by the survey Jesus carried out among his disciples. It showed that Jesus' activity had reached a crucial and decisive moment. As a result of this free decision of human beings after his proclamation of the gospel, Jesus began to rethink his approach. He began to see the establishment of the reign of God as taking place in a different way. From now on the prophecy that speaks of the suffering and death of Yahweh's Suffering Servant (Is 53:1–13) was to be his signpost. This now was the Father's will clearly expressed in Holy Scripture that Jesus accepted, albeit with anguish and fear (Jn 12:27). Human rejection did not prevent God's plan from being carried out. On the contrary, it helped to ensure that it was carried out in a different way, one that revealed even more clearly God's goodness to human beings. There is no use asking: "What would God's reign have been like if people had accepted it right from the beginning?" We do not know. It is a possibility that was not realized.

Temptation in Jesus' Life

No one can deny that Jesus was tempted, since the Gospels mention it explicitly (Mt 4:1–11; Mk 1:12–13; Lk 4:1–13). The Letter to the Hebrews presents temptation or testing as a constant feature of Jesus' life (Heb 4:15). Jesus was tempted in the desert, where Satan tried to get him to follow a different path to accomplish his mission, one different from the one God had shown him. Jesus reacted firmly, with phrases taken from the Bible, and did not allow Satan to achieve his objectives. Satan is the person who diverts us from the path specified by God. Later, Peter was to be called Satan (Mk 8:33), because he wanted to dissuade Jesus from following the path of suffering. Peter thought that such a path was incompatible with the dignity of the Messiah.

In addition to these two occasions on which Satan appears, Luke refers to another when he says: "When the devil had finished every test, he departed from him until an opportune time" (Lk 4:13). What was this opportune time?

Jesus was constantly faced with the choice between taking the path the Father wanted or the path the people wanted. For example, after the multiplication of the loaves, the people wanted to make Jesus a king. They thought he really was "the prophet who is to come into the world" (Jn 6:14) and wanted to turn him into the sort of Messiah they wanted, an earthly political Messiah. It was a temptation for Jesus, but he resisted it by fleeing to the mountain (Jn 6:15).

During the first phase of his activity, Jesus tried to get the people to change their opinions about the Messiah and the reign of God and to accept him as he was, without conditions and without preconceptions. He failed. The people held on to their opinions, and Jesus respected them. Again and again, popular aspirations made Jesus leave one path for another. This is the temptation, the crisis, that marked Jesus' life. This is Satan interfering, trying to divert him from the path marked out by the Father. This is the constant human attempt to fit God into our human aspirations, without allowing God to challenge them. Jesus held firmly to his path, through constant prayer. He did not give way to the easy compromises of power and popular aspirations.

This is how events came to a head. Jesus faced his moment of truth. He realized that it was not possible to change the people's outlook, mainly because of the influence of their leaders, the Pharisees and scribes. They would never accept Jesus' views; that would destroy their social position. Given this, things were clear. Jesus also was not going to change. A conflict was becoming inevitable. The cross appeared on the horizon of his life. His violent death was no longer a mere possibility; it became a certainty.

Scanning the likely prospects in the light of the mission he had received from the Father and in the light of his love and respect for human beings, Jesus began to change the direction of his activity. The decision he was about to make in response to the people's negative reaction would determine his whole future. It was a life-or-death decision. He was obedient to the Father; he chose the path of fidelity that was to lead him to death. It was a firm decision: "He set his face to go to Jerusalem" (Lk 9:51), where he was to be killed. All this, however, did not take place without an inner struggle, without temptation, like those that the Gospels describe taking place on the Mount of Olives. Satan, we might say, constantly reappears in Jesus' life. The transfiguration occupies a central place in this change that took place in Jesus' life.

Crisis and Temptation
in the Lives of the Apostles

Jesus asked his question, "Who do people say that I am?" (Mk 8:27), and was given a reply based on a survey of popular opinion. None of the answers was right. He asked the apostles the same question and Peter replied: "You are the Messiah" (Mk 8:29). The apostles accepted him as he was, without conditions and without preconceptions. At least, so it seemed. They signed the blank check, ready for whatever was demanded. And immediately Jesus began to fill in the blank check, with a sum reflecting the inner decision he had now made.

Jesus began to say what he himself thought of his messianic mission. It was as if he had said: "That's right. I am the Messiah, but you must realize that the Messiah will have to suffer a great deal, will be rejected by the leaders of the people, will be handed over for execution, but will rise again" (Mk 8:31). For the apostles, this revelation was like lightning from a clear sky. They could not make it fit their ideas about the Messiah. Like the majority of the people, they believed in a glorious, majestic Messiah, a severe judge. And here was the man they believed to be the Messiah telling them that, because he was indeed the Messiah, he was going to be mocked, rejected, tortured, and condemned as though he were a criminal. They couldn't take it in. The crisis of faith in the apostles' lives had begun.

Peter, who a little earlier had expressed what they all felt when he said that Jesus was the Messiah, now did the same thing again. "God forbid, Lord!" he said. "This must never happen to you" (Mt 16:22; Mk 8:32). Jesus' reaction was extremely strange: "Get behind me, Satan! You are a stumbling block to me; for you are setting your mind not on divine things, but on human things" (Mt 16:23; Mk 8:33). The conflict had begun, but Jesus stuck firmly to his way of understanding his mission as Messiah and Savior. It would be hard to carry this mission through to the end, because he would face opposition even from his closest friends, quite apart from the opposition of people in general.

But Jesus did not waver. Not only did he say that he had to suffer, but added that they too, the apostles, had to suffer, deny themselves, carry their cross, and follow him (Mk 8:34; Mt 16:24–25). There was to be no doubt or uncertainty. Instead of damping down the conflict, Jesus fanned it to white heat. Anyone who wanted to accompany Jesus must know what they were doing and what to expect.

This was the general setting in which the transfiguration was to take place. Jesus was making the decision to face his mission as Messiah even though it meant winning the glory of God's reign through suffering and death. He had to endure temptation from the people, who wanted something else, and from the apostles, who didn't understand him. He also endured the natural revulsion that death provokes in any normal person. The apostles, in deep crisis, no longer knew what to do. The people wanted to seize Jesus and make him a king, an earthly, political Messiah, but did this because they knew no better and were a flock without a shepherd, deserving pity more than severe judgment (Mk 6:34). This was the real situation of Jesus and the apostles.

The Transfiguration —
In the Lives of Jesus and the Apostles

In the description of the transfiguration we find a reference to "dwellings," "shelters," or "tents," according to the translation: "If you wish I will make three dwellings" (Mt 17:4; Mk 9:5; Lk 9:33). The story is introduced with the time reference: "after six days" (Mt 17:1; Mk 9:2), which has no connection with the previous text. What is the meaning of these two details?

The Jews had a festival called the Feast of Tabernacles, or the Feast of Tents, which commemorated the forty days they had spent in the desert in tents. The festival lasted seven days. During these days the people were supposed to live in improvised tents. If it was not possible to do this for the whole seven days, they had to do so at least on the seventh day. It was a national day, a sort of Independence Day, full of references to the destiny of the nation. In Jesus' time it was also a day when expectation of the Messiah peaked. People expected the Messiah to come on such a day.

The atmosphere was thick with messianic and political hope. The people looked to Jesus, hoping and insisting that he define himself, proclaim himself as the Messiah. The temptation was stronger, keener, and more pressing on the last day of the festival. That is why "after six days," that is, on the seventh day, Jesus sought solitude, as on that other occasion when he fled to the mountain (Jn 6:15). He went up on the mountain to pray (Lk 9:28). Faced with the temptation from the people, Jesus drew strength from God through prayer. He took with him only three apostles, Peter, James, and John. It was there, cut off from everything, that Peter remembered the obligation to make tents, because it was the last day of the festival: "Lord, it is well that we are here. If you wish, I will make three dwellings" (Mt 17:4).

At this point two figures appear, Moses and Elijah, representing the Old Testament, and talk to Jesus about his death in Jerusalem (Lk 9:31). In other words, even the Old Testament, which for the apostles was the supreme expression of God's will, was in agreement with Jesus: he had to suffer because that was part of God's plan, which the prophets had already sketched out. At the same time, Jesus appeared completely glorified, different, transfigured. In this sequence of events the apostles found a means of overcoming their crisis of faith: they saw Jesus completely glorified, with the glory they had dreamed of for the Messiah.

At the same time, the Old Testament, in its two greatest representatives, Moses and Elijah, was saying that Jesus had to suffer. Therefore the passion that Jesus had been talking about, and against which they had rebelled, was indeed part of God's plan. The cross was the path to glory. There was no other path. They were wrong, and Jesus was right. They would have to change their ideas and rethink their position. They were confirmed in this decision by the voice from heaven: "This is my Son, the Beloved; listen to him" (Mk 9:7). This is the beginning of the gradual victory over the crisis of faith produced by the scandal of the cross.

According to Luke's Gospel, the transfiguration had many resemblances to the agony in the garden. In both cases Jesus prayed (Lk 9:28; 22:41). At the transfiguration two men appear talking to Jesus about his passion and death (Lk 9:31), whereas in the agony in the garden an angel appears to strengthen him to accept the passion and death (Lk 22:43). In both cases the apostles fall asleep (Lk 9:32; Lk 22:45). At the transfiguration, while Jesus is praying he appears glorified (Lk 9:29), while in the agony his appearance changes and drops of blood begin to run from his face (Lk 22:44). Thus, in order to lift a little the veil of mystery that surrounds the person of Christ and to understand what happened within him at the moment of the transfiguration, we can refer to the scene of the agony and say this is where we see the really human side of Jesus.

Like any human being, he felt fear and anguish at the thought of death, but he faced it with courage and prayer in order to be faithful to God. His mission had reached a critical moment. In order to escape the calls of the people, who wanted to divert him from his path, he went away from them to be alone with the Father. Praying and reflecting on the Old Testament, he dealt with the situation in the same way that he dealt with the devil in the desert, falling back on the words of Holy Scripture. Jesus' steadfast clinging to the Father received a response in his transfiguration, in the appearance of the two representatives of the Old Testament and the heavenly voice saying: "This is my Son, the Beloved; with him I am well pleased" (Mt 17:5).

When it is all over, Jesus forbids the three to tell the others what they have just seen (Mt 17:9; Mk 9:9; Lk 9:36). Everything has disappeared and there is only Jesus. The Gospels insist on this point: only Jesus! It is as though they wanted to say: from now on the only expression of God's will to human beings is Jesus Christ — Jesus Christ at the moment when he accepted death, in a complete giving of himself to his brothers and sisters. He, in this attitude, is the law that should rule our lives.

This decisive moment marks the beginning of the second phase of Jesus' life that we mentioned earlier.

The Transfiguration in the Gospels

Each evangelist describes the fact in his own way. When three people paint the same friend, each will paint the friend differently, since each of them will see something in the friend that the other two do not see. The difference appears in the little details.

In the same way, Matthew's Gospel (Mt 17:1–8) says that Jesus' face became like the sun. It mentions a bright cloud and says that the disciples' fear came when they heard the heavenly voice. The other two, Mark and Luke, do not have these details and, although they talk about the apostles' fear, they put it in a different context. Emphasizing these little details, Matthew, who was writing for Jewish converts, makes the reader think of Moses, whose face shone like the sun when he came down from the mountain with the ten tablets of the old law in his hand (Ex 34:29–35) and recalls the bright cloud that came down over Mount Sinai when God made known his law through Moses. In this way, Matthew is suggesting that the old law was given through Moses, but the new law is given through Jesus Christ. Jesus himself is the new law: God said: "Listen to him" (Mt 17:5). And just as the people in the Old Testament became afraid when Moses came with the law, so too fear comes at the moment when the new law is given.

Mark's Gospel (Mk 9:2–8) has few features peculiar to itself in the description of the transfiguration. It simply narrates what was said about the event without trying to put across any particular idea of its own. The only picturesque detail, found only in Mark, is the stress on the whiteness of Jesus' clothes when he was transfigured: "dazzling white, such as no one on earth could bleach them" (Mk 9:3).

Luke's Gospel (Lk 9:28–36), as we have already seen, emphasizes the resemblance between the transfiguration and Jesus' agony in the garden.

But before being written down by the three evangelists, this story was transmitted orally by the first Christians. Why did they pass on this fact? All the signs are that there were several reasons:

1. The scandal of the cross was an enormous stumbling block for the evangelization of the Jews (1 Cor 1:23). How could they be persuaded to believe that a man found guilty by two courts and killed scandalously on a cross could be the Messiah? Only if it could be proved that the suffering and the cross formed part of God's plan as described in the Old Testament. The transfiguration addressed this problem and showed the Old Testament as indicating that the cross was the Messiah's path to glory.

2. Christians found in this event a confirmation of their faith in Jesus as Son of God, because God did say: "This is my Son."

3. The story confirmed Jesus Christ's authority as the law and rule for Christians: "Listen to him!"

This is the story of the transfiguration. A careful study of this very familiar episode in Jesus' life has revealed unknown aspects of that well-known life. It has shown us how real is the truth we profess: in Christ, God became incarnate and became a human being like us. This may lead us to look more attentively at "Jesus, the pioneer and perfecter of our faith, who for the joy that was set before him, endured the cross" (Heb 12:2).

16

THE LETTERS OF PAUL
Living the Same Faith in Jesus Christ

Paul did not get on very well with the Jerusalem community. It wasn't his fault. Some Christians there didn't trust him. Apart from still having painful memories of the persecution he had instigated (Acts 9:13, 26), they thought that Paul was too progressive. There was a rumor that he was abolishing traditions and encouraging the Jews of the whole world to abandon their observance of the law of Moses (Acts 18:13; 21:28). He was supposed to have said that circumcision no longer had value (Acts 21:21). This might have elicited reactions like those of some Catholic faithful after Vatican II, when they were told that some practices — such as fasting from midnight before receiving the Eucharist, or abstaining from meat on Fridays, or fulfilling Sabbath obligations on Sunday — were no longer essential elements of Catholic practice.

Paul felt very deeply this lack of confidence on the part of his brothers and sisters in the faith. It was so unjust when he had given his all for love of the Christ in whom they also believed (Gal 2:20; 2 Cor 10:1; 11:22–23; Phil 3:5–8). Apart from being untrue, the accusation against him was a symptom of a hidden problem. It brought to light a very deep difference between Paul and his colleagues in Jerusalem. They had diametrically opposed views on the gospel and the function and place of Jesus Christ in human life.

Paul thought that it was perfectly acceptable that, within the unity of faith, there should be a degree of pluralism in the ways this faith in Jesus Christ was lived out. Converts from Judaism lived this faith, in sincerity and total dedication, while observing the Mosaic regulations (Acts 21:20; 10:14, 28; 11:3). Paul himself, when he thought it opportune, kept the law (1 Cor 9:20). This didn't make him guilty of opportunism, because he was not seeking his own interest.

But he could not stand the arrogance of some of his Jerusalem colleagues who were trying to set up the Jewish way of living the gospel as the only valid and authentic one and to impose it on all as the obligatory path to be followed by anyone wishing to share in the salvation won by Christ (Acts 15:1, 5, 24). Paul thought that pagans who converted to Christianity ought to be able to live the same faith in their own way, differently from Jews, but with the same utter sincerity and commitment. It was this point that exposed the difference. The others did not have Paul's openness of mind and challenged his initiative. They may have acted in good faith, motivated by badly formed consciences. Paul, however, did have doubts about their sincerity (Gal 2:4–5; 4:17; 6:12; Phil 3:2). Whatever their motives, they worked actively and in an organized way to achieve their aim.

Doubts and Internal Struggles Produced by the Conflict

All this produced huge confusion within the church (Acts 15:2). No one was sure. Who was right? Paul or the Jerusalem group hiding behind the name of the apostle James (Gal 2:12)? Even Peter, the leader of the church, was perplexed and uncertain, unable to see immediately the best course to take in what was above all a practical problem, and he allowed himself to be influenced by the Jerusalem group (Gal 2:11–14).

The church was at a crossroads and no one knew the right course to take. This hadn't been foreseen. Christ had left nothing in writing, and earlier rules were inadequate to solve this totally new problem, which called for creativity. It was difficult to choose: if the more moderate line were adopted, there would be no danger of persecution (Gal 6:12; 5:11), but there would also be no pagans coming into the church if they had to submit to the rite of circumcision, and the church would be reduced to a Jewish sect and would be eroded by time. If Paul's line were followed, the Jewish and Roman worlds would make the church a target (Acts 13:45; 13:50; 14:2, 5; 16:20), but the faith would be open to everyone without distinction. What was to be done? Should the church run the risk of attracting general hostility and jeopardize the survival of the faith through trying to go too fast, or should it take things more slowly, with the risk that the faith would die out through obsolescence?

Paul took the first view and fought for it. He suffered a great deal for this conviction. His adversaries did everything to reduce Paul's influence. They tried to challenge his authority, claiming that the gospel he preached was a private doctrine of his own and not that of the apostles Peter and James (Gal 2:6–9; 1:19–23). If his authority were destroyed, the whole basis of his work would be undermined. Paul had to defend himself and show that there was no difference between himself and those two great apostles (Gal 2:1–10). He did everything he could to destroy the impression that he was an iconoclast, out to destroy law and tradition (2 Cor 11:21–23; 12:11; Acts 25:8; 24:14–15; 1 Cor 9:20; Rom 3:31; 10:4). It is possible that the reaction of the others to Paul was motivated merely by fear of persecution. It is difficult to judge at this distance. Paul, at least, took that view: "Only that they may not be persecuted for the cross of Christ" (Gal 6:12). He called them "false believers" (Gal 2:4; 2 Cor 11:26, 12–13).

Paul's Conviction
Translated into Practical Attitudes

Paul cared little whether a person was circumcised or not, a Christian from a Jewish background or a pagan background (Gal 6:15; 5:6; 1 Cor 9:20). He did not forbid anyone to keep the law of Moses. But he also could not tolerate the claims of others that this law was necessary for a person to be a Christian. The salvation Christ brought was open to all and so, according to Paul, all that was needed was faith in Jesus Christ, understood as total commitment to him (Gal 3:22; 2:15–19, 21). In Christ's sight everyone is equal. Everything else, observances, regulations, and that vast number of rules, fell into the secondary category of instruments and means.

That is why, when it suited him — that is, to become a Jew to the Jews — Paul kept the law of Moses (1 Cor 9:20). He even made a point of circumcising Timothy, to smooth relations with the Jews (Acts 16:3), but he firmly refused to do the same with Titus, when the others tried to make it an issue of principle (Gal 2:3–5; 5:2).

The same applied to the Jewish observances about food and drink. Paul thought that in this whole area what was important was conscience (Rom 14:1–5). People should do as they wished, but everyone should always follow conscience and do everything for the Lord (Rom 14:6–9), since, in the end, "the kingdom of God is not food and drink" (Rom 14:17). People had to be really free (Gal 5:1). However, when the others tried to turn these secondary matters into questions of principle, Paul reacted strongly, even challenging Peter himself (Gal 2:11–14), and denounced their claims as contrary to God's will, matters of appearance (Col 2:23). Above all, they were no more than human rules (Col 2:22).

Paul detested uniformity of practice imposed in the name of faith. He did not like people who, because they understood nothing of the central issue, set themselves up as defenders of secondary principles and tried to use these to measure other people's orthodoxy. Just as he said, "The reign of God is not food and drink," we might say today: "The reign of God is not a matter of communion in the hand or in the mouth, married or celibate priests, colors of vestments, white or brown robes, confession once a month or once a year, a liturgy with one reading or three, whether the eucharistic fast should be fifty minutes or sixty, whether the response to 'The Lord be with you' should be 'And also with you,' or 'He is in our midst,' or a whole host of other questions that obscure the main point." The reign of God is "righteousness and peace and joy in the Holy Spirit" (Rom 14:17). What is really important is "faith working through love" (Gal 5:6). Everything else is good, valid, and useful as long as it can lead to and express this. If not, it is worthless; it certainly "does not come from the one who calls you" (Gal 5:8).

On another occasion Paul adopted a course of action that must have cost him dearly. On his return to Jerusalem after his third missionary journey to the pagan world, he agreed to take a group of men to the Temple to fulfill a promise made according to the law of Moses. It was a tactical move suggested by some of his allies in Jerusalem to give the others the impression that Paul was not against the law (Acts 21:20–24).

But on another occasion, when the issue was merely eating habits, Paul challenged Peter publicly (Gal 2:11–14). For the sake of Jewish traditions and conventions, Peter had allowed himself to be coopted by the Jerusalem group and had given up associating with Christian converts from paganism, taking meals only with converts from Judaism. This made the pagans feel that they were being reduced to a lower category of Christians and obliged by this situation to observe the same conventions. Paul reacted very strongly to this situation: "If you, though a Jew, live like a Gentile and not like a Jew, how can you compel the Gentiles to live like Jews?" Paul said this "before them all" (Gal 2:14).

We see that even if great issues are at stake, the battle is always decided, then as now, on very ordinary things, irritating, trivial matters, but it is here that the battle is won or lost. We cover a mile an inch at a time.

Freedom in Christ

The most important thing of all to Paul was his freedom. He was free from the law (Gal 3:13), free from every compulsion in order to be able to follow in every dimension this new consciousness born of commitment to Christ (Gal 5:1; 2:4). The compulsion now did not come from outside, but grew from within. Nothing would make Paul surrender that freedom (Phil 3:7–9), and he would not let anyone prevent the pagans from living that same freedom (Gal 2:4–5).

Not even Peter, the highest leader of the church, had the authority to do that (Gal 2:14). Not even the "big chiefs" or "super-apostles" in Jerusalem (2 Cor 11:5; 12:11). Paul stood up to them bravely because, as he wrote, "I am not at all inferior to these super-apostles" (2 Cor 12:11) because "I think that I too have the Spirit of God" (1 Cor 7:40).

It was in the light of this outlook that Paul made his decisions, but not without previously consulting the other apostles (Gal 2:1–2), though they never had any criticism to make of him, at least on fundamentals. Perhaps in practice they could not understand Paul's methods at all. In fact there were many people who couldn't follow Paul in his openness, because they had not gone through the same struggle and the same experience. He was able to respect the consciences of others.

Because he was really free, he made himself the slave of all (1 Cor 9:19). He saw in everyone, however weak or closed, a "believer for whom Christ died" (1 Cor 8:11). And if, perchance, his free approach risked leading anyone astray, he was prepared never to eat meat again, if in that way he could help that brother or sister (1 Cor 8:13). He practiced what he wrote to the Galatians: "You were called to freedom, brothers and sisters; only do not use your freedom as an opportunity for self-indulgence, but through love become slaves to one another" (Gal 5:13). Love made him respect other people's consciences. He merely asked that they should not make his work more difficult by imposing restrictions that had nothing to do with faith in Christ, and that they should not hide under the cloak of faith and good order their own lack of courage to face the outside world and persecution (Gal 6:12).

Another point we should note is that all this, for Paul, did not remain as words or on paper. He had the courage to teach others in practice and to accept the consequences. He had the courage to tell the Galatians, a simple and poorly educated community: "Live by the Spirit...and do not gratify the desires of the flesh" (Gal 5:16). The "desires of the flesh" were worries about material observances connected with food and drink, about festivals and rules, and above all about circumcision in the flesh.

Nor did he stop there. After giving clear instructions to others, he himself did not waver when difficulties arose with other authorities. Paul's commitment to Christ meant in practice commitment to others. He did not make theological distinctions in order not to get involved in quarrels. He did not make much distinction between theory and practice. He treated faith as a supremely practical attitude and argued from his own real-life commitment: "From now on, let no one make trouble for me; for I carry the marks of Jesus branded on my body" (Gal 6:17). He was referring to the suffering and torture he had endured for the sake of others.

The Solution to the Problem: Accept Pluralism

As time passed, confusion increased in the church. It became more and more difficult for Christian converts from paganism and Christian converts from Judaism to live together (Acts 15:1–5). It was an urgent task to solve this problem and reach a clearer view of the gospel. A meeting was called in Jerusalem, which went down in history as the first ecumenical council (Acts 15:6). The discussion was long (Acts 15:7), but at the end Peter spoke and settled the issue: what really saves and frees us, he declared, is faith in Jesus Christ (Acts 15:11). He said this, not to please Paul, but because he himself had seen and understood, through his own experience and signs from God, that this was the right course (Acts 15:7–9; 10:44–48). Now everyone understood. There was no ban on observance of the law of Moses; all that was banned was the imposition of this observance on converts from paganism (Acts 15:10).

James supported Peter's decision (Acts 15:13–19), and both distanced themselves once and for all from those who spread the contrary view (Acts 15:24). They took care to make this point very clear in the final communiqué:

> Since we have heard that certain persons who have gone out from us, though with no instructions from us, have said things

to disturb you and have unsettled your minds, we have decided unanimously to choose representatives and send them to you, along with our beloved Barnabas and Paul, who have risked their lives for the sake of our Lord Jesus Christ. (Acts 15:24–26)

Once there was acceptance in principle of plurality in the living faith in Jesus Christ, there was an attempt to translate it into practice and give it a degree of structure. Principle is one thing, practice another. In the application of the general rule, the apostles followed common sense. It was, for example, impossible to insist that a convinced Jew like Peter or James should live like Christian converts from paganism. And this was not necessary. Nor could Paul be forced to adapt to the rules of Jewish life.

For this reason Paul and Barnabas were given responsibility for the communities established in the pagan world. Peter and James would look after the communities in the Jewish world (Gal 2:7–9). All, however, had the right to live their faith in Christ in the sacred freedom of their consciences, but for the sake of community harmony the converts from paganism were required to keep four rules suggested by James (Acts 15:20; 21:25).

So peace returned, at least as a real possibility, a peace based on respect and acceptances of mutual differences. The Christians had been able to discover and accept the will of God in all that confusion. And, strange as it seemed, this realistic acceptance of the mutual differences laid the foundation for a much more intimate and real communion than the one that the others had tried to achieve by imposing on all the same model of living faith in Jesus Christ.

In the council, the conservative Jerusalem Christians, abandoning their demands, as it were, cut the umbilical cord and allowed Christ really to be born for the whole world. By that magnanimity, which cannot have been easy, they won the grateful recognition of the Christians who had come from paganism. This gratitude later produced a beautiful gesture of unity, the great collection in the churches of the pagan world for the poor of the Jerusalem community.

Pluralism Produces the Impulse to Unity

The Jerusalem Christians, by their painful concession, freed the Christian message to circulate in the pagan world. And it was in the pagan world, probably in Corinth (2 Cor 8:10), that the initiative started to return the favor (Rom 15:27). There a solidarity campaign was organized that won the sympathy and active support of all the communities of Galatia, in Asia Minor (1 Cor 16:1), Macedonia in northern Greece (2 Cor 8:1), and Achaea in southern Greece (2 Cor 9:2). There was even a degree of competition between them to see who could give the most money (2 Cor 9:2). And they were generous, despite their poverty (2 Cor 8:2–3), because we hear of "a generous gift" (2 Cor 8:20). This was a general mobilization of the pagan churches in support of their needy brothers and sisters in Jerusalem. Paul put everything into this work. He became an expert fund-raiser, persuading others to give generously (2 Cor 8–9).

This solidarity campaign should not be confused with any ordinary collection. It is an eloquent sign that the Holy Spirit is never defeated by new events. The Spirit is never trapped by human ideas. The Spirit creates and is able to produce new things when human beings run out of ideas and lose heart in the face of the harshness of life.

And of course, once the difference between pagans and Christians was made official, once the facts were accepted and reality admitted at this first council, with the ink still dry on the new agreement, a new problem immediately appeared — as always happens. How was unity to be maintained in these conditions? Still worse, the Jerusalem Christians, recognizing and accepting the voice of God in events, had to watch the slow shift of the church's center of gravity to the pagan world. They knew that they would be a small minority, but what would be their place and their future in the church?

They all followed the same Christ, professed the same faith, the same God, the same baptism, the same Holy Spirit (Eph 4:4–6), but life took different forms. From the same trunk sprouted quite different branches, which grew increasingly different from each other with time. And yet, in these branches, for all their variety and difference, there ran the same sap that produced in all of them the same leaves and the same fruits, the fruits of charity, given practical shape in the wide-ranging solidarity campaign. This was, by all accounts a spontaneous initiative, not something imposed (2 Cor 8:3, 10), that united the pagan communities more than before and gave the Jerusalem community a much greater sense of belonging to the church, a much greater sense than before. The campaign was even part of the official recognition of the pluralism that existed in the church (Gal 2:10). It was a way of translating the council's decisions into practice.

The campaign was not so much to give an impression of unity to others; the world wasn't looking on to applaud these Christian initiatives. It wasn't to build a front to hide deep divisions. On the contrary, it grew out of a realistic acceptance of differences, out of pluralism itself. It was the grateful response of the Christian converts from paganism to the generosity of their coreligionists in Jerusalem, who had given them the freedom to live their faith according to their own inspiration and situation (Rom 15:26–27). The disunion was overcome, because they had been able to discover the sense of unity at the deepest and most solid level of pluralism, where love can prove its creativity. Such a campaign would have been impossible before the Jerusalem council, when they were still quarrelling over ideas, with one group trying to impose its opinion on the others. Then, the campaign would have been one more instrument to enable one group to dominate the other.

Now that diversity was accepted it formed the soil in which unity could thrive and every flower could unfold in its own space, with its own nutrients, and show its own qualities and colors, displayed in the window of the church to delight the whole community. The campaign showed the extent of each Christian's commitment to Christ and to fellow Christians. It was a barometer of their faith, hope, and charity, not cheap charity to appease their consciences.

Conclusion

Not all the converted Jews were capable of seeing things in this way. Some did not understand the huge opening that had taken place in the council and continued afterward to make life as difficult as possible for Paul. But a person who has won a war doesn't worry about minor skirmishes. These arguments, painful as they were, were unable to quench Paul's deep sense of gratitude. He was able to distinguish between what was the initiative of a few, however dangerous and disagreeable, and an initiative of the church.

All this is now far in the past, dead and buried. But today there is a similar situation of conflict in the church, and all the signs are that it is also a symptom of a deep difference about the meaning of the gospel for today. Could it be that, then as now, we are preventing Christ from being born for the world by keeping him imprisoned in thought patterns that have little to do with faith? Perhaps it's time for us to show generosity, like the Jerusalem Christians. Perhaps we should be realistic and accept pluralism in the way we live the faith, the same faith, in Jesus Christ. Or are we afraid of facing reality and persecution?

17

FAITH IN THE RESURRECTION

"If God is for us, who is against us?"

We have talked a lot about the resurrection, right from the very first page. This created an expectation: what can this faith in the resurrection be? Many things can be said in many ways about the resurrection. I am not going to say everything. I can't. I shall say merely enough to answer the question I have raised: "What can faith in the resurrection mean for us today?"

Trying to Understand the Resurrection

Today there is a lot of argument about the resurrection. It provokes a whole series of questions: What will God do on resurrection day? Will we have the same bodies? The same size? Will ugly people stay ugly? What about the children who have died? Will they stay children forever? And if we are all adults, won't it be a boring life without the beauty of children? And people who died in explosions, when nothing at all was left of their bodies? How will God deal with them?

So questions keep coming up, creating useless arguments that can't be settled. One question produces another. They are like a child dashing from flower to flower, gradually getting further and further from the house. When she finally stops, she is lost and doesn't know which way she came from or which way to go. The child starts to cry. These questions about the resurrection are a bit like the child's crying. They are a sign that we're lost, far from home, far from the real meaning of the truth. We are lost, not on the difficult paths of faith, but in the spider's web of our own thoughts, which have completely emptied the resurrection of meaning. We no longer know what to make of it in our lives.

Many people have enough common sense to say that these problems cannot be of God's making and simply complicate a life that is difficult enough already.

Others don't believe in the resurrection because they can't find sufficient evidence to convince them. They say that it's impossible for anyone to prove that Christ's resurrection is a fact by historical investigation because of the many problems involved.

Other people begin to study the resurrection wanting to know exactly what happened on that Easter Sunday, what Christ's glorified body was like, how the disciples experienced the appearances, and how to explain the contradictions about these matters in the Gospels.

Others again study the resurrection to try to defend it against the difficulties brought against it. In this way they want to make this truth a little more acceptable to people today.

Studying the Resurrection: Where to Begin?

I think that, for any Christian who claims to believe, we cannot start an account of the resurrection by trying to prove the fact of Jesus' resurrection with scientific arguments and trying to disprove the arguments against it. Faith in the resurrection is something that has such a deep effect on life and has such profound repercussions on all that we do that it cannot be dependent on a few shaky arguments that not everyone accepts. It must have a more solid basis.

Moreover, if we adopt this attitude we have already taken up a position of superiority to the resurrection, at least psychologically, since the resurrection will depend on arguments we offer. When the resurrection depends on my arguments, for a few moments I control this truth. It exists, and goes on existing, thanks to my arguments. I am not easily going to let this resurrection, which was under my control and depended on me, become superior to me, with its radical demands for life. Besides, the Bible doesn't base its case on a defense of the resurrection.

To begin the study of the resurrection with an analysis of what happened on the first Easter Sunday, in my view, is to go in a door that doesn't lead to the center of the house. If we take this approach, we start out by reducing the resurrection to an isolated fact in the past, from a bygone age. We distance ourselves from the resurrection. We will then find it hard to go on to see what it could mean for our lives. This wasn't the approach of the first Christians. Paul's letters, which are earlier than the Gospels, mention the resurrection on almost every page, but there is hardly any mention, indeed only one (1 Cor 15:1–4), of the historical form in which the appearances and the events of Easter Sunday took place.

To the questions we ask today about the resurrection, Paul's answer would be: "Stupid! Have you ever seen a tree or a plant that looks like its seed? Have you ever seen anyone sowing plants or trees? They sow the seed from which the plant or tree will grow. In the same way, you, living today, you with your life, are like a seed from which, when you die, a new life will grow. That new life will be different, spiritual, created by God's power. Look after the seed, and let God do the rest" (free summary of 1 Cor 15:35–50).

So we are left with the question: "What did faith in the resurrection mean for Paul?"

The Difference between Us and the First Christians

There is a very big difference between our attitude to the resurrection today and the way the first Christians lived this same truth in their lives.

For most of those who believe in the resurrection today, their faith has something to do with the past and with the future. It has to do with the past: as we say in the Creed, "We believe that Jesus Christ was crucified, died, and was buried. He descended into the realm of the dead, and rose on the third day." Through faith in the resurrection, we accept that almost two thousand years ago a tomb was found empty and Jesus rose and appeared a number of times to the apostles. It has to do with the future: in the Creed we say, "We believe in the resurrection of the body." Through faith in the resurrection, we believe that one day, we don't know when, all the dead will rise.

Faith in the resurrection holds these two poles very firm, one in the past and the other in the future. What about the present? Is there a wire that connects one pole to the other and, as it passes through the present, lights up the lamp of life, lets us see the road surface and starts the engine of existence? What use do people who are alive today make of their faith in the resurrection in their lives? Is there any resurrection in their lives?

For most of us Christians today, to all intents and purposes the resurrection has little to do with our lives here and now. It is one of those difficult mysteries of the faith, hidden in the wake of the past and the future, that we're not very sure what to do with in everyday life.

The way the New Testament talks about this same truth is very different. The perspective is different.

If I am to talk about life, I must have life: I must be alive. If Martians existed, they could study our life on this planet, but it would be purely theoretical knowledge, from outside. A simple, uneducated laborer from a remote rural area could speak with much more authority about life on Planet Earth than a Martian, no matter how intelligent. A blind person who has never seen light can imagine what light is like, do accurate and complex calculations, but a child whose eyes can see the light knows more than the blind person, even if the child cannot put into words all his experiences and feelings about light.

It's the same with the New Testament when it speaks of the resurrection. Faith in the resurrection was the necessary condition for talking about the life that sprang from the resurrection. The first Christians did not regard themselves as superior to the resurrection and able to prove it, nor did they take their distance from it in order to appreciate it. Nor were they interested, at least at the beginning, in knowing what exactly happened on the first Easter Sunday, and they didn't start their study of the resurrection by trying to defend it. If we are alive we don't have to prove we were born, nor do we have to argue for the existence of our parents. The resurrection didn't need defending. It was the light that enabled them to see and understand life.

Faith in the resurrection was the environment within which they lived and out of which they spoke. It was like the air they breathed. Both those who talked about the resurrection and those who listened to them lived within this new environment. Faith in the resurrection was the root of everything, just as the life we have is the root of everything we do in life. A branch cannot detach itself from the tree to get a good look at the tree. That would kill it. Nor does it need to prove to others that it is attached to the trunk of the tree. All it needs to do is produce leaves. These are the proof that it is attached to the trunk and the root. When the sun is high in the sky, no one worries about proving the existence of the sun. What we are anxious about is using its light and heat to improve our health. It is this second sort of concern that gave rise to the New Testament.

These are two very different ways of approaching and living the same truth of faith. Today we situate the object of faith in the resurrection in the past and in the future. The first Christians situated it in the present. The way the New Testament talks about the resurrection contains many elements that can help us to rethink our way of seeing and living the resurrection.

The emergence of faith in the resurrection is something so new and different that it doesn't fit our criteria. Accordingly, before studying this truth and criticizing and examining it with our questions, even before trying to defend it with our arguments, it is a good idea to let the New Testament speak for itself and listen to what it understood by faith in the resurrection and how it lived it in life. Otherwise we may find ourselves creating difficulties where none exist, or defending things that don't need defending, because they have nothing to do with faith in the resurrection.

The Starting Point for Faith in the Resurrection

In order to appreciate the full scale and novelty of something that appears in our lives, we first need to analyze the previous situation. It is in the comparison of the two, the comparison between the before and the after, that we see the value of the new thing that has appeared. That is why we shall first analyze the soil in which the seed of faith in the resurrection was planted and grew, to see if this soil still exists in our world today.

The two disciples of Jesus, Cleopas and his friend, who were making their way along the road toward Emmaus (Lk 24:13ff), epitomize what had happened in the disciples' lives after Jesus died. They also epitomize what was happening in the lives of Christians making their way along the road of life at the time Luke wrote this section of his Gospel: they were persecuted people, no longer able to inject into their lives the faith in the resurrection, because death had killed their hope, and they could no longer find the living Christ in whom they had believed. They epitomize what is happening in the lives of many people today.

"We had hoped that he was the one to redeem Israel...and it is now the third day..." (Lk 24:21). This was the two disciples' bitter complaint. With Jesus' death, something had died in their lives, something of fundamental importance. Life no longer had any meaning for them. Before, their lives had grown so united to Jesus that they could no longer imagine life without him (Jn 6:68–69). They were ready to die with him (Jn 11:16), to suffer for him (Mk 10:38–39), to die for him (Mk 14:31), because without him everything would lose its meaning. For love of him, they had abandoned everything they owned (Mk 10:28). Jesus had become the axle on which the wheels of the apostles' lives turned.

Jesus' death broke this axle. It fell, tragically, like an insurmountable barrier between the present and the ideal of the future they had cherished. It was better to leave Jerusalem (Lk 24:13), for each of them to return to the old familiar routine (Jn 21:3). Too bad. It had been an illusion, utopianism, alienation, to believe in Jesus and the message he preached. Now it was all over: it was now the third day. His death had brought them back to hard reality with a jolt.

On the other hand, once the veil had been lifted on the future and they had had the chance, during the three years they had spent with Jesus, to see the huge possibilities implicit in human life, the desire remained. After this future had been closed off by Jesus' death, the world seemed darker than before. No other future any longer attracted them. Death had destroyed all aspirations and killed any initiative for the future.

And this death was not just the cross. It was a situation concentrated in the cross that led to the cross for anyone who wanted to follow Christ's path. The forces of death were stronger than ever: Roman imperialism, which had sealed the death sentence with a word, the soldiers who had carried out Governor Pilate's sentence, in the absence of any power that could prevent them; the scribes, who had been delighted by the execution; the Pharisees and the Pharisaism that had brought it about by manipulating public opinion; the shifting attitudes of the people and so many other factors. All this built up and combined in a single force against Jesus (Acts 4:24–28) and succeeded in conquering him. By killing Christ, they had killed the future in the apostles' hearts. Death was personified in that situation as a terrifying force threatening any initiative the disciples might take to continue doing what Jesus had done. Everything was over. The shadows of death had taken up residence in life, making hope impossible and threatening everything and everyone with oppression.

The apostles panicked in the face of this force, and fled (Mk 14:50–52). They even barred the doors of their house (Jn 20:19). There was nothing more to be expected of these terrified men. They had been defeated by the crushing weight of life.

Jesus' death killed something in the apostles, just as the death of a husband or wife kills something in the surviving spouse, or a friend's death kills something in us who are left. The apostles were more dead than Christ himself. The spring had dried up and the water had stopped flowing. The generator had been destroyed and the light had gone out.

This was also the situation of Christians making their way along the road of life around the year 75, the time when Luke was writing his Gospel. For some time they had believed in Jesus Christ. He was said to be alive, in the midst of the community. He was said to have conquered death, and those who believed in him were supposed to share in this power that conquered death. But where was he? Where was this victory? The Roman empire continued to persecute those who believed in Christ. It would not allow Christians to open a new road into the future, one that gave a new meaning to human life. Christians were dying like common criminals in prisons and in the arena. Where was Christ? "We had hoped that he was the one to set Israel free, but now. . . ." An impassable barrier had come down between the present and the future. Death, personified in the structures of the Roman empire, was killing hope in Christians' hearts. What use was there in continuing to believe?

Today as well, many people make their way like this along the road of life: people without much hope, defeated by the crushing weight of life, which kills hope and destroys the future. Forces against which individuals feel powerless, which they cannot control, and which vastly overwhelm them keep life imprisoned, unable to grow. They seem to be trying to reduce the whole human race to complete slavery. What individual human being can do anything against economic power, against the power of advertising and public opinion, against the power of ideology and the totalitarian state, against the power of the shifting attitudes of the masses, against the power of fashion and social custom, against the power of irony and sarcasm, against the power of the organization, which gives privileges to some and excludes others, even against the power of economic theories, which sometimes seem contradictory?

Everything is made for human beings. "The human person is the measure of all things," as the old saying had it. But hope dies in human hearts, so great are the barriers and the limits we come up against in life, whether personal or in the family, whether social or international. Awareness increases, but so, at the same time, does lethargy. Our numbers increase, but so do emptiness, despair, and isolation. As the power of the waters increases, so does the power of the dam that tries to hold them back. These today are some of the outposts of death, which spreads its arms over life, covering everything with the veil of mourning and threatening everything with oppression.

We lack the resources to deal with all this. Death, this death personified in a situation, is too strong for us. On the horizon the last lamp still alight goes out. We all take our own precautions so as not to be carried away by the void and by total frustration. We all look for a place in the sun. Many people have stopped believing in anything or anyone. They regard as ridiculous and childish the timid initiatives taken to break the iron band that is choking life to death. They adapt and become satisfied slaves, happy and peaceful, locked in a golden cage, but unaware of their situation. The old struggle for survival has returned today, at a higher and more civilized level. Survive at all costs. . . . Is it still worth believing in anything?

In the midst of all this, we Christians make our way with our faith in the resurrection, attached to one fact in the past and another in the future. How can we use our faith to spark hope in human hearts?

Our own situation is not so different from that of the apostles after Christ's death. As in Luke's day, we go on our way with our faith under our arms, not quite sure what to do with it. We can't find the space to implant it in life, and so the precious plant finally dies in its turn without bearing fruit. The problem is that we are still not aware of the constraints and the oppression within which we live.

Some people solve the problem like this. The resurrection, they say, has to do only with the situation that will obtain after death.

They try to work in this world in such a way as to secure resurrection in heaven, after death. They regard the world as just a workshop in which the vehicle that is life is repaired, so that it can get into heaven. A workshop is not a place where people live; that's not what it's for. It doesn't occur to them that their faith can have some relevance to the life we live here and now.

The New Dimension Created by Faith in the Resurrection

But — and this is what is absolutely new about the resurrection — on the third day after Jesus' death the women who went to the tomb and the eleven men had the clear and incontrovertible experience that Jesus was alive (Lk 24:5, 34). It was Jesus himself, the same Jesus whose life they had shared for three years (Acts 10:40–41). The appearances confirmed it (Mk 16:9–14; 1 Cor 15:1–4). It was Jesus. He had crossed a barrier that no human being had ever before crossed. This Christ, victorious over death, was now with them, their friend. It was plain to see, although they had had some difficulty in believing immediately in this new and unexpected event (Lk 24:10–11, 37–43; Jn 20:25).

Now there was no longer any reason to feel defeated by events. They too had risen. The veil hiding the future had opened again and now would never close. A new power had come into their lives, the power of God, a power so strong that it was able to bring life out of death (Eph 1:19–20). This power was linked to the living person of Jesus Christ, invisible in itself, but visible in its effects. It was a power stronger than all that previously had killed the hope within them. All the barriers that had stifled life and killed hope were now overthrown: the power of Roman imperialism, of Pharisaism, of public opinion, of the wavering view of the masses.

The powers of death were defeated. The war was won, even though fighting was continuing. It was just a matter of time.

Nothing could frighten them any longer: they were able to face the people, the Jews, the Sanhedrin, the Romans, the Pharisees, torture, and imprisonment (Acts 2:14; 4:8, 19, 23–31; 5:29, 41). The life that had been born in them had already passed through death; it was already a new and victorious life (Eph 2:6). Even though they might have to yield to the onslaught of death, life would no longer die (1 Cor 15:54–58). Now it made sense to resist, not to accept the situation, but to act to transform it.

Even so, Christians, making their way along the road of life, persecuted by the Roman empire, asked the question: "Where can we find this living Christ? Where can we find this power he communicates?" Luke answered by telling the story of the two men traveling along the road toward Emmaus. They discovered Christ, and recognized him "in the breaking of the bread" (Lk 24:35). It is when Christians come together around the Eucharist, when the bread is broken and distributed, where they celebrate and make present the death and resurrection of the Lord (1 Cor 11:26), that there is, or ought to be, the source from which flows that new water that can irrigate the tree of life and enable it to produce fruit. It is this community around the table that opens eyes (Lk 24:31) and allows Christ's voice to be heard, whether in the words of the Bible (Lk 24:32) or in the anonymous companion who accompanies us on the road of life (Lk 24:15–16, 35).

Luke identifies these three channels of communication with Christ and his power: the man or woman alongside us, the Word of God, and the coming together of friends around the same faith and the same ideal in the Eucharist. This makes us realize how far current liturgical renewal still has to go before it achieves its goal. Through these three instruments, Christians will find ways to overcome the crisis and rediscover in their lives the meaning of faith in the resurrection, their faith in Christ in their midst. To believe in the resurrection is not just to accept a fact from the past and another in the future, but is, first and foremost, an attitude to life arising out of the discovery of a friend, alive in our lives, thanks to the power of God.

The Resurrection —
Yesterday, Today, Tomorrow

The resurrection of Jesus Christ is not a fact that started a motor about two thousand years ago that is still running. The resurrection is not something that happened and is now over. Jesus, as at every moment, hears the voice of God calling him to life (Jn 5:19–21; 6:57). God raises him and gives him new life in a permanent act. It's like electricity: it's there as long as the generator keeps turning. As soon as the generator stops, the light goes out in our homes. To take an absurd and impossible example, as soon as God stopped calling Jesus to life, Christ, the light of the world (Jn 9:5), would go out, and the church, the people of God, the sacraments, faith, all this would cease to exist.

The act of God that raises Jesus is comparable to the act of creation: on the day God stopped uttering the divine creative word, we would fall into nothingness, whether or not we realized it. As soon as God stopped uttering the divine saving word, which culminates in the resurrection, our faith would be in vain, empty of all meaning (1 Cor 15:14–15, 17–19).

The action of God that raises Jesus is not like the action that winds up a watch or starts a motor. The watch or the motor, once started, carry on on their own, independently of their owner. God's action is like the bell that rings as long as I keep my finger on the button. It's like a communications satellite that picks up transmissions from other countries. As soon as the transmission from the other country stops, the satellite stops picking up and transmitting signals, and our television screens go blank. As soon as God ceases to speak the word that raises Jesus Christ, Christ falls silent. If that happened, Christ would be nothing, would no longer be revelation, and the screen of our faith would go blank; our words and witness would become empty and hollow. They would be lies, a worthless check (1 Cor 15:15). In that case, a better policy would be: "Let us eat and drink, for tomorrow we die" (1 Cor 15:32).

But God does not stop pressing the button, will never cut off transmissions, will never stop calling Jesus to life. God does not deceive or frustrate. God is faithful and is sufficiently strong to carry on doing what God has started. No power can stop God. God always conquers. This is one of the pillars of our faith. What does it rest on?

The deepest foundation, the very root of our faith in the resurrection, is the goodwill of God, the goodwill of Someone who has made an irrevocable commitment to us. Faith in the resurrection does not depend on a blind and impersonal law; it has nothing to do with the philosophical arguments for the immortality of the soul; it is not based on a calculation of ours based on historical studies that have proved the historicity of Jesus' resurrection, nor does it depend on proofs that have refuted the contrary arguments. Faith in the resurrection springs from the friendly word that Someone spoke in our favor. Just as a word from a friend can affirm a person, restore our sense of self-worth, and open us to a new hope, in the same way God's friendly word touches human beings in our hearts, restores our sense of self-worth, raises us to a new life, and makes us live forever.

In raising Jesus from the dead, God gave a practical example of goodwill toward human beings. God expressed the irresistible power of that saving and liberating will and affirmed its fidelity, making us realize how far we can trust in God's goodwill toward us, to the point of being able to do the impossible, to the point of hoping that life can be born out of death.

God had been demonstrating this goodwill since the beginning, by calling Abraham and freeing the people from Egypt. God showed through history that when we have the courage to make a commitment to God, we will find what we seek, we will find happiness. The full content of this word that began to ring in Abraham's ears and the complete power it possesses appeared in Christ's resurrection. In Christ, a human being like us who lived in complete openness and obedience to the Father attained the final goal in the resurrection. And God not only raised him, but also brought him to God's side, giving him all power and placing the fate of humanity in his hands (Phil 2:8–11). Now, eternally, one of our brothers is at God's side, as a complete and final proof that when

God makes a promise, God keeps it (Is 40:7–8), and that we can indeed trust in what God says and promises (Heb 4:14–16; 5:5–10). Christ's resurrection is the permanent expression of God's irrevocable commitment to us. It is the permanent and supreme proof of the guarantee that accompanies the promise. It is God's "new and eternal covenant" with human beings.

Believing in the resurrection, therefore, is believing, not in a thing, not in arguments, but in Someone who acts in us and through us, with immense power, capable of bringing life out of death and making old things new, guiding us toward a future of vast dimensions.

Believing in the resurrection means starting now to overcome, through hope that anticipates the future, the limits that were overcome or broken by the resurrection of the crucified Jesus. No limit, no barrier, no difficulty, nothing in this world, will be able to quench the life and hope kindled in this way in human hearts.

Believing in the resurrection has nothing to do with flight or alienation from the world in order to reach the next world or with basing ourselves on a past event that is now over. The object of faith in the resurrection is not situated either in heavenly eternity or in the impenetrable past, but in the future of the earth in which Christ's cross was rooted and remains rooted to this day. The past fact, attested by the apostles, is the foundation. But on this foundation rests the huge edifice of life that will not die, which is reborn from the ashes of death, anticipating the new world that appears out of the hands of those who believe in it.

Believing in the resurrection is summed up by Paul in the following words:

> If God is for us, who is against us? . . . Who will separate us from the love of Christ? Will hardship, or distress, or persecution, or famine, or nakedness, or peril, or sword? . . . No, in all these things we are more than conquerors through him who loved us. For I am convinced that neither death, nor life, nor angels, nor rulers, nor things present, nor things to come, nor powers, nor height, nor depth, nor anything else in all

creation, will be able to separate us from the love of God in Christ Jesus our Lord. (Rom 8:31, 35, 37–39)

The list is complete: nothing can separate us from God and from our future, because Christ, who, through the resurrection, conquered all those powers, is at God's side interceding for us who believe in him (Rom 8:32–34; Heb 5:7–9).

Conclusion: A Challenge

The first Christians' attitude to the resurrection shows that the fundamental problem of faith in the resurrection is not outside us, in possible historical or scientific difficulties. It is within ourselves: are we or are we not capable of the courage to believe in a God who frees and saves with a power greater than the forces of death? This resurrection power operates and shows itself only where there is faith in it. There is no push-button to activate this power of God; it is a free power, placed at our disposal. It is like the power of friendship: it works only on the basis of mutual trust and faith of one person in another.

Paul, anxious for Christians to become aware of this, prays for them and asks the Father that they may all come to understand "what is the immeasurable greatness of his power for us who believe, according to the working of his great power. God put this power to work in Christ, raising him from the dead and seating him at God's right hand in the heavenly places, far above all rule and authority and power and dominion, and above every name that is named, not only in this age but in the age to come" (Eph 1:19–21). Where this awareness takes root in human beings, it activates an irresistible force that will never rest until the powers of death have been conquered by the forces of life.

The high point of faith in the resurrection is not in the past or in the future, but in the present. It is the tree grown from the seed planted in the past that today indicates an enormous harvest in the future. It roots human life in a deep peace, but waves its branches in radical dissatisfaction with the present state of the world, a dissatisfaction that cannot be at peace with a world in which the oppressive power of death holds sway.

The key point of faith in the resurrection is that we should discover in our lives this ever-present power of God who is a God of the living. Only in this way will we too rise and, once risen, realize the scope of faith in the resurrection. The scientific arguments will not give faith in the resurrection its importance, but the lived experience of the resurrection will give importance to the arguments we discover to defend it. The only truly convincing proof of the resurrection is life that rises again and is renewed today, that overcomes the powers of death today and enables the repressed and shackled powers of life to be discovered and released to give us all happiness and hope. This is the proof that there is a power stronger than death acting in human beings, the power of the risen Christ. Where are these signs of the resurrection in our lives to give backing to our words about the resurrection?

Much more could and should be said to make our account of the resurrection complete. All I have done here is to open a small window to give an idea of the tremendous power of faith in the resurrection to transform human life.

EPILOGUE

The Bible and the People

From my vantage point in speaking about the Bible, I see a door, the door through which the world gains access to the Bible. From my window, I have observed this door, watched the people going in, and I have studied its history, which is also the history of this book. That history, described in this Epilogue, is very simple and somewhat symbolic. It is a parable that expresses perfectly the message of this book.

The Parable of the Door

In the village there was a house. It was called the People's House. It was very old and well built. It had a fine wide door opening on to the street that the people used.

It was a strange door. Its threshold seemed to remove the separation between the house and the street. People who went in through the door felt they were still in the street. People who passed by in the street felt welcomed and involved by the house. No one realized this fact because it was something as natural as the light and heat when the sun shines.

The house was part of the people's life, thanks to that door that made the house one with the street and the street one with the house. It was the meeting place, where everything happened, where everything was discussed, where people met. The door stayed open day and night. Its threshold was worn by years of use. Lots of people went through it, in fact everybody.

One day two scholars arrived. They came from outside. They weren't from the village. They didn't know the house; they had just heard about its great age and beauty and had come to see it. They were professors who knew the value of old things. They saw the house and right away realized how precious it was. They asked permission to stay. They wanted to study.

They searched and found a side door. They used that door to go in and out for their studies. They didn't want to be disturbed by the noise and bustle of the people at the front door. They wanted the quiet they needed for their thinking.

They stayed inside the house, far away from the people's door, in a dark corner, absorbed in the investigation of the house's past.

When the people came into their house, they saw the two scholars with big books and complicated equipment. As they came close to them, the simple people would fall silent. They kept quiet so as not to disturb them. The people were very impressed. "They're studying the beauty and the past of our house," they said. "They're professors!"

The studies progressed. The two scholars discovered beautiful things that the people didn't know, even though they saw them in their house every day. They were allowed to strip a few walls, and discovered ancient paintings showing the history of the people's life that the people didn't know about. They carried out excavations at the base of the pillars, and were able to piece together the history of the building of the house, which no one remembered.

The people didn't know about the past of their lives and their house because the past was inside them, and of course their eyes didn't see it, but they saw everything else and looked to the future.

At night, when work was over, the two scholars, among the people, described their discoveries. The people's admiration for their house and their professors grew.

They told the people that some people from other countries had spoken and written against the house, but that they had come to study and defend the people's house. They were writing long articles in a foreign language, which were published in big cities that the people had never heard of. The people even began to learn the names of these dangerous enemies who went about saying that the house was worthless. "They're evil," they said. "They don't like us. They're against the house where we're happy."

Time went by. Now, when the people came into the house, they started to keep quiet. Such a rich and noble house, the subject of so much talk and discussion the world over, deserved respect. It was different from the bustling life of the street outside. They ought to respect it a bit more. This wasn't a place for talking and dancing. That was what everyone said, and how everyone behaved.

And some people from that village had stopped going in by the noisy front door. They preferred the silence of the scholars' side door. They avoided the noise of the people. They started going into the house, not to meet and talk to other people, but to learn more about the beauty of their house, the People's House. They were given explanations by the professors about the house they knew so well, but now felt they didn't know.

So, little by little, the People's House stopped being the people's. All the people preferred the professors' door. There they were given a booklet explaining the rare and ancient things discovered in the house.

The people became convinced that they really were ignorant. It was the professors who knew and understood what the people had better than the people themselves. So everybody thought.

Now when they went into their own house, the people were silent and shy. It was as if they were in a strange house belonging to the past, which they didn't know. They looked carefully and studied, booklets in hand, in little groups, moving round in the semi-darkness. By now they no longer remembered the old days, when they had joked and danced together in the place where they now studied, with serious looks, imitating the professors, holding their booklets and learning the text.

Gradually the front door was forgotten. A gale closed it. No one noticed. But it wasn't completely closed. A small gap remained.

Grass grew in front of the door. Bushes grew up and covered the entrance, because no one used it. Even the look of the street changed. Now it was just a street and nothing more. It was dismal and deserted, a dead end; passersby no longer stopped to chat.

The side door was the people's entrance. They went in and looked, impressed and entranced. All these riches that they had never known about!

Inside, the house grew darker, because no light came from the street any more. Instead there were lamps and candles, but the artificial light changed the colors.

Time went by. The excitement of discovery cooled. The number of visitors coming to the house by the side door, the professors' door, fell. The people's door at the front no longer existed. No one remembered it any more.

Educated people, a mere handful, with eminent visitors from other places, continued to come to the People's House, through the professors' door. Inside, they held their meetings and discussed the ancient features of the house, the historical aspects.

The ordinary people, whose lives were hard, went by in the deserted and dismal street. They weren't interested in the past. They didn't understand the professors' disputes. They got on with their lives, nothing more. But something seemed to be missing. They didn't know what, because they didn't remember. What was missing was a house for the people.

The professors, delighted with the discoveries, continued their studies. They even started a school to educate the children of the village in the lore of the past. They were to be their successors as defenders of the People's House. So they thought.

But one of the scholars started to worry about the increasing lack of interest among the people. Most of the people had stopped coming. He noted that the people's life was no longer the same. It was less happy, different from when he arrived. People now thought only about themselves. They didn't get together any more. True, they tried to meet in other places, but it didn't work. The planned meetings even increased their differences. There was something missing, but he didn't know what. He tried to find out.

He wondered, "Why have the people stopped coming to their own house? Why have they stopped coming here to learn about the things that the two of us have discovered and defended for them? Why have they stopped coming here to meet and chat, dance and joke, talk and sing?" He had no answer to his questions.

The other scholar had noticed nothing of all this, because he was absorbed in his studies of the past. He even started to criticize his colleague. "You're not concentrating. Your research is suffering; it's getting very superficial." He insisted that his colleague should devote more energy to the study of the past and less attention to the people in the street. After all, he was the team leader.

One night an old beggar who had no house, nowhere to live, went into the bushes at the side of the street, looking for somewhere to sleep. There he saw, without knowing what it was, a small gap and went through it. He found himself on the threshold of a huge house. It was such a nice house that it made him feel at home straight away. He felt he was in the street, and yet he was well housed.

The following night he went back. He kept going back. He told his friends, all poor beggars like himself. He told them the secret of what he had found. They went with him. They all went in, through the narrow gap in the front door, which the wind had blown shut one day, without closing it completely.

With so many people going in and out of the front door, the grass got trodden down and the bushes beaten back. A narrow track appeared on the ground, and a new path was created.

Because there were so many friends who wanted to get in, they tugged at the door and it gave. The entrance became a little wider, letting the people through and the sun in. The house was lit up inside and became more beautiful. They felt more comfortable. The people were very happy.

News of the discovery spread like wildfire among the simple people. They didn't say anything to the others. It was their secret. "That house is ours," they said. But the discovery couldn't be kept secret. That was a naive idea of the simple people who had no ulterior motives.

In the mornings, at the official opening time of the side door for the eminent visitors, the cleaners found inside traces of the presence of the simple people. They even heard them laughing and talking. They sounded happy and relaxed; they weren't bothered by the historical features, and they hadn't paid to get in. They laughed like people who felt at home in the house that was starting to become once more the People's House.

The news was reported to the two scholars. One got angry. The other said nothing. The first complained: "How can people be so stupid?" he shouted. "They'll damage our house. It's a sacrilege! What about our work? All the years of research? What's left of it?" He talked as though he was the owner of the house. The other retorted: "It's not your house!" The two of them argued about the house and the people.

The second scholar hid at night in a corner of the house. He saw the people come in without asking permission, to dance and joke, talk and sing, to feel at home and meet others. He liked to see this happiness in the house, and for a moment forgot about the ancient treasures. He enjoyed it so much that he joined the circle and danced. He danced and joked, talked and sang, all night long. It was something he'd not done for a long time. He'd never felt so happy in his life.

It was then that he discovered that everything he had spent so much time studying had been made by the people, to make their life happy. Now he discovered the answers to his questions. The mistake was the side door. The side door had turned the people away from the front door, separated the street from the house and the house from the street, made the house darker and strange to the people, made the street deserted and dismal, a dead end.

He too started to go in through the front door. He did that every night. The people got to know him and welcome him, because they didn't make distinctions among the people who mixed with them. He was one of the people.

Going in through the front door, he saw the riches and beauty of the house from a new and unfamiliar angle. Seen in the light that came from the street and the people's happiness, the house revealed beautiful things that the academic books didn't include and the machines couldn't pick up.

He began to see the house as a majestic mountain suddenly lit up by the sun's free reddish-yellow rays at the dawn of a new day. Everything changed, although nothing had changed. Everything was as before, but everything was different. A new hope was born.

He began to study his books with new eyes and discovered things that his colleague never dreamed of. His enjoyment of his work increased, but his colleague didn't believe him.

Being among the people and sharing their happiness, the scholar talked to the people about the riches of the house. He talked about the beautiful features of the house that he had discovered with the light that came from books and the past and with the light that came from the street and the people's happiness. He talked as the opportunity arose. His voice wasn't arrogant or boring. He didn't silence the people with the weight of his learning and knowledge. He taught the people in their happiness and increased their pleasure in life.

And he said to himself, "Looking at the hard lives the people have, we can't talk, we can only keep quiet. We have to forget the ideas of the educated people and become humble and start to think...."

•

One of our hopes for the future is that the front door will become visible again, that the bushes that have grown up in front of it will be cleared, that the door will be opened wide, that the people will be given back the happiness they lost, that the people will be given back what was theirs.

Another hope for the future is that the look of the street will change, that the fine entrance will give it back its beauty, that the light from the street will once more get into the People's House and allow its true beauty to appear and replace the artificial color.

For the future we hope that the side door will be closed, closed not because it's not useful, but so that everyone, both the scholars and the visitors, the educated people and the poor people, can all enjoy the real pleasure that the house gives when it is everyone's house.

For the future we hope that the entrance will be at the front again, that the scholars will go in that way, among the people, mixing with them, and that in this way knowing about the riches of the house will stop alienating people from the house, that the students trained in the professors' school will not forget that they belong to the people, that they will give back to the people the life and happiness they received from the people.

For the future we hope that ever more rigorous studies will be conducted into the beauty and the riches of the People's House, but that they will be conducted in the light that comes from the street and the people's happiness, and that in this way the studies will help to make that happiness even greater. It should be a happiness that springs from the life the people live now, from the life of the past that the professors study, and from the life of tomorrow that we are all looking forward to.

The only remaining problem was the scholar who got angry and thought that the house belonged to him. But the people decided to go and talk to him and say: "Without us the house would never have been built! Without us you would never have been born."

•

This is the parable of the door. It tells the history of the explanation of the Bible to the people. It also describes the history of this book and is a summary of it; it describes how it originated and its sources. It came into being at night, in the middle of the people's happiness. It came into being during the day, in the deserted and dismal street. It came into being by night and day, among the books and complicated equipment in a dark corner of the People's House.

The book seeks to make the hope that was born then come

true. It seeks to help the people to rediscover the front door and make the house once more one with the street and the street one with the house. The door is fine and wide, always open. Its threshold is worn by the feet of all those who have passed through, in the silence of the ages, looking for God and their brothers and sisters.